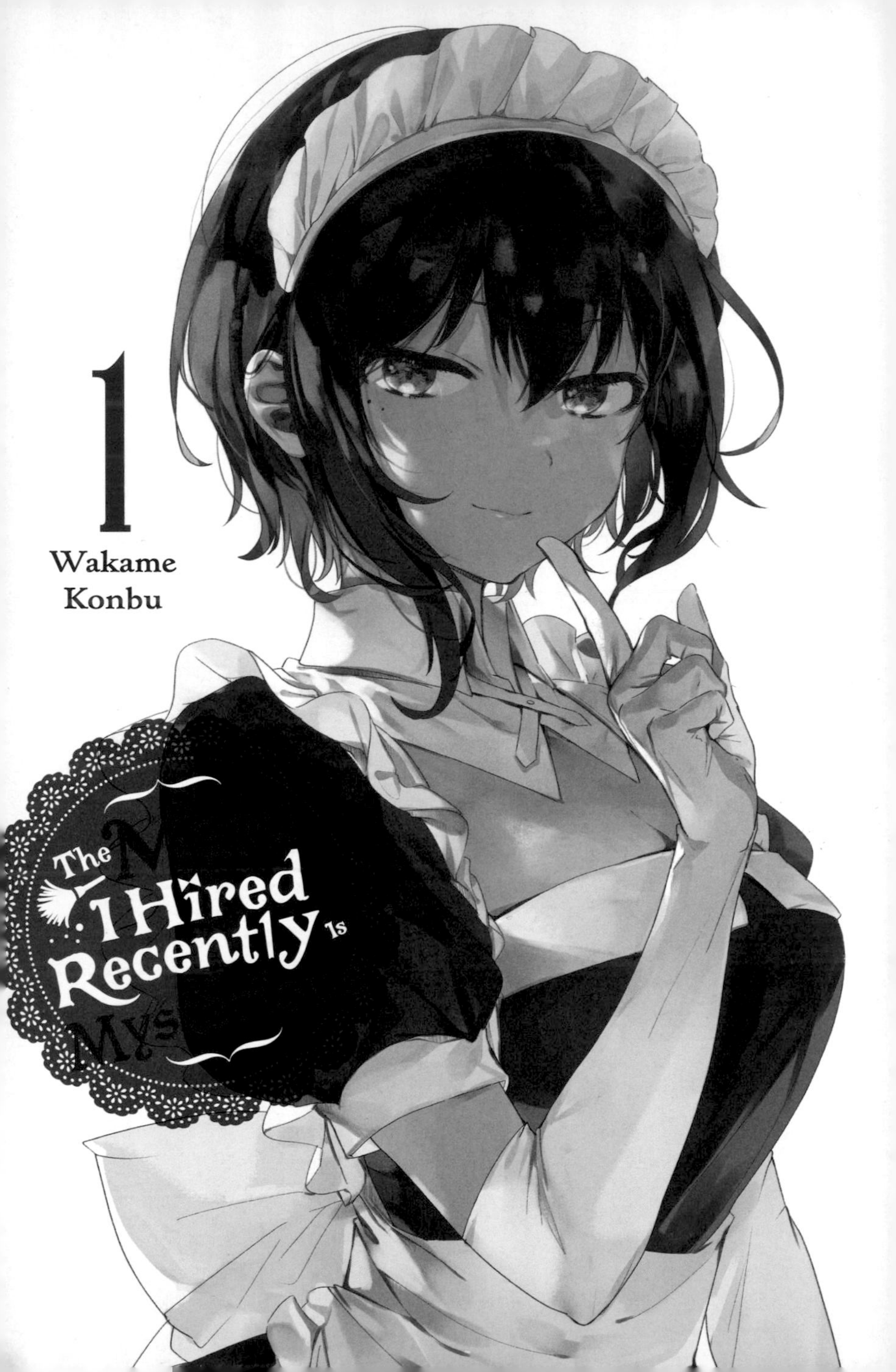
1
Wakame
Konbu
The M
I Hired
Recently Is
Mys

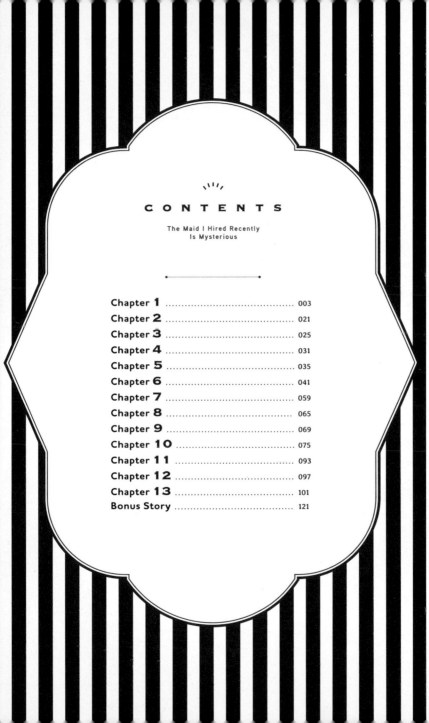

CONTENTS

The Maid I Hired Recently
Is Mysterious

Chapter 1 003

Chapter 2 021

Chapter 3 025

Chapter 4 031

Chapter 5 035

Chapter 6 041

Chapter 7 059

Chapter 8 065

Chapter 9 069

Chapter 10 075

Chapter 11 093

Chapter 12 097

Chapter 13 101

Bonus Story 121

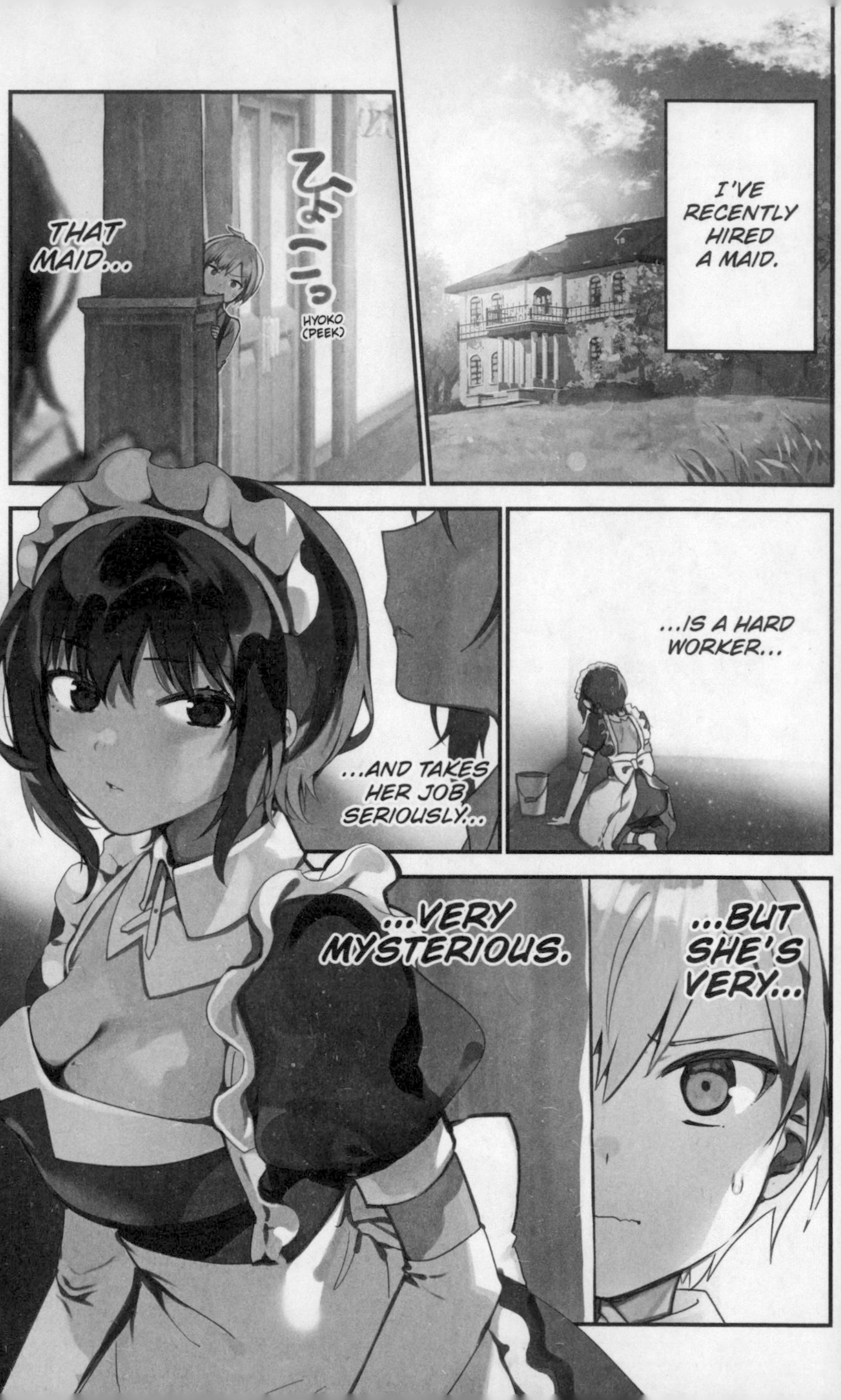
I'VE RECENTLY HIRED A MAID.
THAT MAID...
ひょこっ
HYOKO (PEEK)
...IS A HARD WORKER...
...AND TAKES HER JOB SERIOUSLY...
...BUT SHE'S VERY...
...VERY MYSTERIOUS.

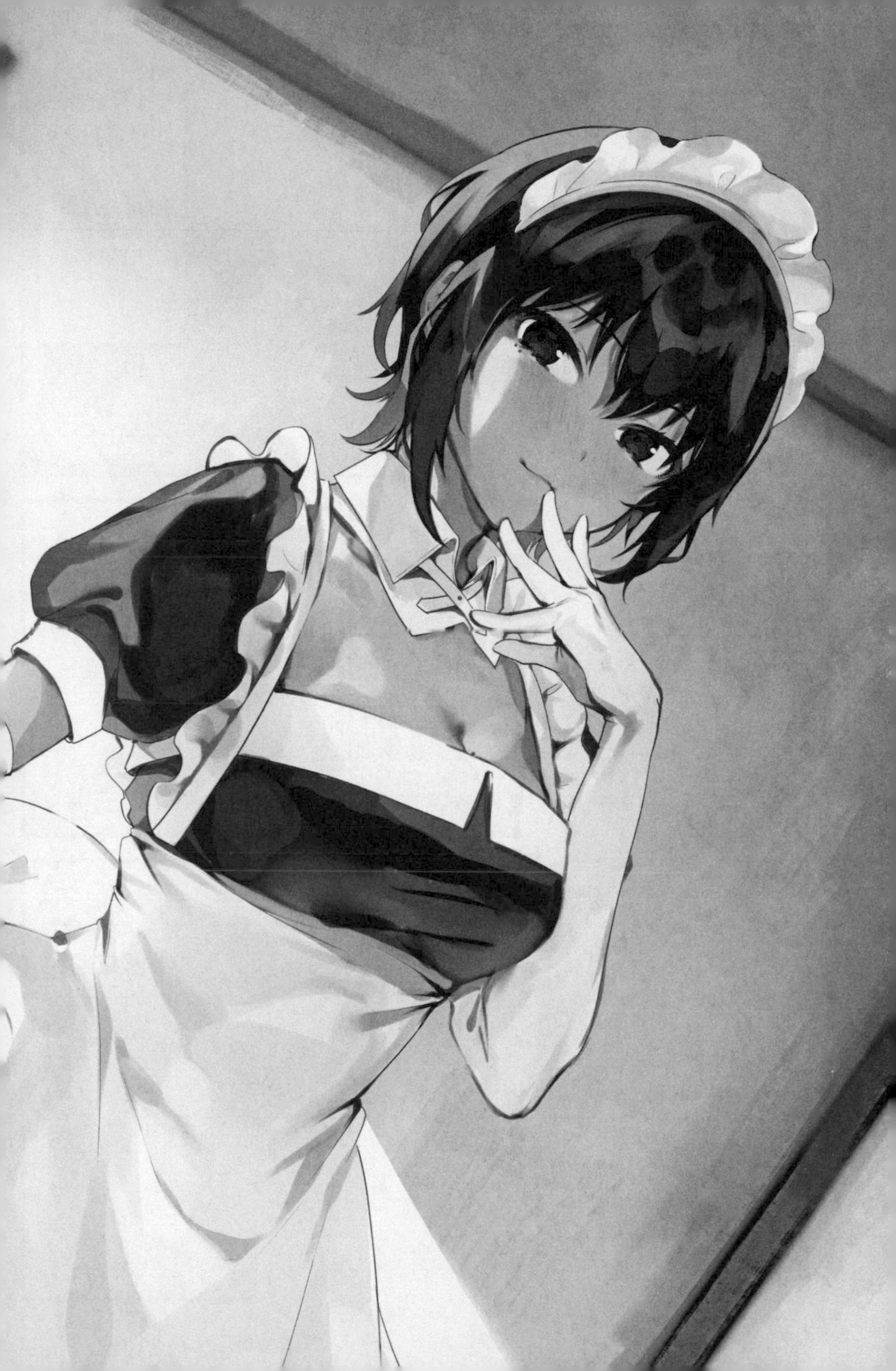

CHAPTER 1

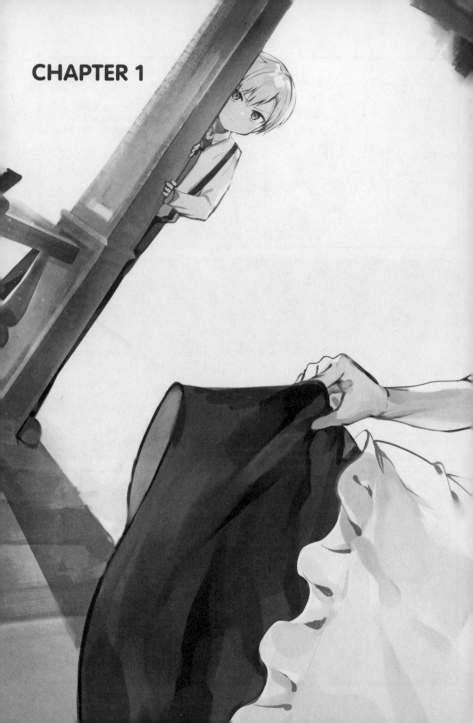

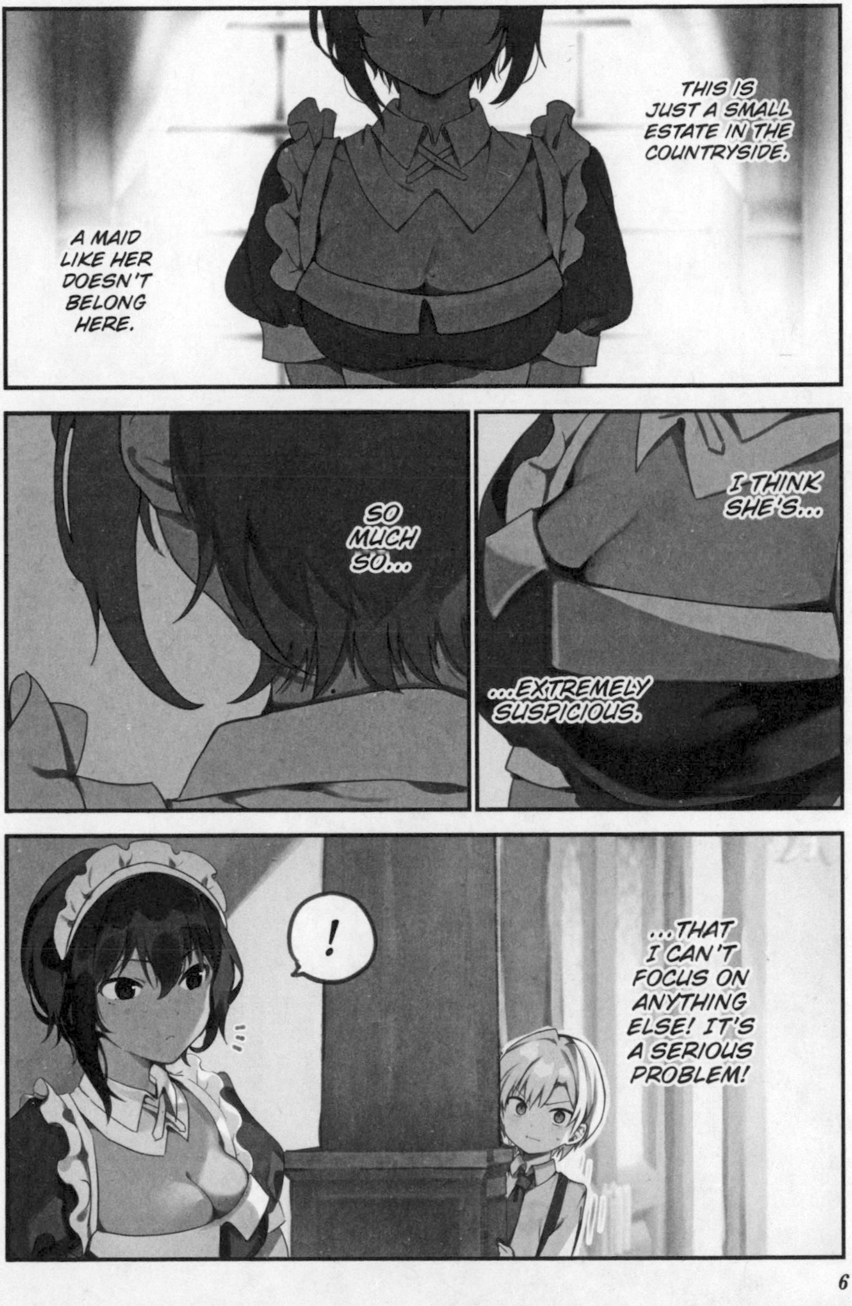
THIS IS JUST A SMALL ESTATE IN THE COUNTRYSIDE.
A MAID LIKE HER DOESN'T BELONG HERE.
I THINK SHE'S...
...EXTREMELY SUSPICIOUS.
SO MUCH SO...
...THAT I CAN'T FOCUS ON ANYTHING ELSE! IT'S A SERIOUS PROBLEM!
!

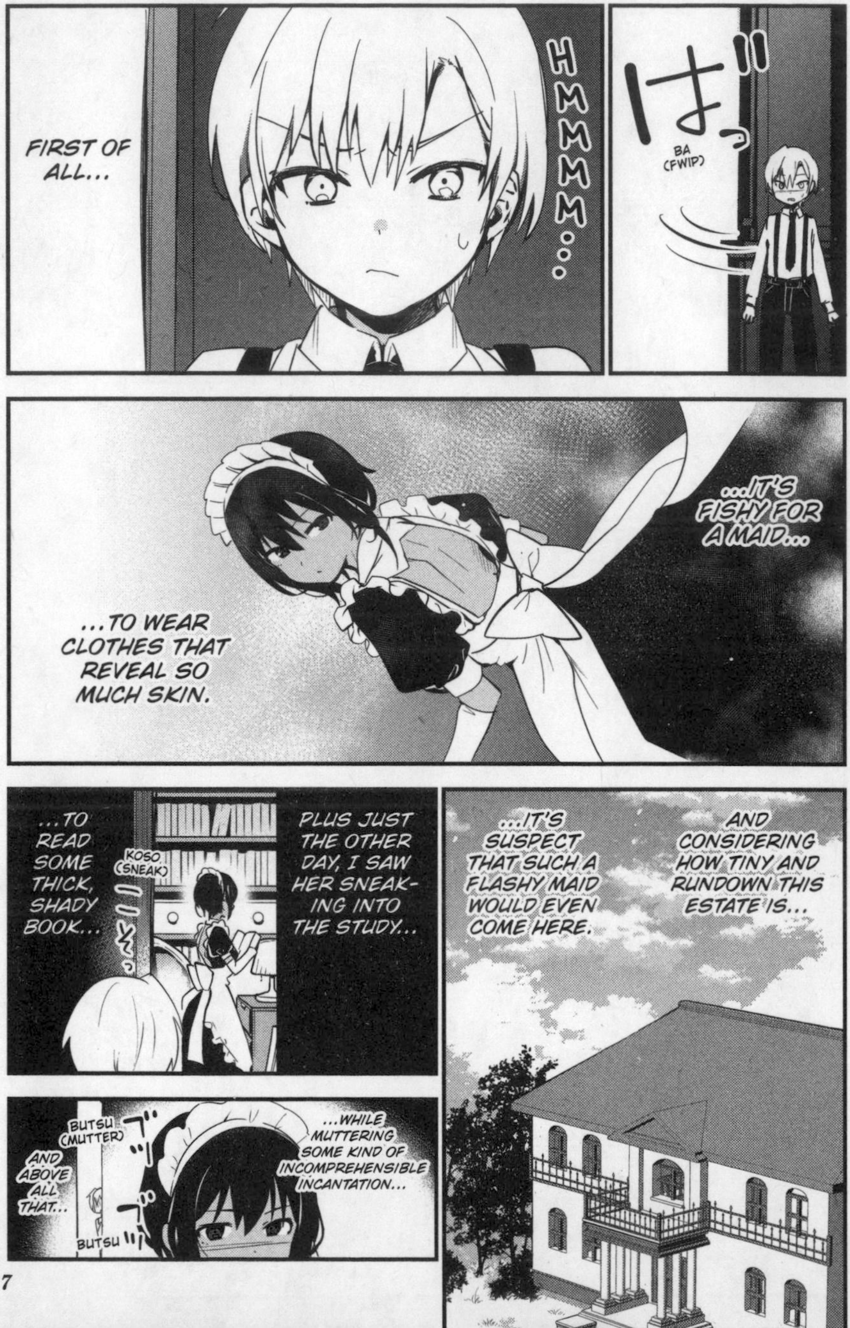
ばっ
BA (FWIP)
HMMMM...
FIRST OF ALL...
...IT'S FISHY FOR A MAID...
...TO WEAR CLOTHES THAT REVEAL SO MUCH SKIN.
AND CONSIDERING HOW TINY AND RUNDOWN THIS ESTATE IS...
...IT'S SUSPECT THAT SUCH A FLASHY MAID WOULD EVEN COME HERE.
PLUS JUST THE OTHER DAY, I SAW HER SNEAKING INTO THE STUDY...
KOSO (SNEAK)
...TO READ SOME THICK, SHADY BOOK...
...WHILE MUTTERING SOME KIND OF INCOMPREHENSIBLE INCANTATION...
BUTSU (MUTTER)
BUTSU
AND ABOVE ALL THAT...

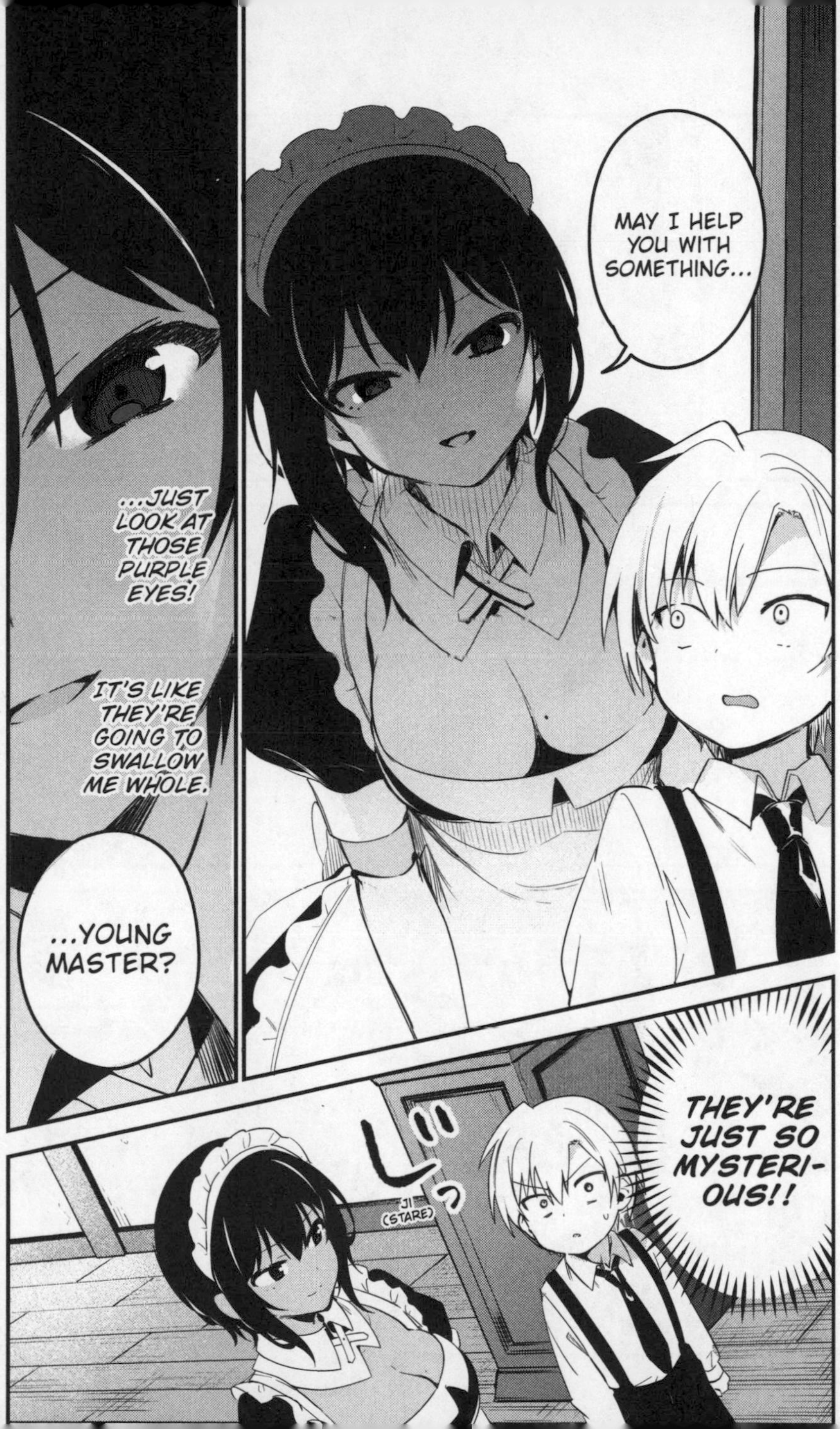
MAY I HELP YOU WITH SOMETHING...
...JUST LOOK AT THOSE PURPLE EYES!
IT'S LIKE THEY'RE GOING TO SWALLOW ME WHOLE.
...YOUNG MASTER?
THEY'RE JUST SO MYSTERI-OUS!!
JI (STARE)

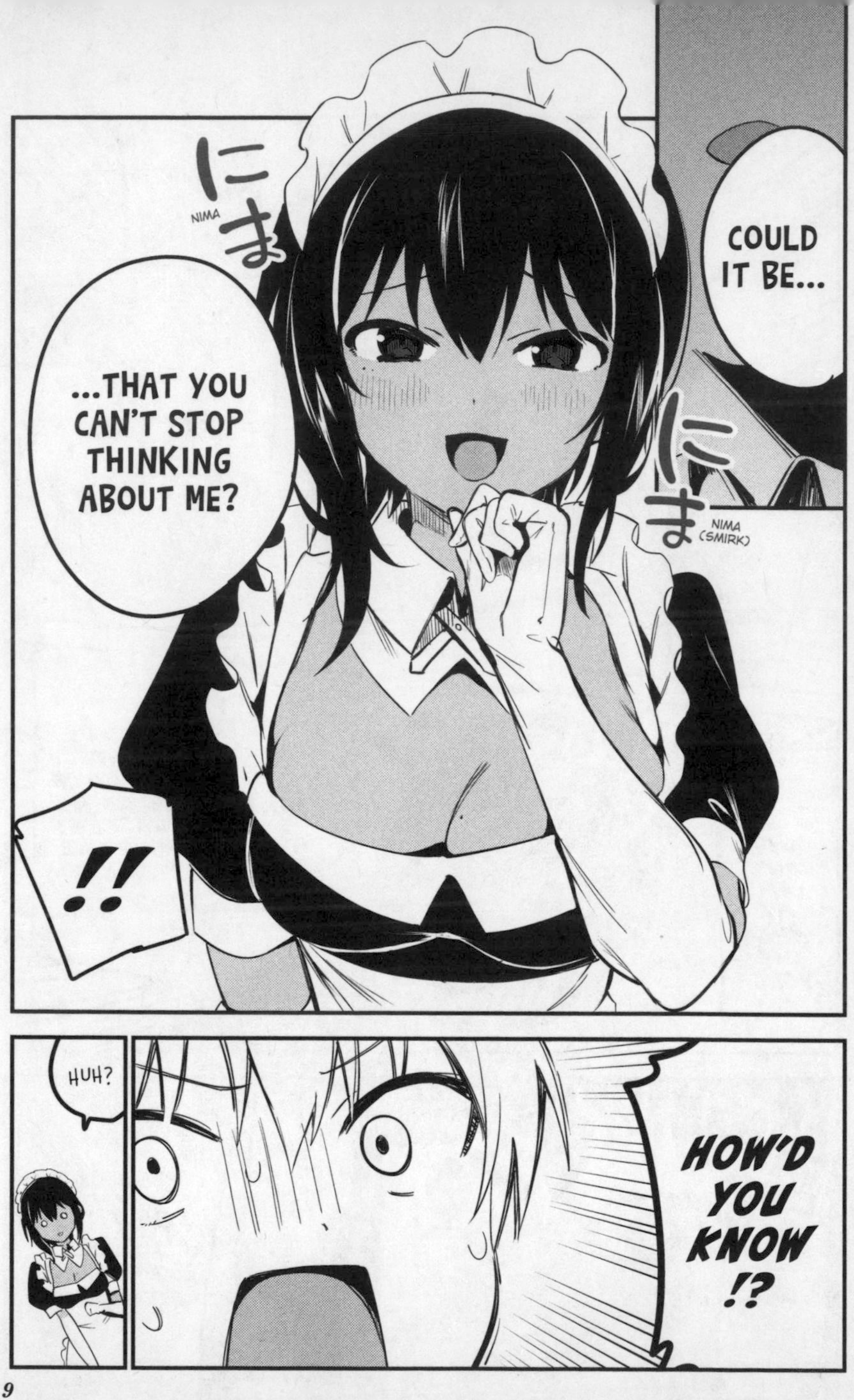
COULD IT BE...
にま
NIMA (SMIRK)
...THAT YOU CAN'T STOP THINKING ABOUT ME?
にま
NIMA
!!
HOW'D YOU KNOW !?
HUH?

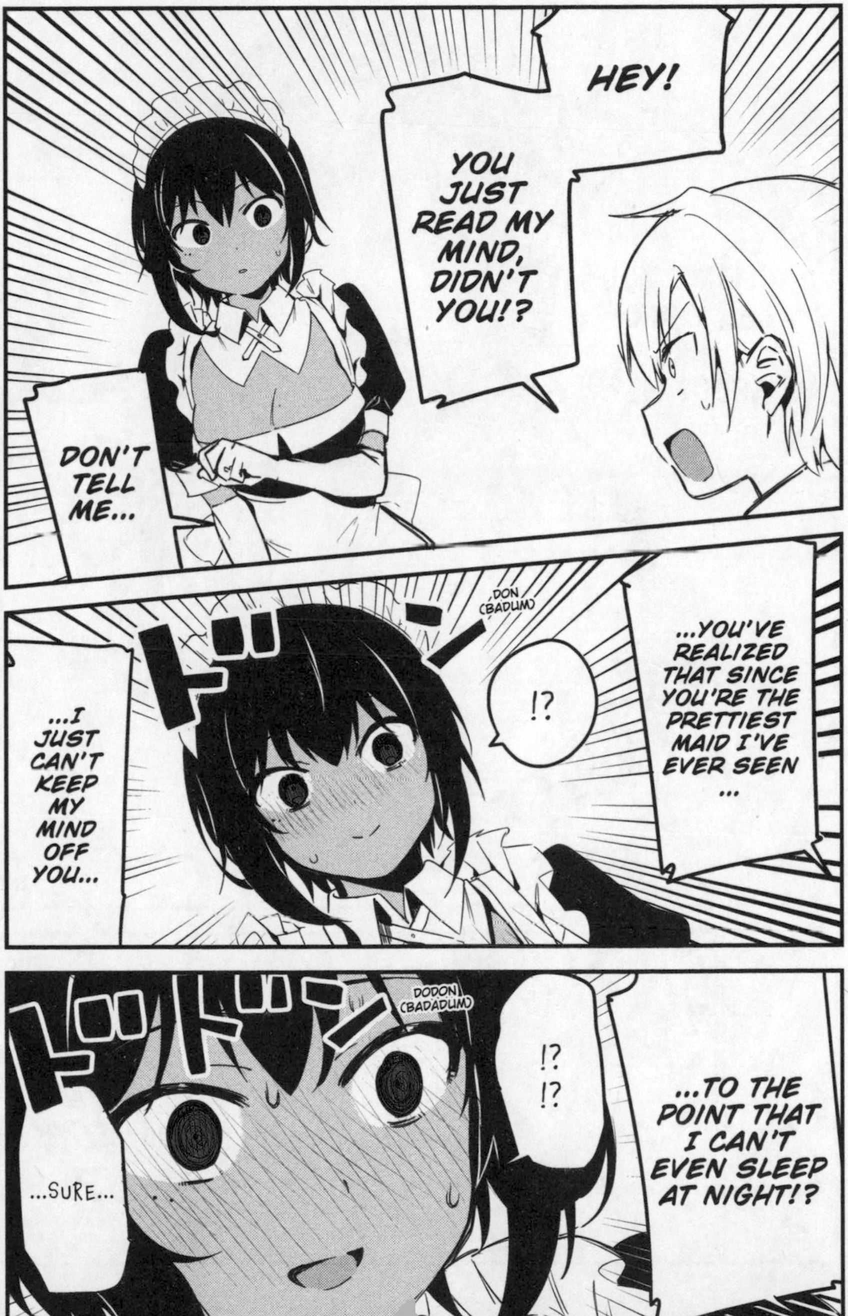
HEY!
YOU JUST READ MY MIND, DIDN'T YOU!?
DON'T TELL ME...
...YOU'VE REALIZED THAT SINCE YOU'RE THE PRETTIEST MAID I'VE EVER SEEN...
DON (BADUM)
!?
...I JUST CAN'T KEEP MY MIND OFF YOU...
...TO THE POINT THAT I CAN'T EVEN SLEEP AT NIGHT!?
!? !?
DODON (BADADUM)
...SURE...

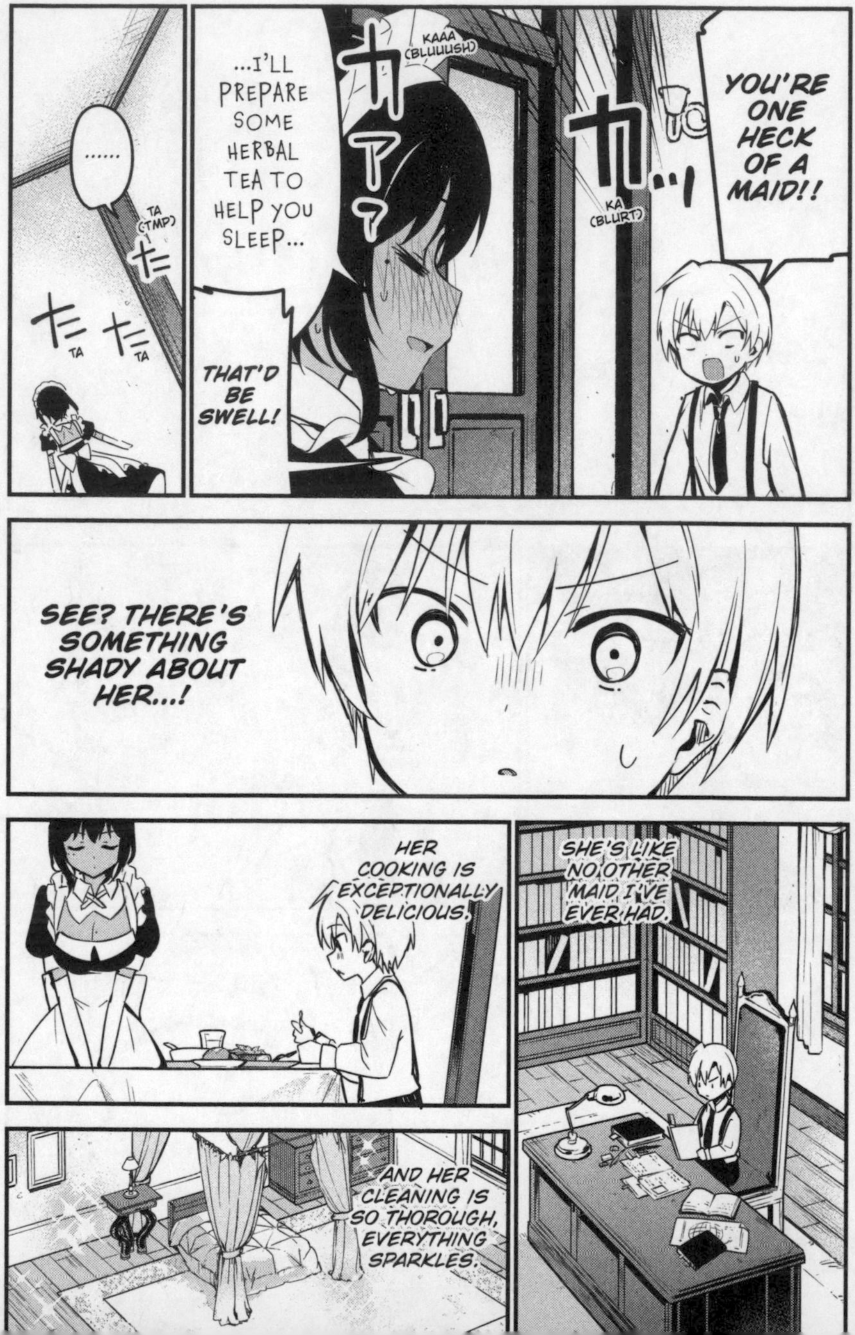
YOU'RE ONE HECK OF A MAID!!
KA (BLURT)
KAAA (BLUUUSH)
...I'LL PREPARE SOME HERBAL TEA TO HELP YOU SLEEP...
THAT'D BE SWELL!
......
TA (TMP)
TA
TA
SEE? THERE'S SOMETHING SHADY ABOUT HER...!
SHE'S LIKE NO OTHER MAID I'VE EVER HAD.
HER COOKING IS EXCEPTIONALLY DELICIOUS.
AND HER CLEANING IS SO THOROUGH, EVERYTHING SPARKLES.

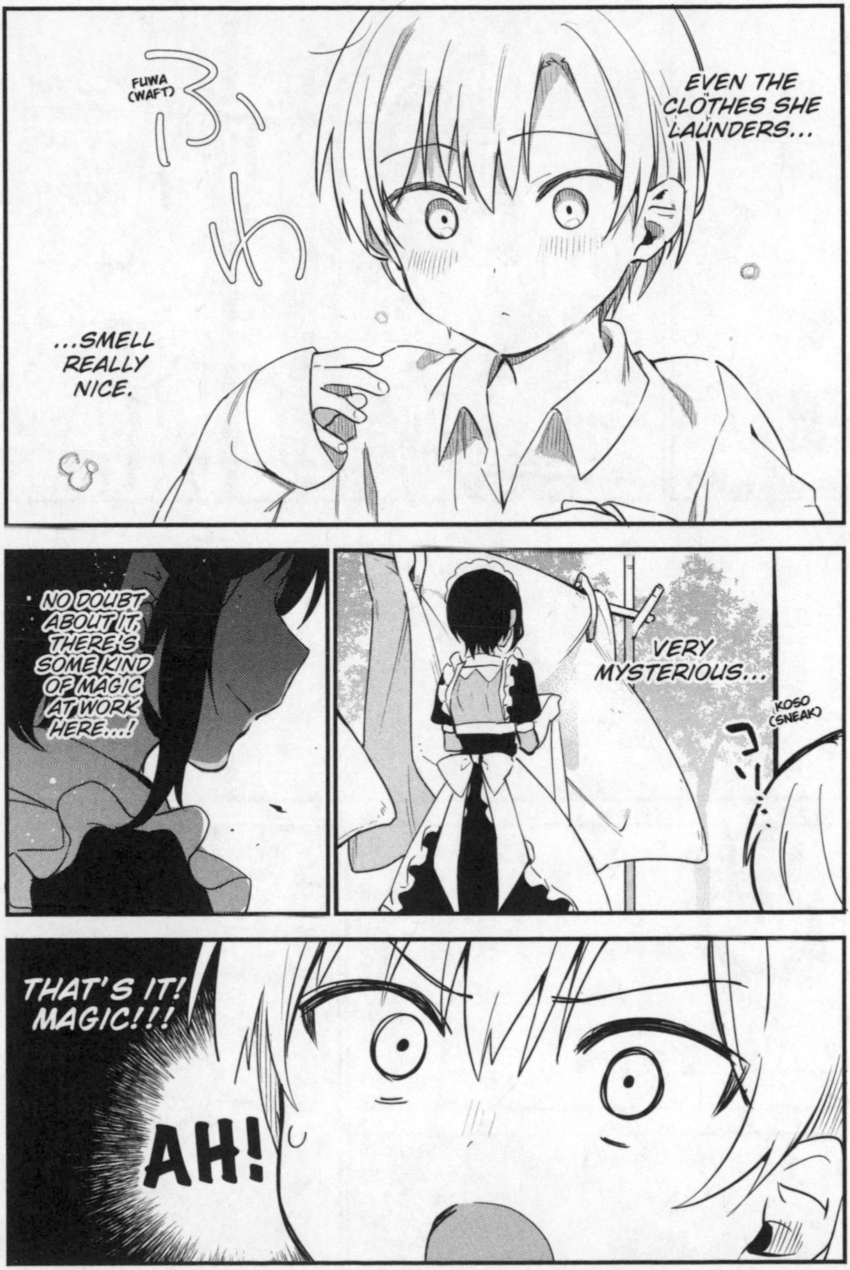
EVEN THE CLOTHES SHE LAUNDERS...
FUWA (WAFT)
...SMELL REALLY NICE.
VERY MYSTERIOUS...
KOSO (SNEAK)
NO DOUBT ABOUT IT. THERE'S SOME KIND OF MAGIC AT WORK HERE...!
THAT'S IT! MAGIC!!!
AH!

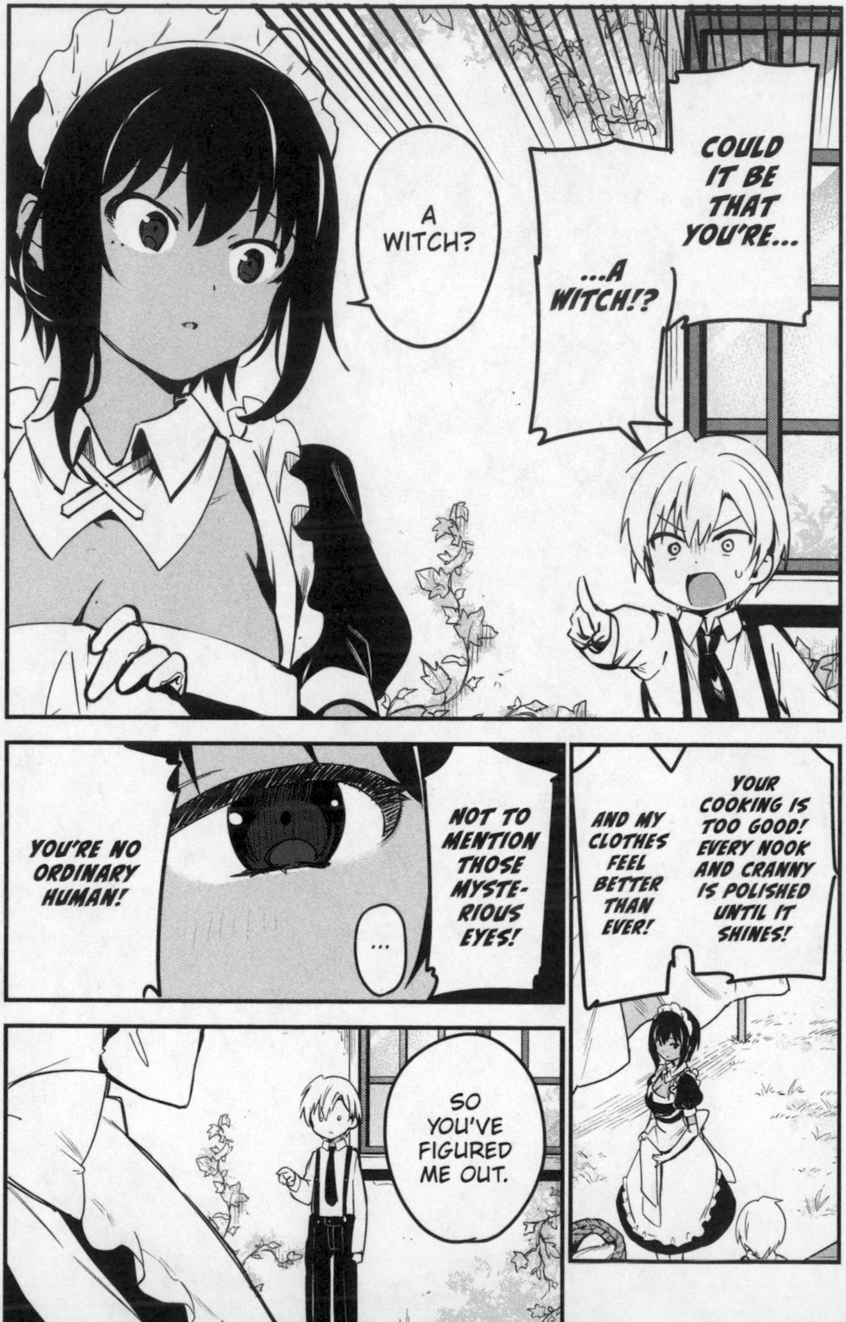
COULD IT BE THAT YOU'RE...
...A WITCH!?
A WITCH?
YOUR COOKING IS TOO GOOD! EVERY NOOK AND CRANNY IS POLISHED UNTIL IT SHINES!
AND MY CLOTHES FEEL BETTER THAN EVER!
NOT TO MENTION THOSE MYSTE-RIOUS EYES!
YOU'RE NO ORDINARY HUMAN!
...
SO YOU'VE FIGURED ME OUT.

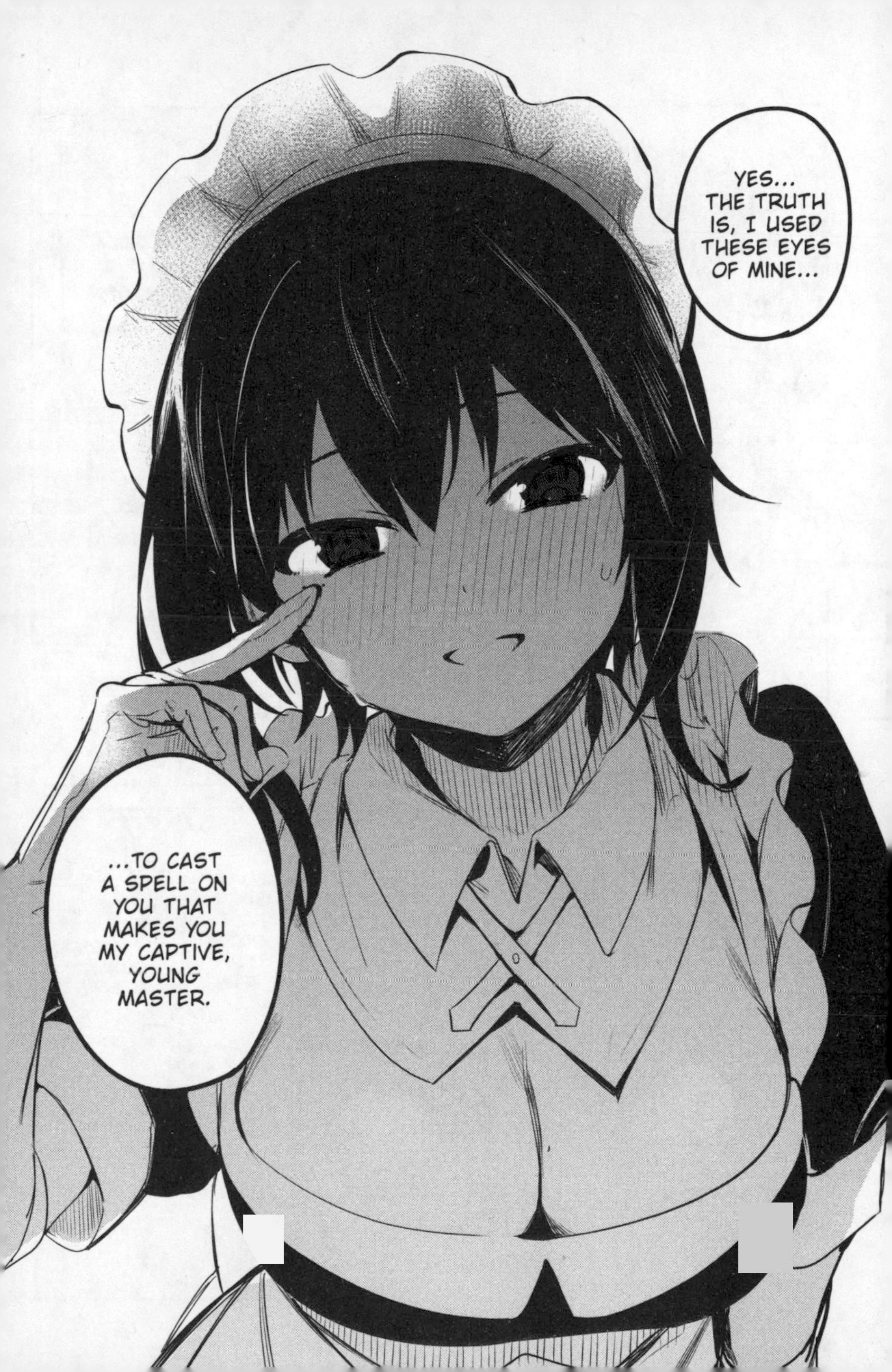
YES... THE TRUTH IS, I USED THESE EYES OF MINE...
...TO CAST A SPELL ON YOU THAT MAKES YOU MY CAPTIVE, YOUNG MASTER.

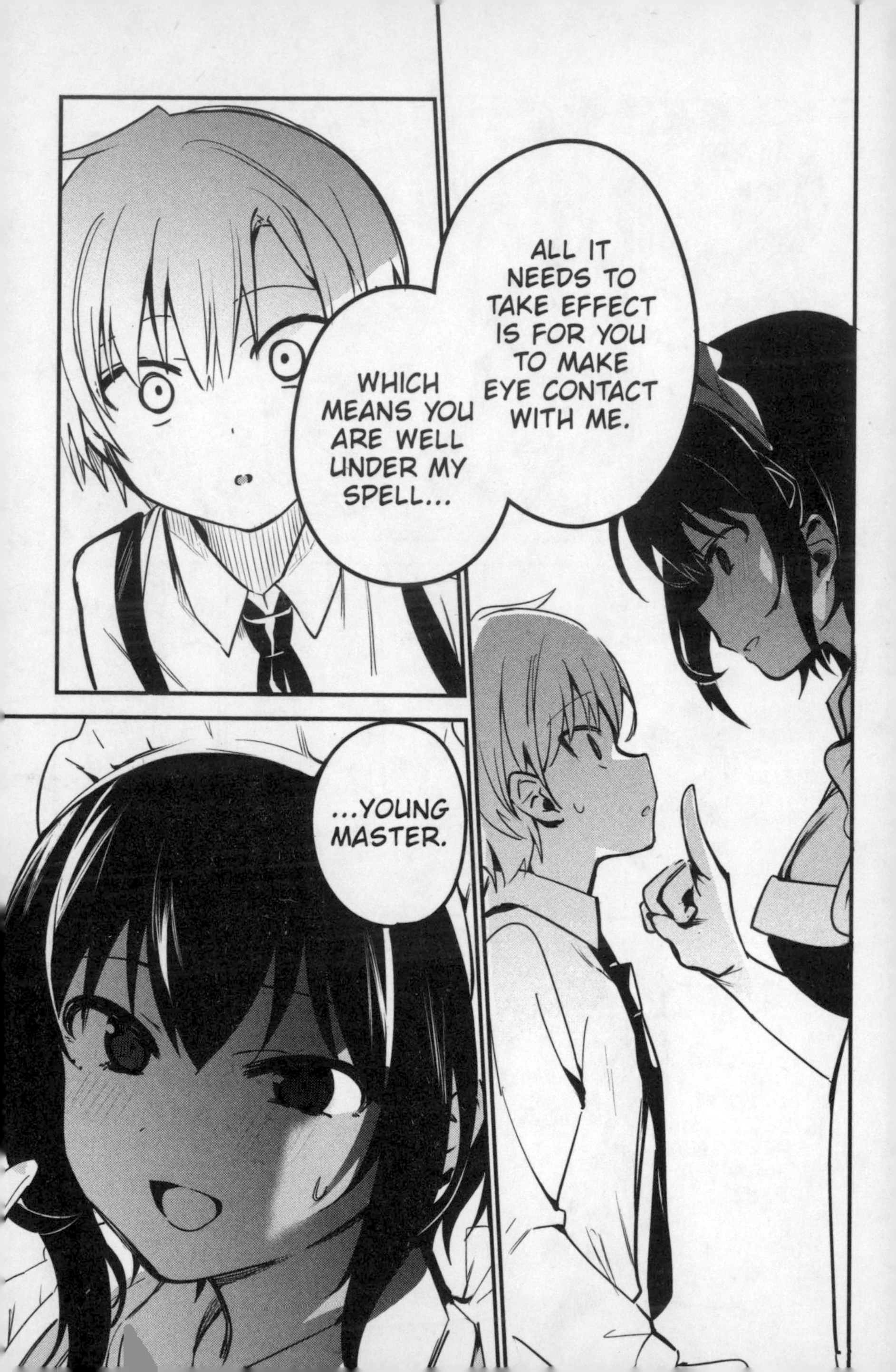
ALL IT NEEDS TO TAKE EFFECT IS FOR YOU TO MAKE EYE CONTACT WITH ME.
WHICH MEANS YOU ARE WELL UNDER MY SPELL...
...YOUNG MASTER.

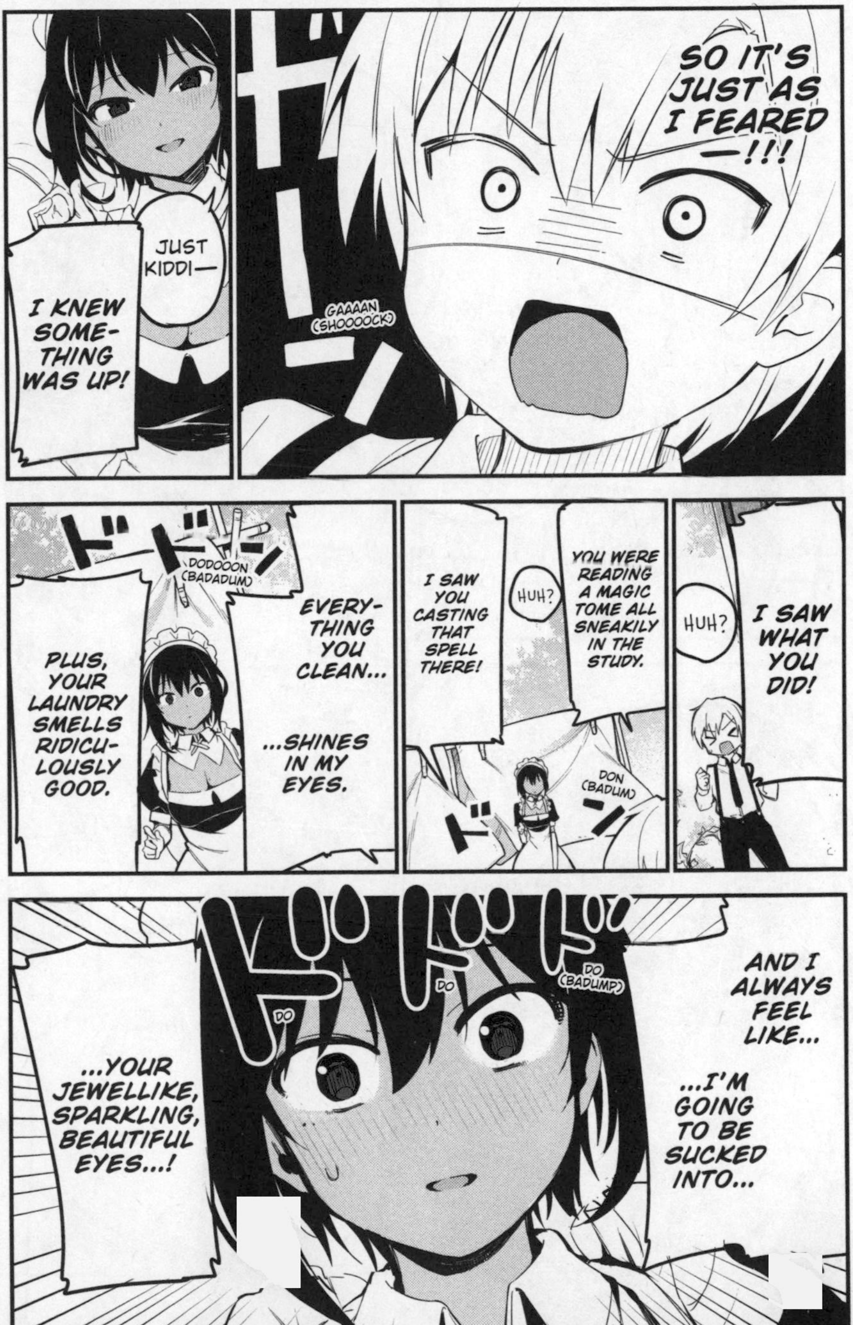
SO IT'S JUST AS I FEARED—!!!
GAAAAN (SHOOOOCK)
JUST KIDDI—
I KNEW SOMETHING WAS UP!
I SAW WHAT YOU DID!
HUH?
YOU WERE READING A MAGIC TOME ALL SNEAKILY IN THE STUDY.
HUH?
I SAW YOU CASTING THAT SPELL THERE!
DON (BADUM)
EVERYTHING YOU CLEAN...
...SHINES IN MY EYES.
PLUS, YOUR LAUNDRY SMELLS RIDICULOUSLY GOOD.
DODOOON (BADADUM)
AND I ALWAYS FEEL LIKE...
...I'M GOING TO BE SUCKED INTO...
DO DO DO (BADUMP)
...YOUR JEWELLIKE, SPARKLING, BEAUTIFUL EYES...!

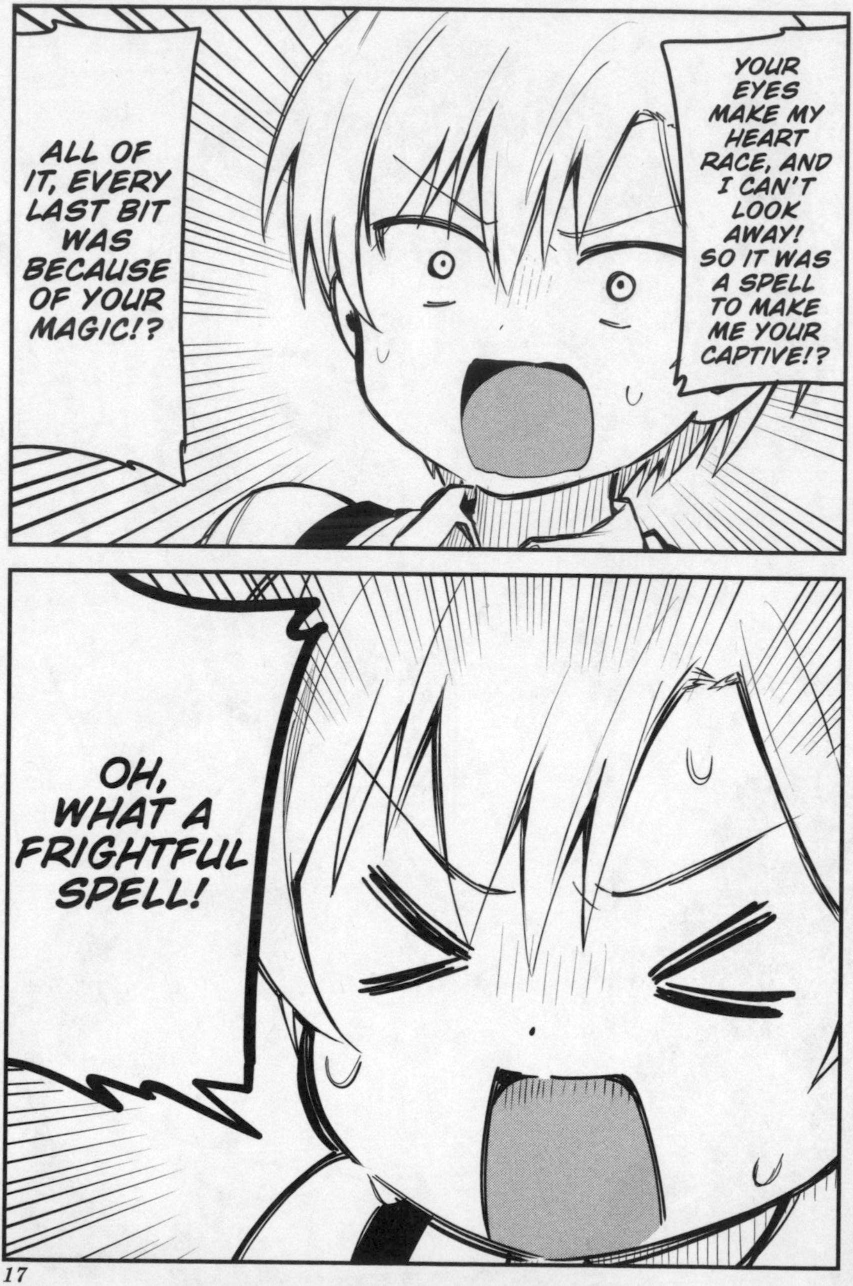
YOUR EYES MAKE MY HEART RACE, AND I CAN'T LOOK AWAY! SO IT WAS A SPELL TO MAKE ME YOUR CAPTIVE!?
ALL OF IT, EVERY LAST BIT WAS BECAUSE OF YOUR MAGIC!?
OH, WHAT A FRIGHTFUL SPELL!

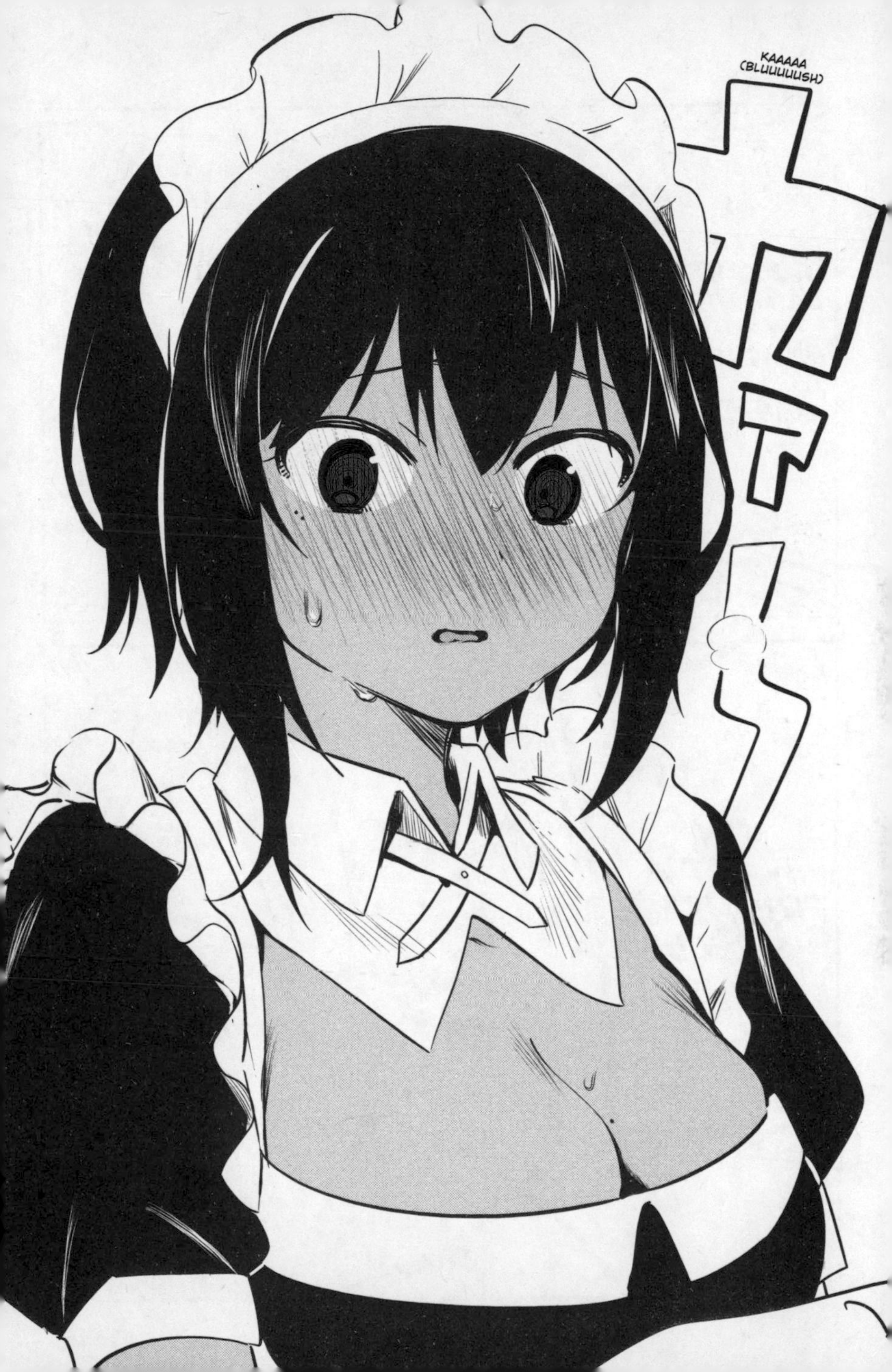
KAAAAA
(BLUUUUUUSH)

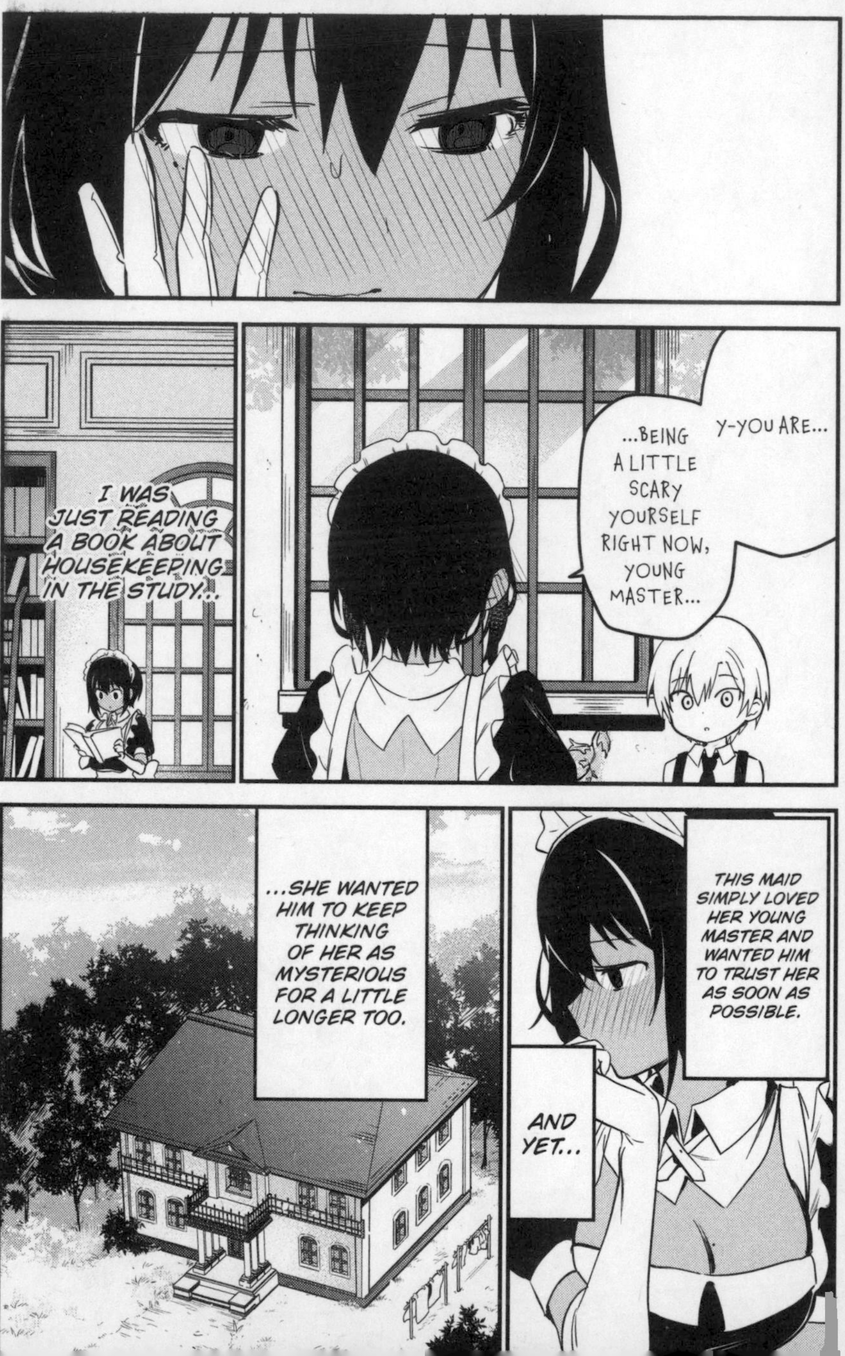
Y-YOU ARE...
...BEING A LITTLE SCARY YOURSELF RIGHT NOW, YOUNG MASTER...
I WAS JUST READING A BOOK ABOUT HOUSEKEEPING IN THE STUDY...
THIS MAID SIMPLY LOVED HER YOUNG MASTER AND WANTED HIM TO TRUST HER AS SOON AS POSSIBLE.
AND YET...
...SHE WANTED HIM TO KEEP THINKING OF HER AS MYSTERIOUS FOR A LITTLE LONGER TOO.

The Maid I Hired Recently Is Mysterious

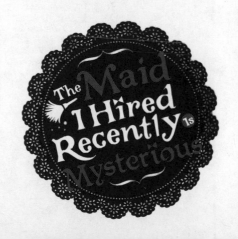

CHAPTER 2

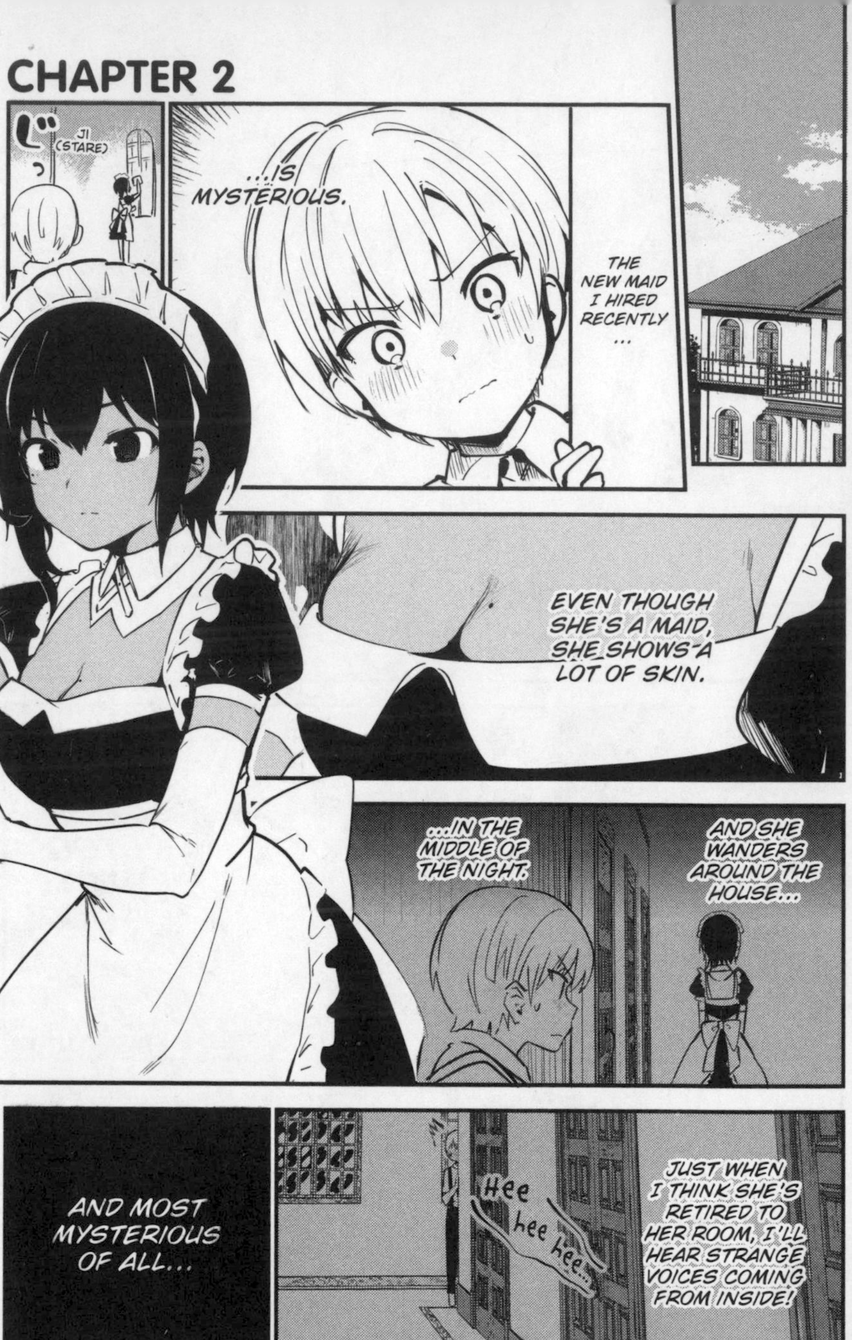
THE NEW MAID I HIRED RECENTLY...
...IS MYSTERIOUS.
じっ
JI (STARE)
EVEN THOUGH SHE'S A MAID, SHE SHOWS A LOT OF SKIN.
AND SHE WANDERS AROUND THE HOUSE...
...IN THE MIDDLE OF THE NIGHT.
JUST WHEN I THINK SHE'S RETIRED TO HER ROOM, I'LL HEAR STRANGE VOICES COMING FROM INSIDE!
Hee hee hee...
AND MOST MYSTERIOUS OF ALL...

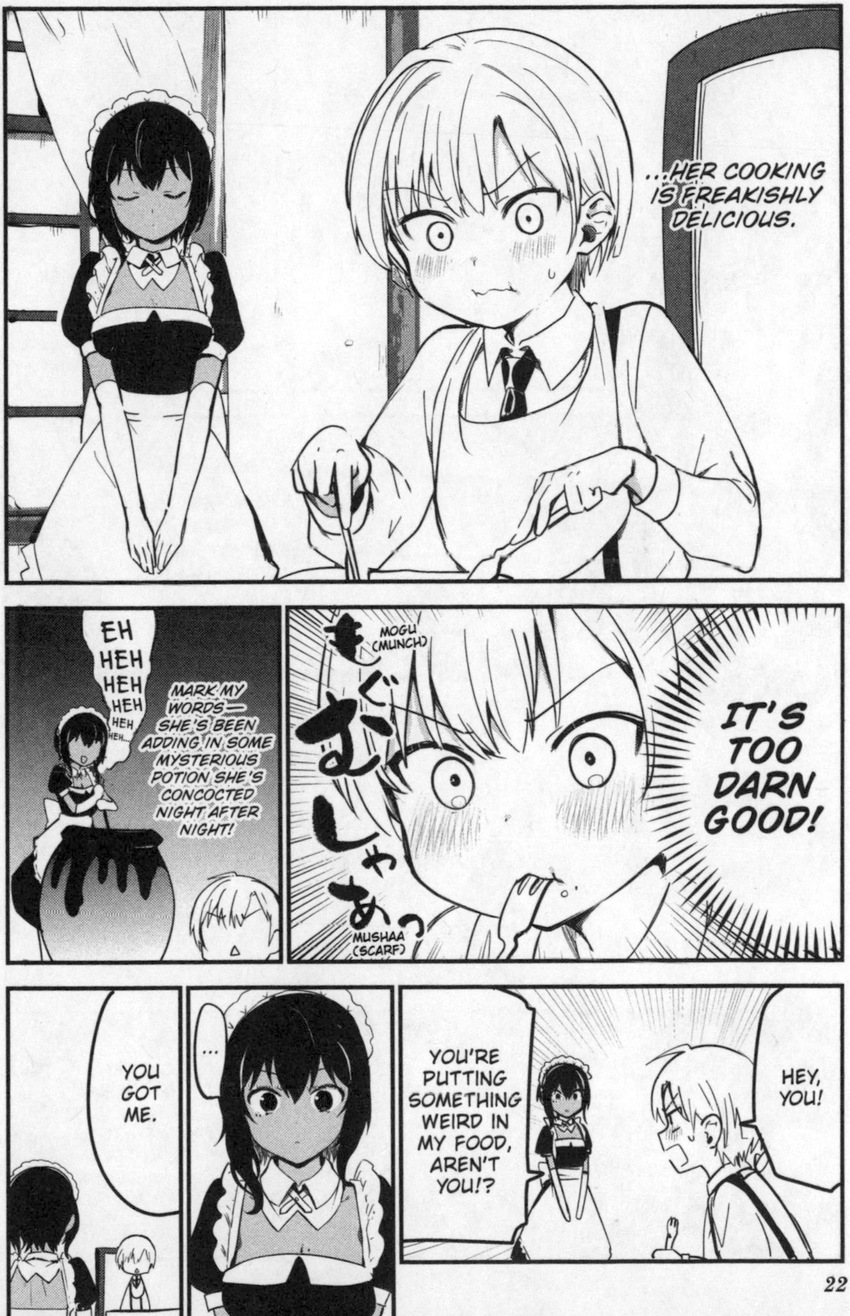
...HER COOKING IS FREAKISHLY DELICIOUS.
もぐ
MOGU (MUNCH)
むしゃあっ
IT'S TOO DARN GOOD!
MUSHAA (SCARF)
EH HEH HEH HEH HEH HEH...
MARK MY WORDS—SHE'S BEEN ADDING IN SOME MYSTERIOUS POTION SHE'S CONCOCTED NIGHT AFTER NIGHT!
HEY, YOU!
YOU'RE PUTTING SOMETHING WEIRD IN MY FOOD, AREN'T YOU!?
...
YOU GOT ME.

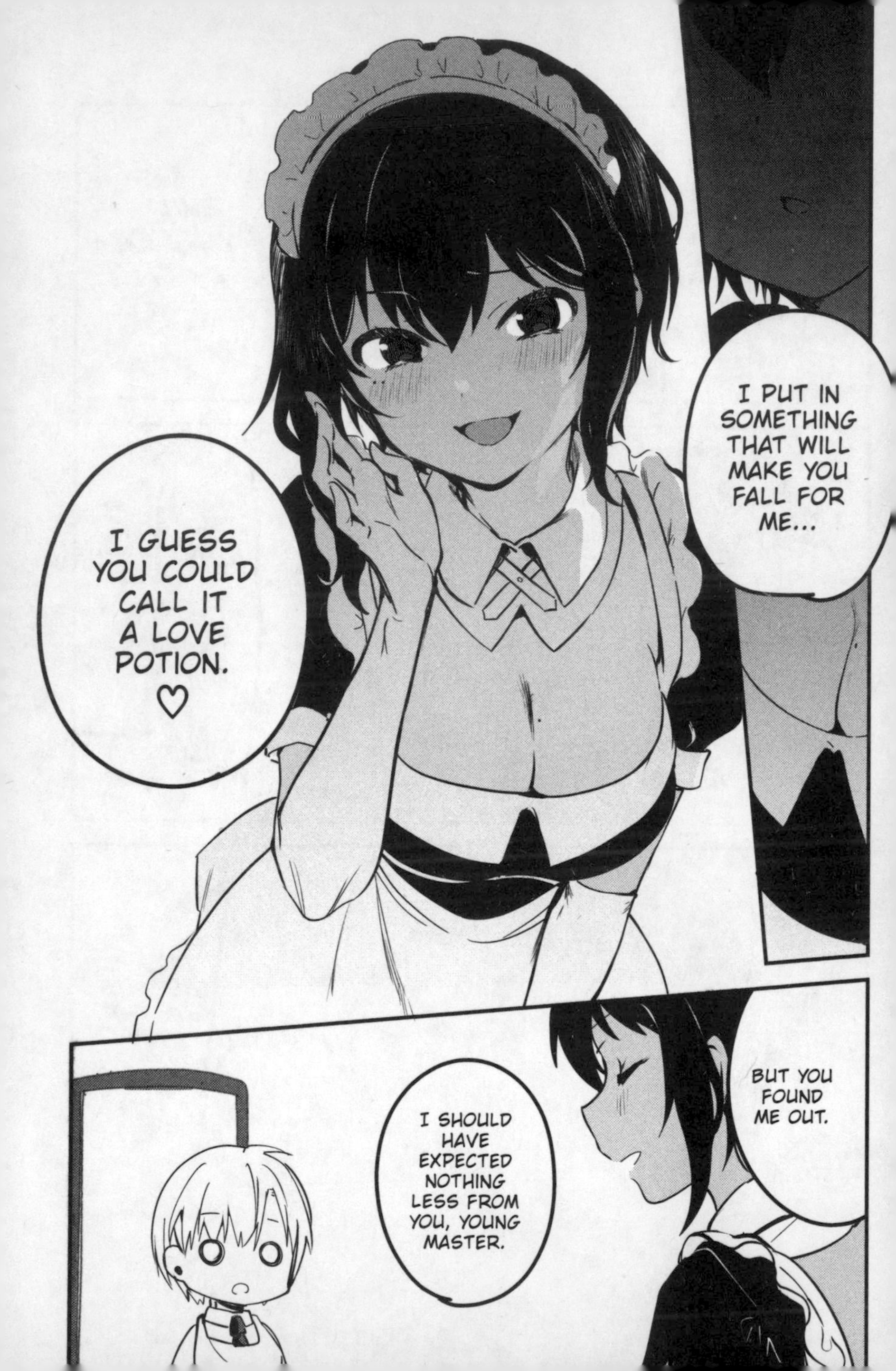
I PUT IN SOMETHING THAT WILL MAKE YOU FALL FOR ME...
I GUESS YOU COULD CALL IT A LOVE POTION. ♡
BUT YOU FOUND ME OUT.
I SHOULD HAVE EXPECTED NOTHING LESS FROM YOU, YOUNG MASTER.

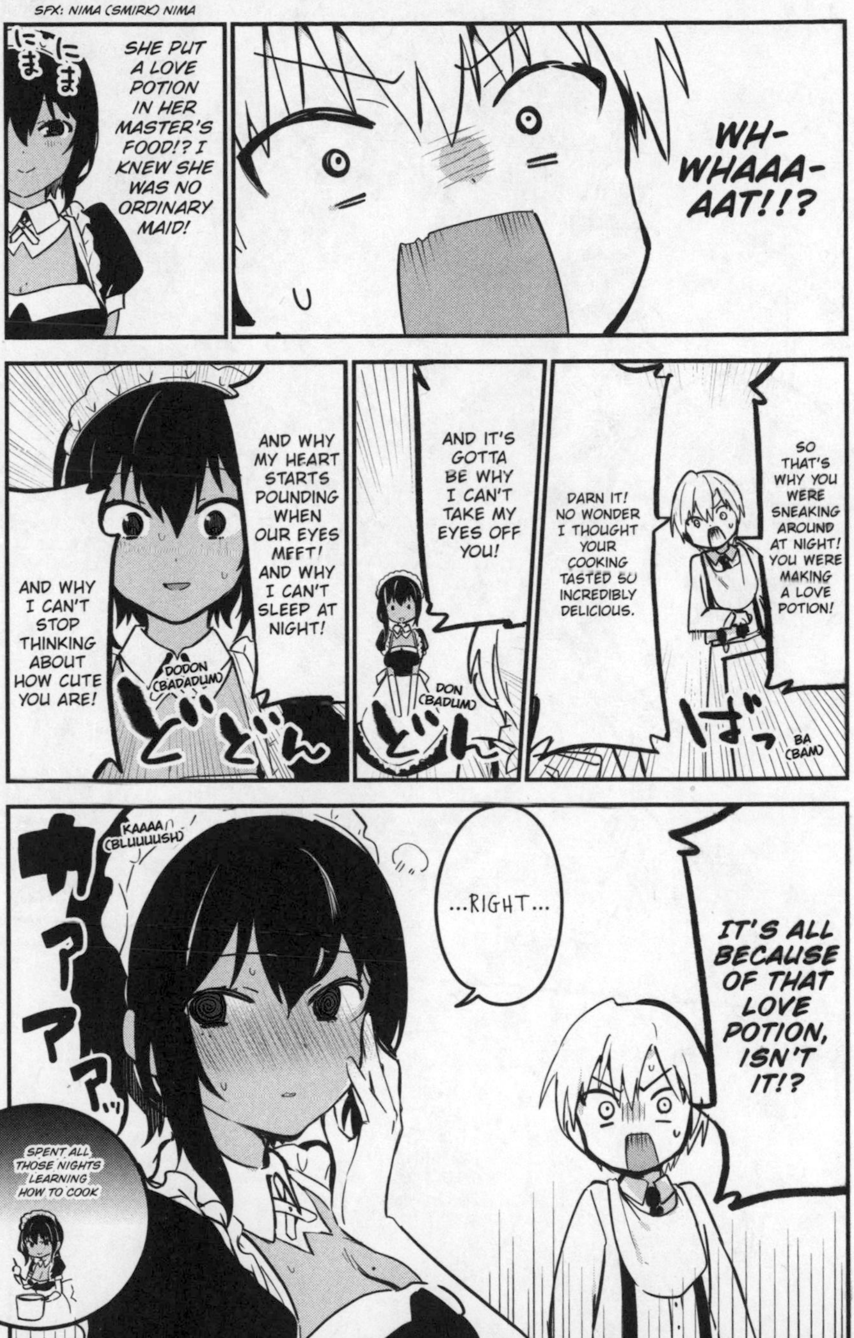
SFX: NIMA (SMIRK) NIMA
WH-WHAAAA-AAT!!?
にまにま
SHE PUT A LOVE POTION IN HER MASTER'S FOOD!? I KNEW SHE WAS NO ORDINARY MAID!
SO THAT'S WHY YOU WERE SNEAKING AROUND AT NIGHT! YOU WERE MAKING A LOVE POTION!
DARN IT! NO WONDER I THOUGHT YOUR COOKING TASTED SO INCREDIBLY DELICIOUS.
ばっ
BA (BAM)
AND IT'S GOTTA BE WHY I CAN'T TAKE MY EYES OFF YOU!
どん
DON (BADUM)
AND WHY MY HEART STARTS POUNDING WHEN OUR EYES MEET! AND WHY I CAN'T SLEEP AT NIGHT!
AND WHY I CAN'T STOP THINKING ABOUT HOW CUTE YOU ARE!
どどん
DODON (BADADUM)
IT'S ALL BECAUSE OF THAT LOVE POTION, ISN'T IT!?
...RIGHT...
カァァァッ
KAAAA (BLUUUUSH)
SPENT ALL THOSE NIGHTS LEARNING HOW TO COOK

CHAPTER 3

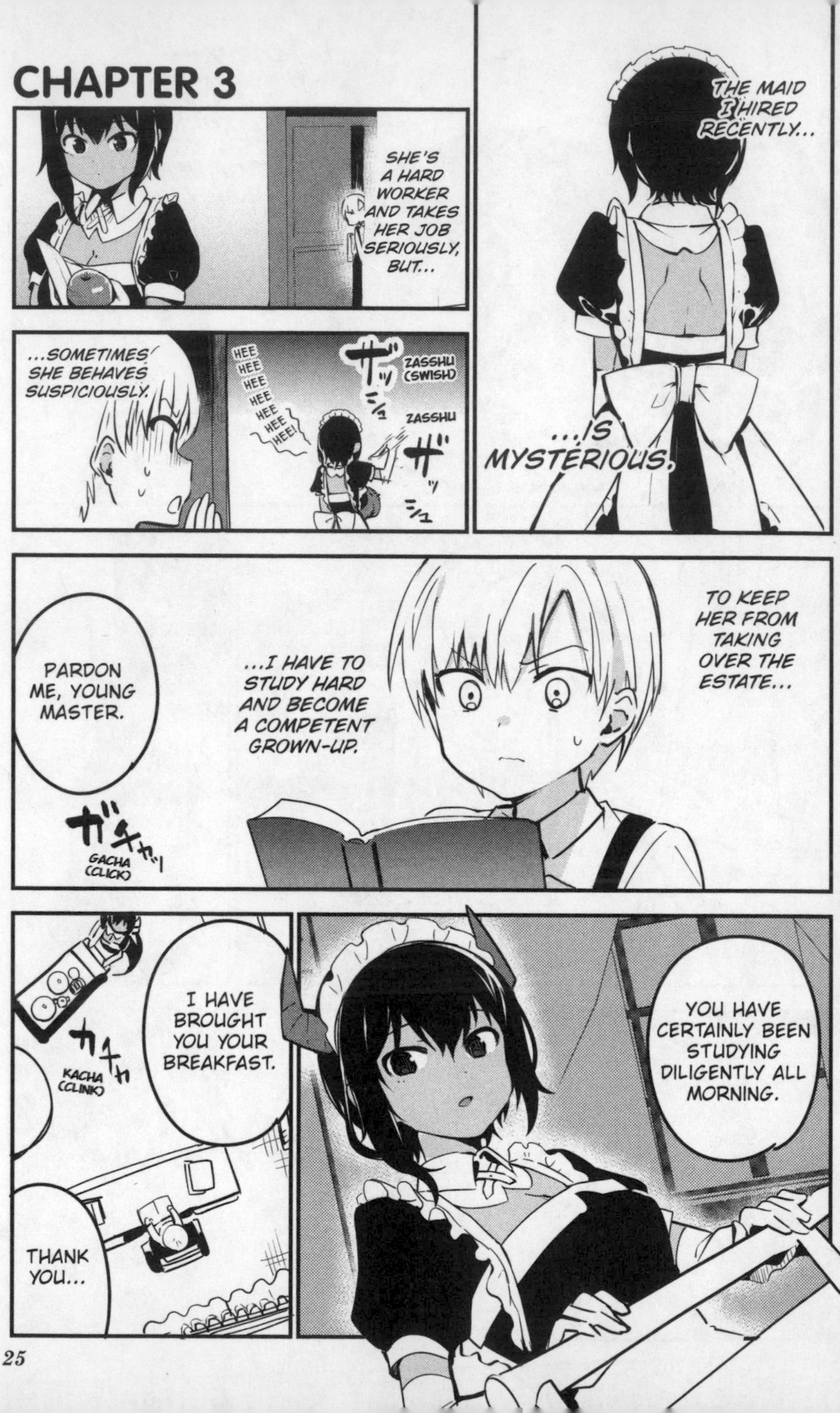
THE MAID I HIRED RECENTLY...
...IS MYSTERIOUS.
SHE'S A HARD WORKER AND TAKES HER JOB SERIOUSLY, BUT...
ZASSHU (SWISH)
ZASSHU
HEE HEE HEE HEE HEE HEE HEE!
...SOMETIMES SHE BEHAVES SUSPICIOUSLY.
TO KEEP HER FROM TAKING OVER THE ESTATE...
...I HAVE TO STUDY HARD AND BECOME A COMPETENT GROWN-UP.
PARDON ME, YOUNG MASTER.
GACHA (CLICK)
YOU HAVE CERTAINLY BEEN STUDYING DILIGENTLY ALL MORNING.
I HAVE BROUGHT YOU YOUR BREAKFAST.
KACHA (CLINK)
THANK YOU...

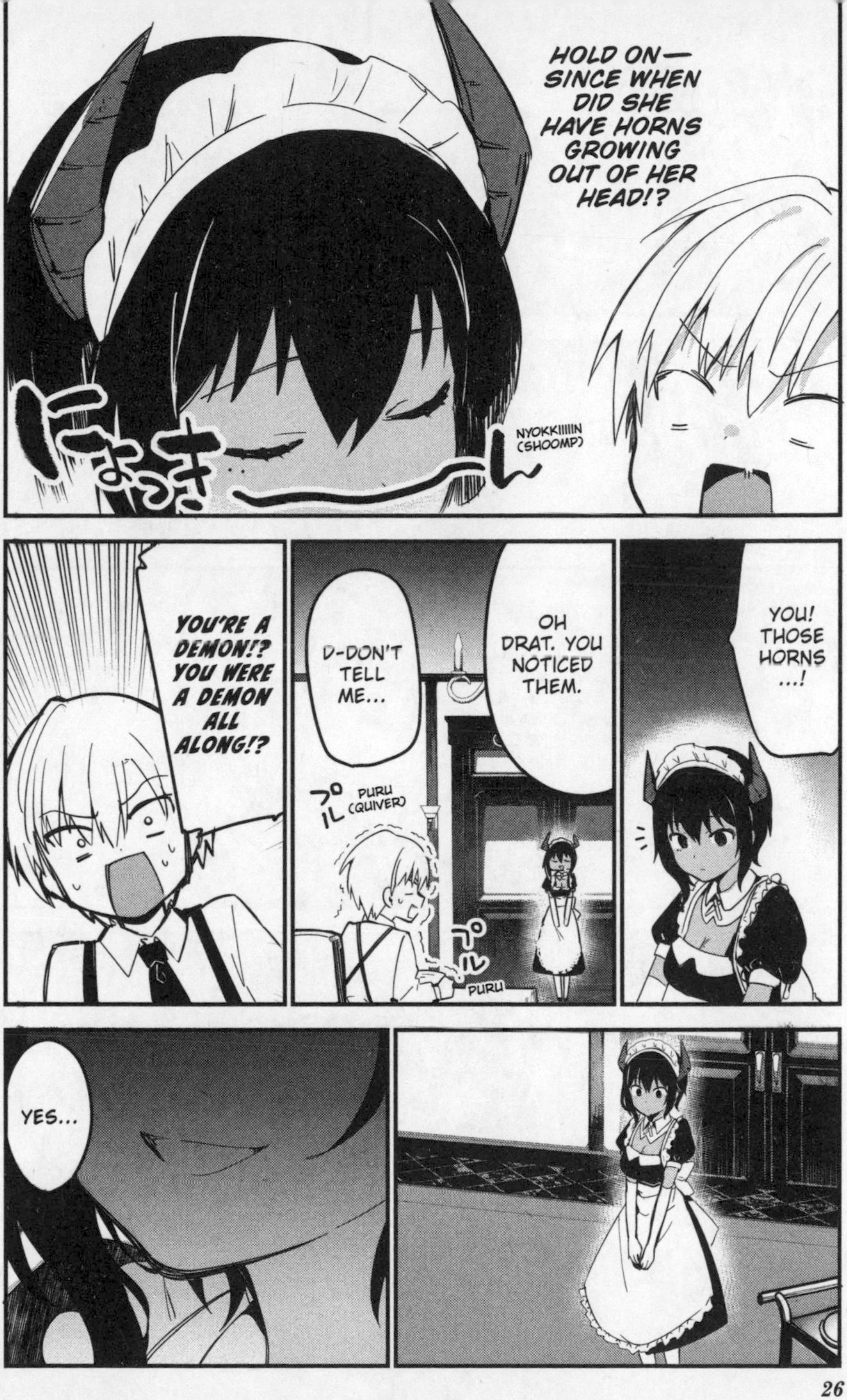
HOLD ON— SINCE WHEN DID SHE HAVE HORNS GROWING OUT OF HER HEAD!?
NYOKKIIIIIN (SHOOMP)
YOU! THOSE HORNS ...!
OH DRAT. YOU NOTICED THEM.
D-DON'T TELL ME...
プル
PURU (QUIVER)
プル
PURU
YOU'RE A DEMON!? YOU WERE A DEMON ALL ALONG!?
YES...

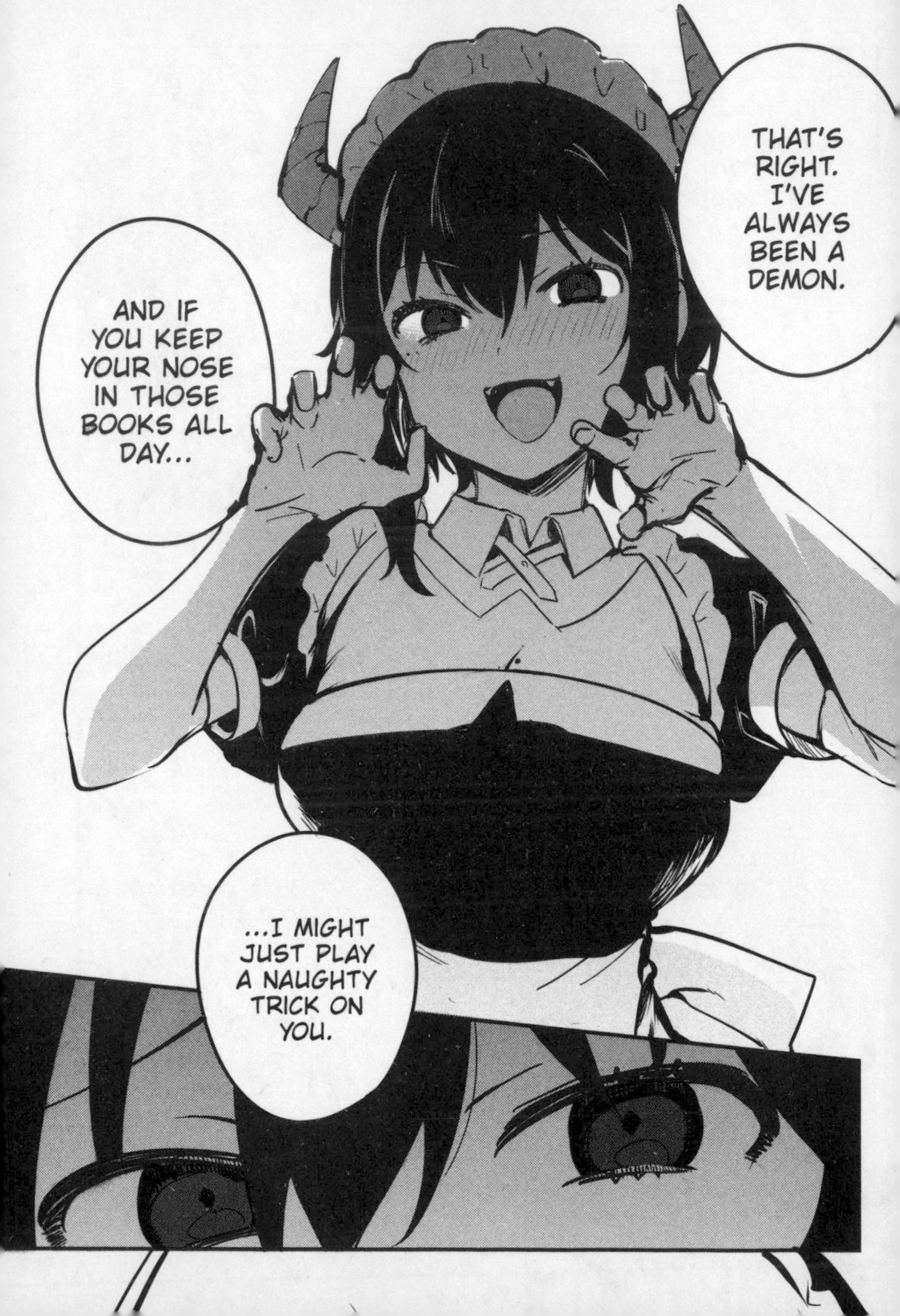
THAT'S RIGHT. I'VE ALWAYS BEEN A DEMON.
AND IF YOU KEEP YOUR NOSE IN THOSE BOOKS ALL DAY...
...I MIGHT JUST PLAY A NAUGHTY TRICK ON YOU.

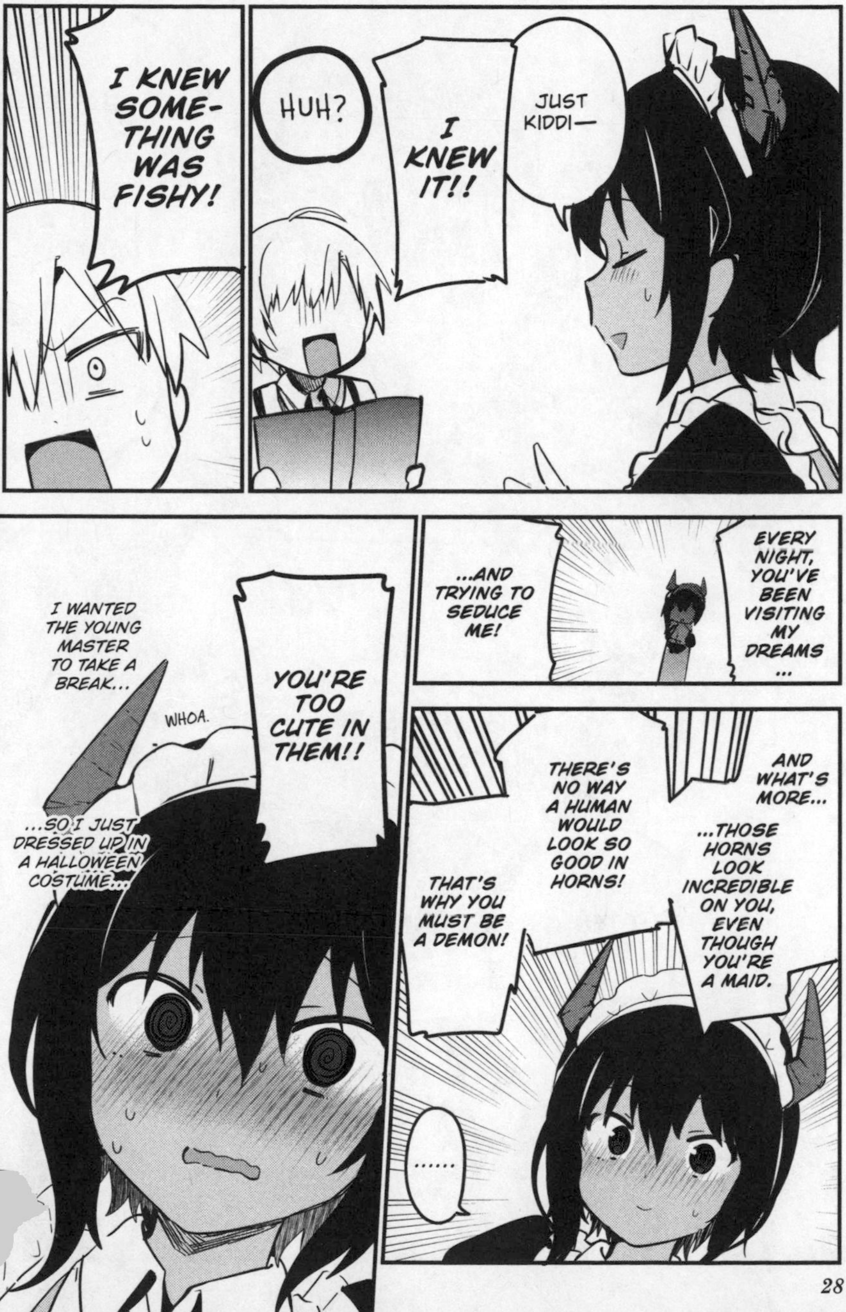
JUST KIDDI—
I KNEW IT!!
HUH?
I KNEW SOME-THING WAS FISHY!
EVERY NIGHT, YOU'VE BEEN VISITING MY DREAMS...
...AND TRYING TO SEDUCE ME!
AND WHAT'S MORE...
...THOSE HORNS LOOK INCREDIBLE ON YOU, EVEN THOUGH YOU'RE A MAID.
THERE'S NO WAY A HUMAN WOULD LOOK SO GOOD IN HORNS!
THAT'S WHY YOU MUST BE A DEMON!
......
YOU'RE TOO CUTE IN THEM!!
WHOA.
I WANTED THE YOUNG MASTER TO TAKE A BREAK...
...SO I JUST DRESSED UP IN A HALLOWEEN COSTUME...

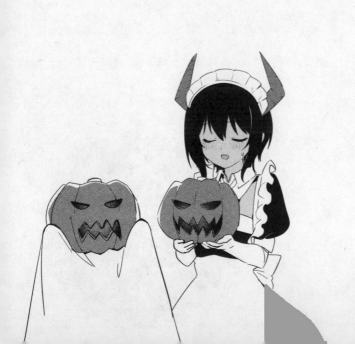

The Maid I Hired Recently Is Mysterious

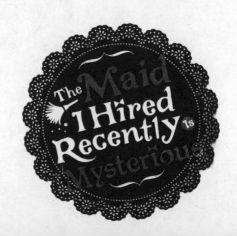

CHAPTER 4

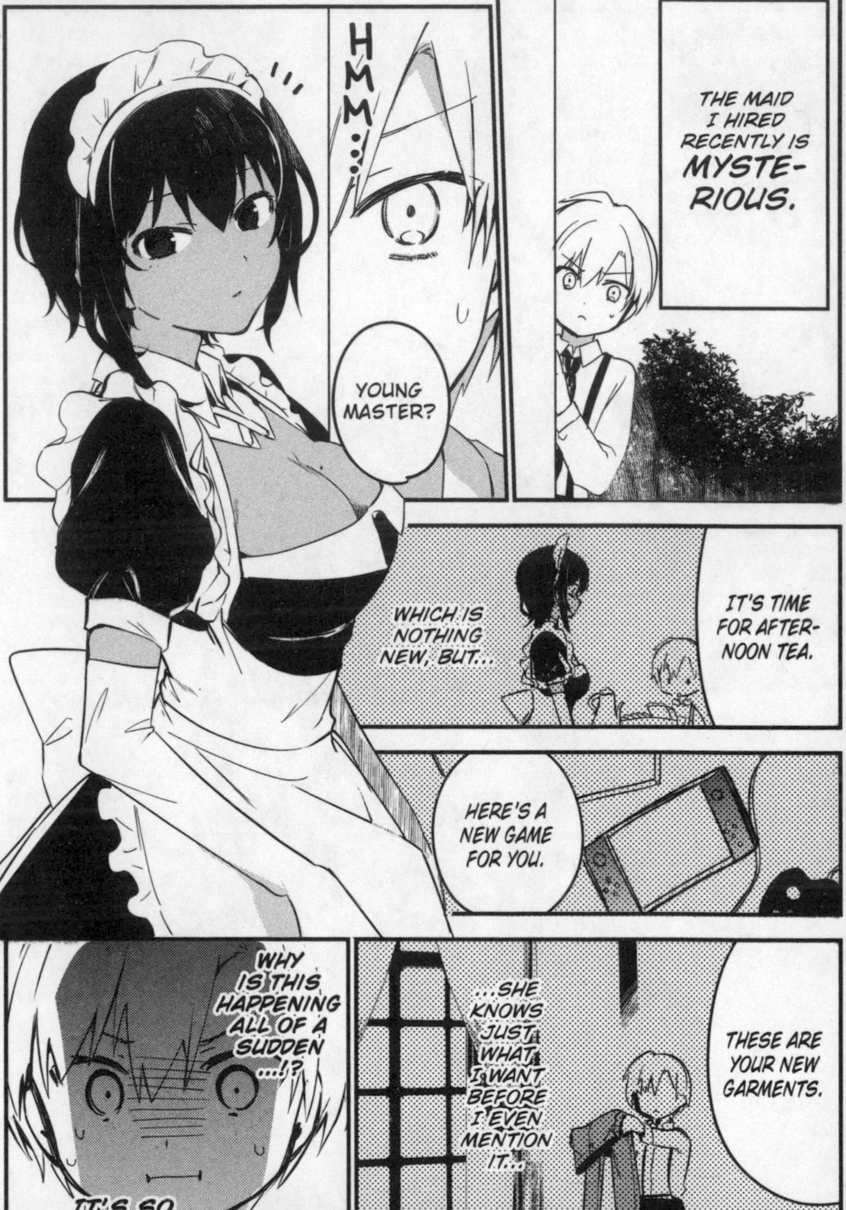
THE MAID I HIRED RECENTLY IS MYSTERIOUS.
HMM...!
IT'S TIME FOR AFTERNOON TEA.
WHICH IS NOTHING NEW, BUT...
HERE'S A NEW GAME FOR YOU.
YOUNG MASTER?
THESE ARE YOUR NEW GARMENTS.
...SHE KNOWS JUST WHAT I WANT BEFORE I EVEN MENTION IT...
WHY IS THIS HAPPENING ALL OF A SUDDEN ...!?
IT'S SO MYSTERIOUS...!!

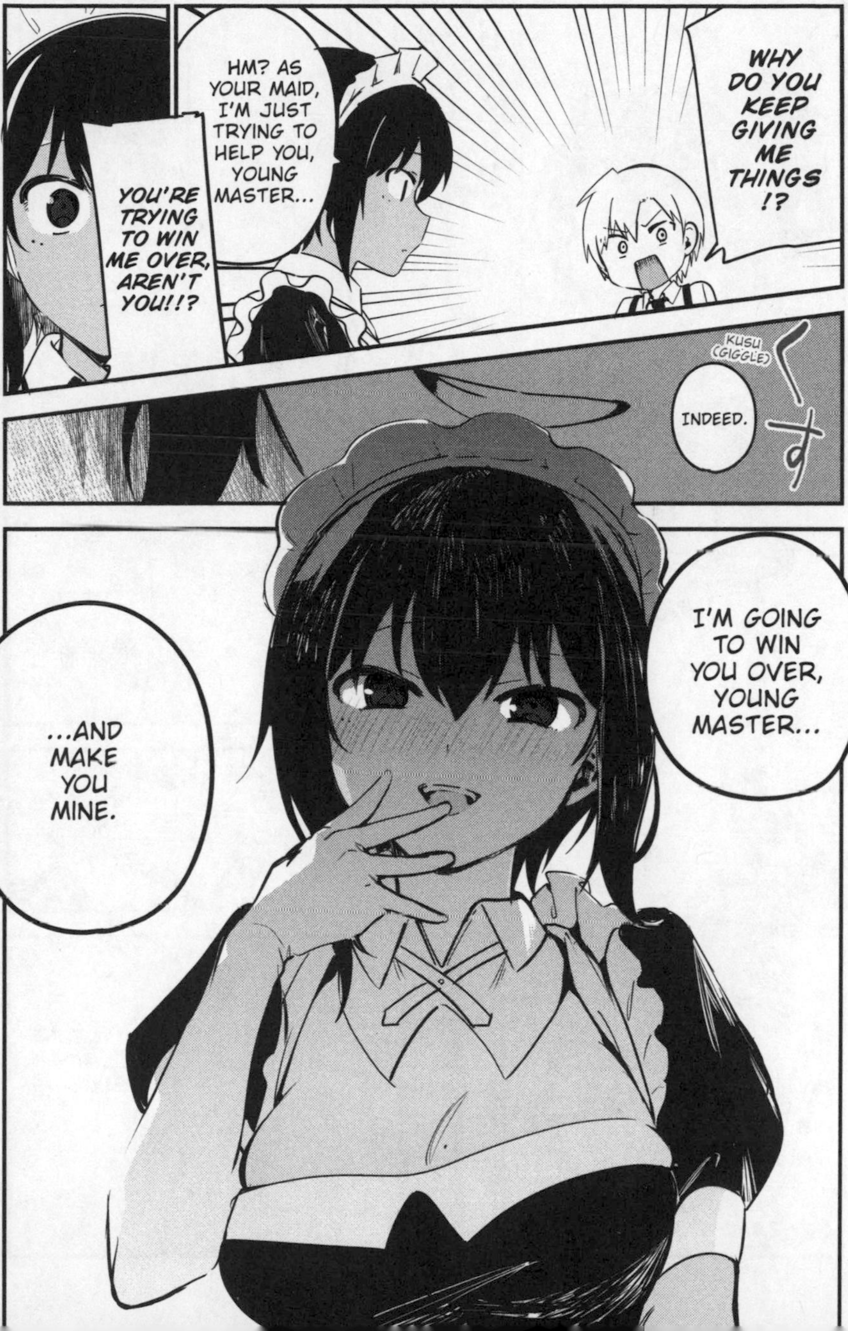
WHY DO YOU KEEP GIVING ME THINGS!?
HM? AS YOUR MAID, I'M JUST TRYING TO HELP YOU, YOUNG MASTER...
YOU'RE TRYING TO WIN ME OVER, AREN'T YOU!!?
くす
KUSU (GIGGLE)
INDEED.
I'M GOING TO WIN YOU OVER, YOUNG MASTER...
...AND MAKE YOU MINE.

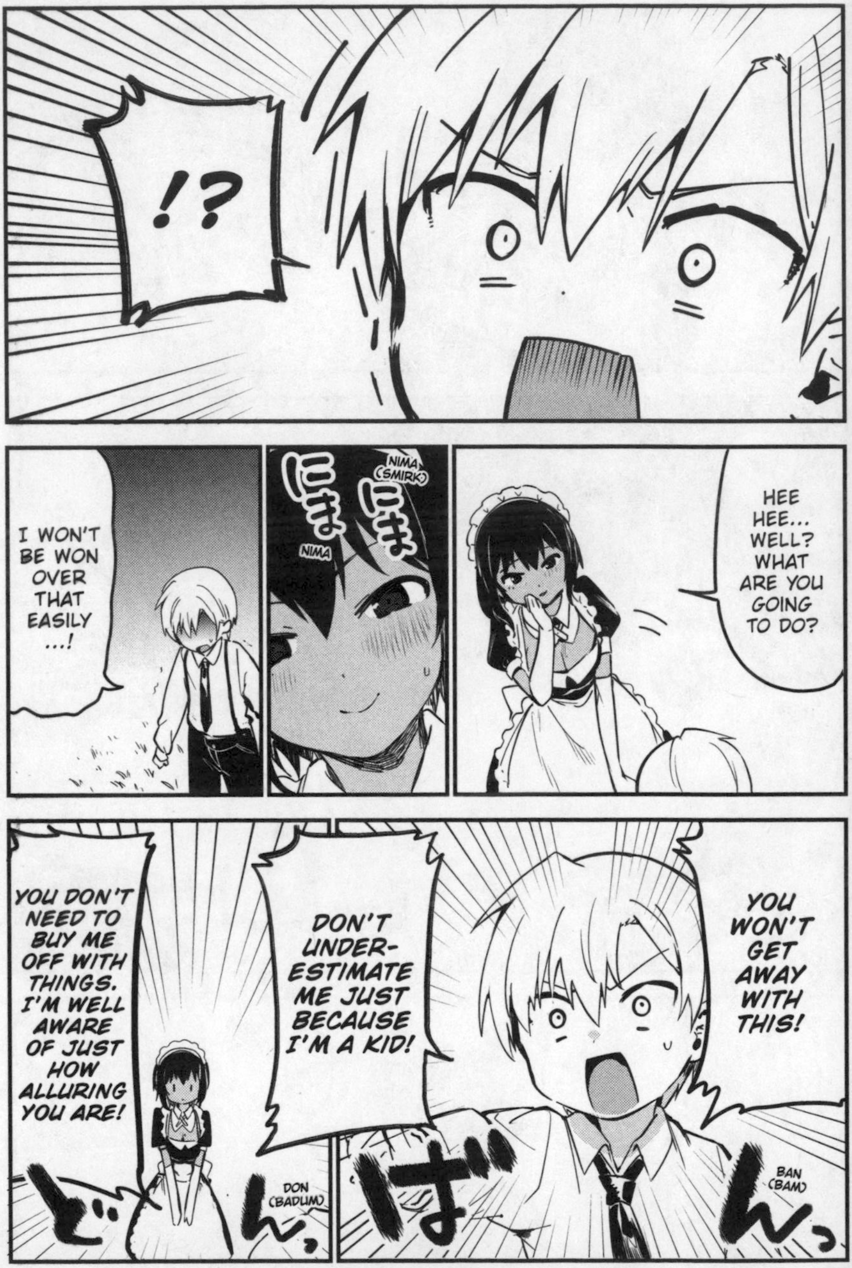
!?
HEE HEE... WELL? WHAT ARE YOU GOING TO DO?
にまにま
NIMA (SMIRK)
NIMA
I WON'T BE WON OVER THAT EASILY...!
YOU WON'T GET AWAY WITH THIS!
DON'T UNDER-ESTIMATE ME JUST BECAUSE I'M A KID!
ばんっ
BAN (BAM)
YOU DON'T NEED TO BUY ME OFF WITH THINGS. I'M WELL AWARE OF JUST HOW ALLURING YOU ARE!
どんっ
DON (BADUM)

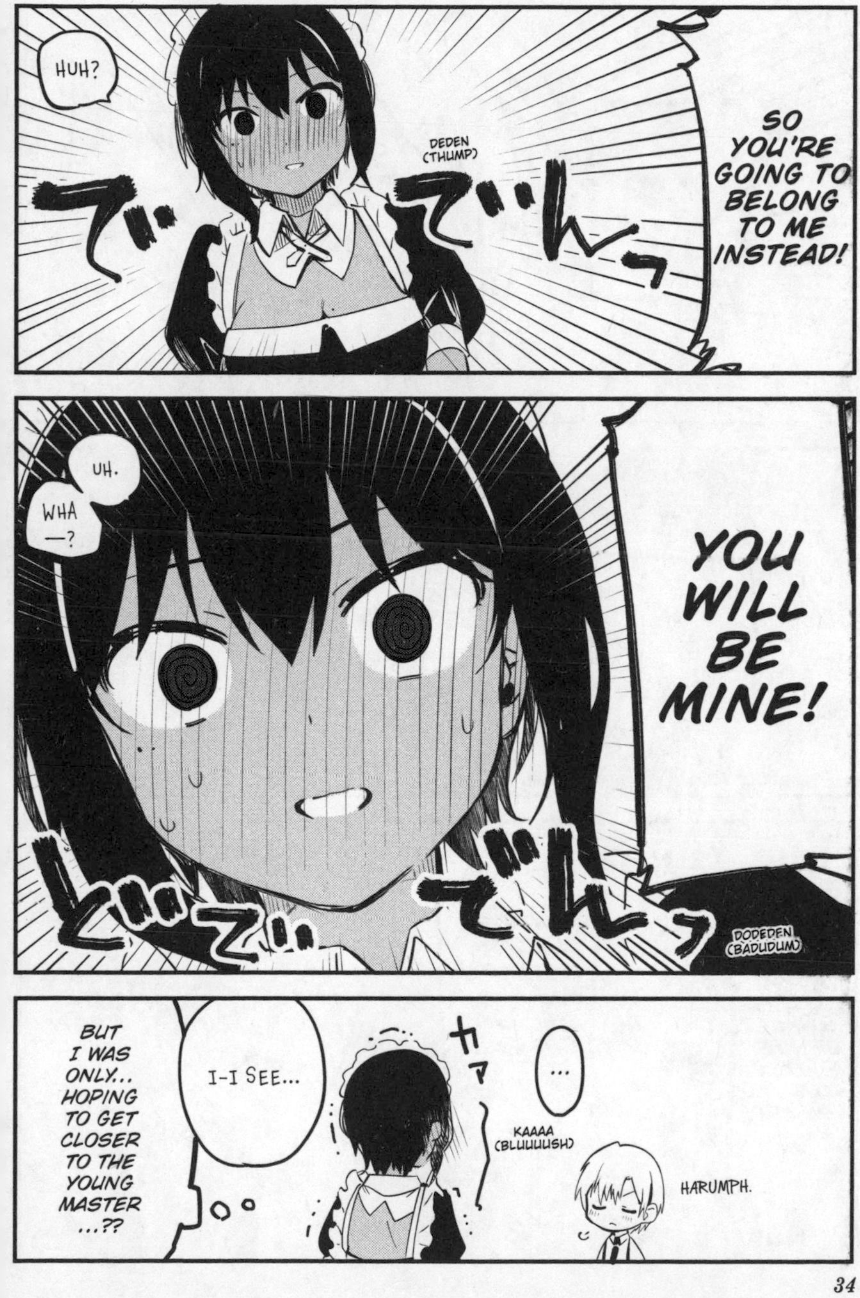
SO YOU'RE GOING TO BELONG TO ME INSTEAD!
DEDEN (THUMP)
HUH?
YOU WILL BE MINE!
UH.
WHA—?
DODEDEN (BADUDUM)
...
HARUMPH.
KAAAA (BLUUUUSH)
I-I SEE...
BUT I WAS ONLY... HOPING TO GET CLOSER TO THE YOUNG MASTER ...??

CHAPTER 5

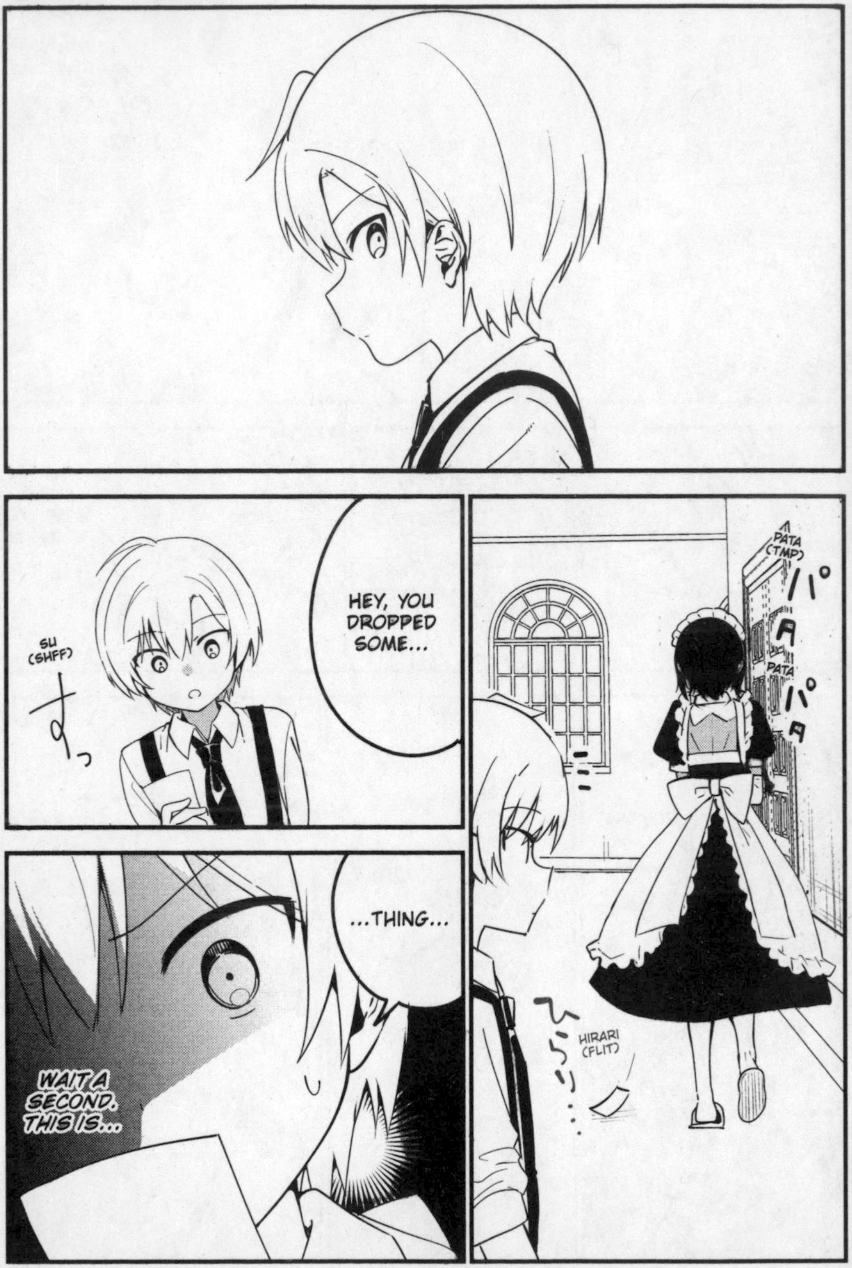
PATA (TMP)
パタ
PATA
パタ
ひらり…
HIRARI (FLIT)
HEY, YOU DROPPED SOME...
SU (SHFF)
すっ
...THING...
WAIT A SECOND. THIS IS...

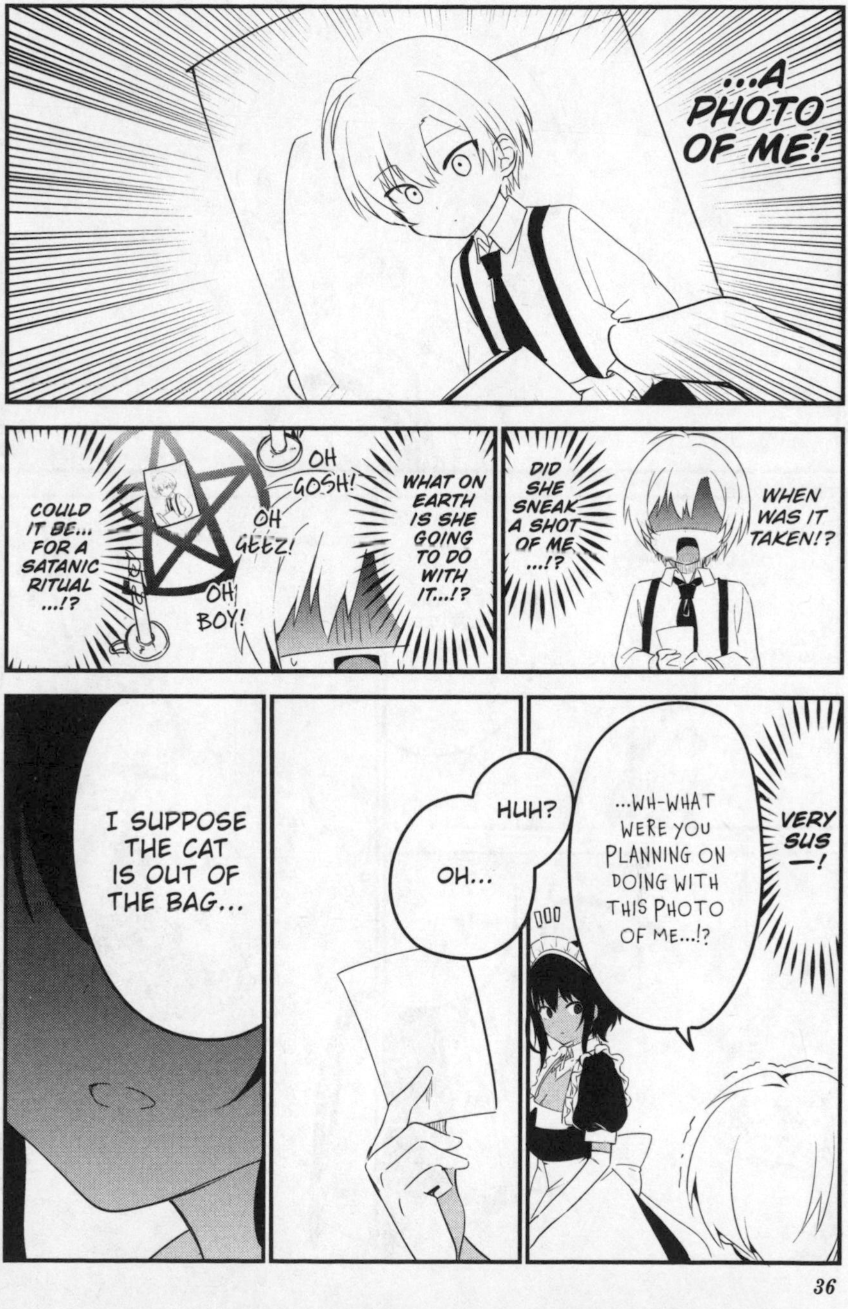
...A PHOTO OF ME!
WHEN WAS IT TAKEN!?
DID SHE SNEAK A SHOT OF ME ...!?
WHAT ON EARTH IS SHE GOING TO DO WITH IT...!?
OH GOSH!
OH GEEZ!
OH BOY!
COULD IT BE... FOR A SATANIC RITUAL ...!?
VERY SUS —!
...WH-WHAT WERE YOU PLANNING ON DOING WITH THIS PHOTO OF ME...!?
HUH?
OH...
I SUPPOSE THE CAT IS OUT OF THE BAG...

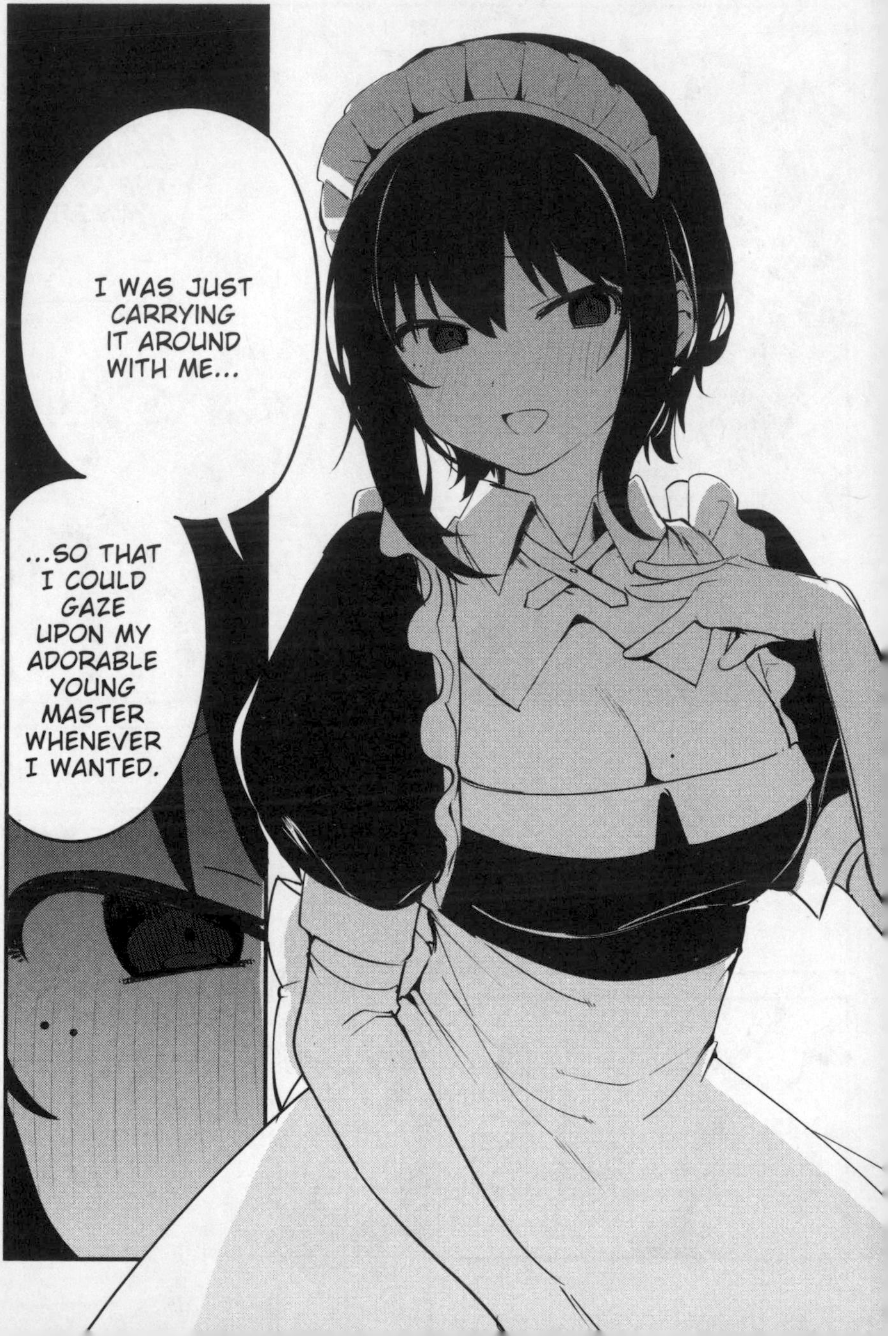
I WAS JUST CARRYING IT AROUND WITH ME...
...SO THAT I COULD GAZE UPON MY ADORABLE YOUNG MASTER WHENEVER I WANTED.

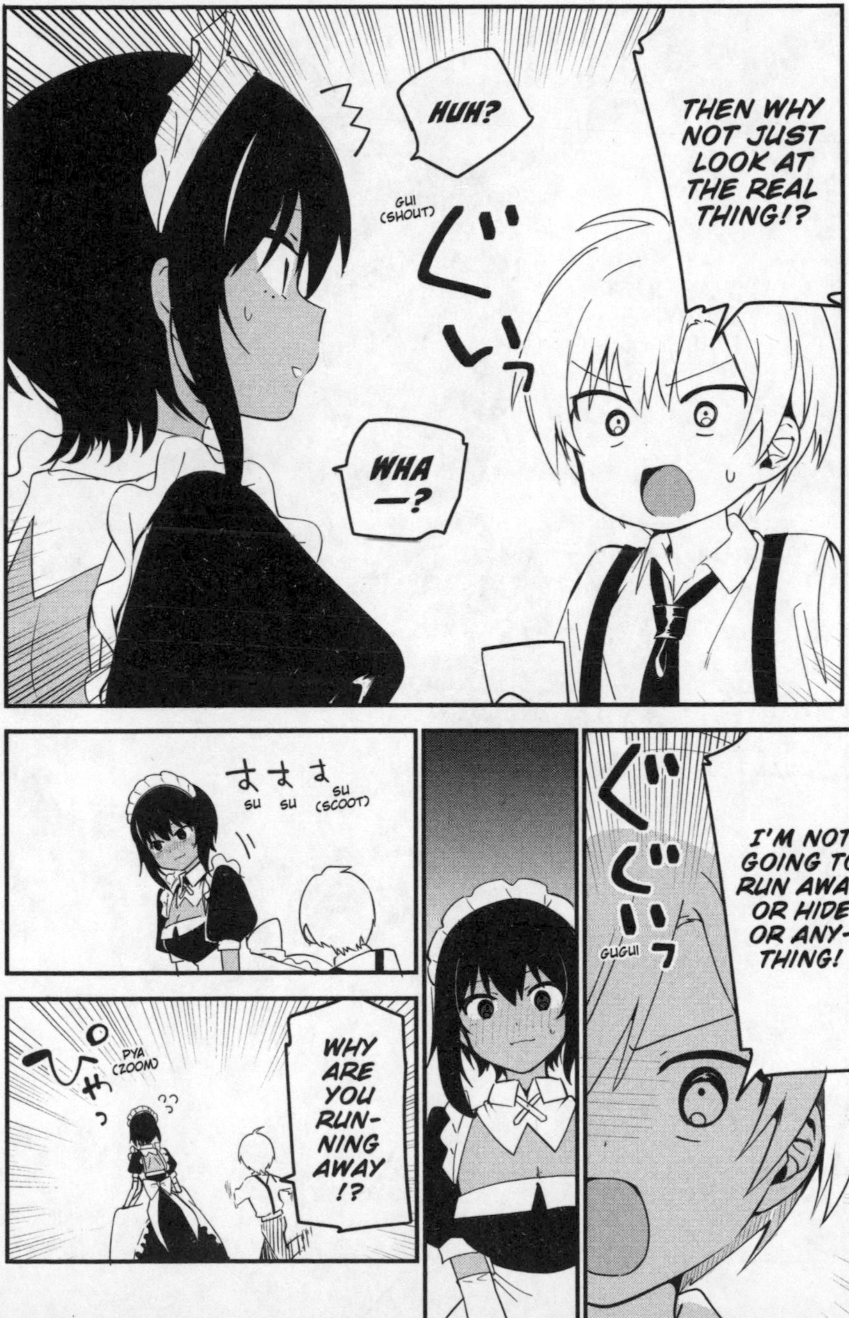
THEN WHY NOT JUST LOOK AT THE REAL THING!?
HUH?
ぐいっ
GUI (SHOUT)
WHA—?
I'M NOT GOING TO RUN AWAY OR HIDE OR ANYTHING!
ぐぐいっ
GUGUI
すすす
SU SU SU (SCOOT)
WHY ARE YOU RUN-NING AWAY!?
ぴゃっ
PYA (ZOOM)

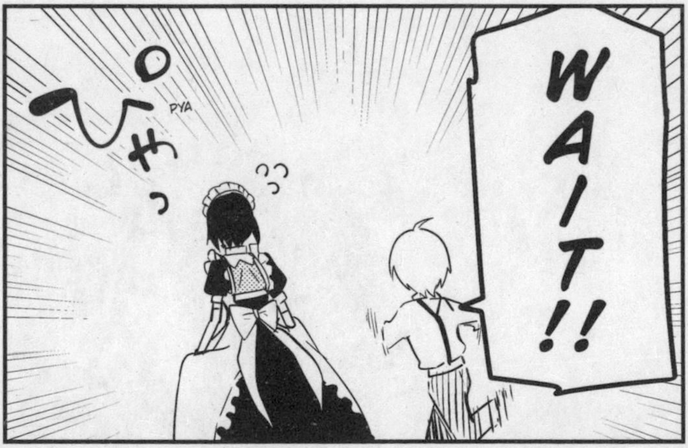
WAIT!!
ぴゃっ
PYA

The Maid I Hired Recently Is Mysterious

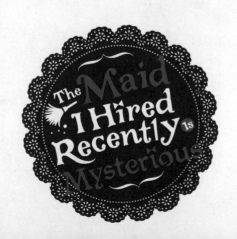

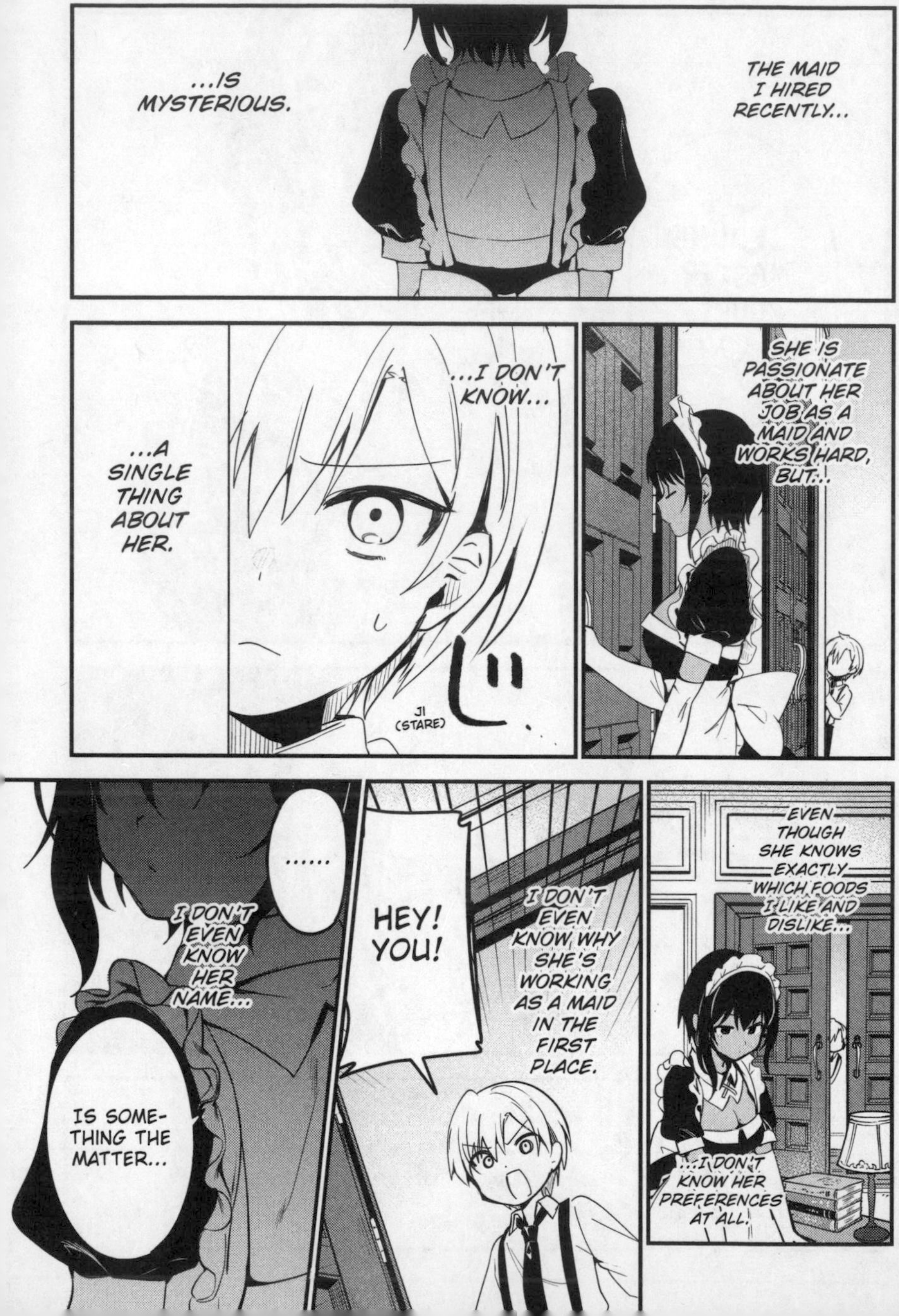
THE MAID I HIRED RECENTLY...
...IS MYSTERIOUS.
SHE IS PASSIONATE ABOUT HER JOB AS A MAID AND WORKS HARD, BUT...
...I DON'T KNOW...
...A SINGLE THING ABOUT HER.
JI (STARE)
EVEN THOUGH SHE KNOWS EXACTLY WHICH FOODS I LIKE AND DISLIKE...
...I DON'T KNOW HER PREFERENCES AT ALL.
I DON'T EVEN KNOW WHY SHE'S WORKING AS A MAID IN THE FIRST PLACE.
HEY! YOU!
......
I DON'T EVEN KNOW HER NAME...
IS SOME-THING THE MATTER...

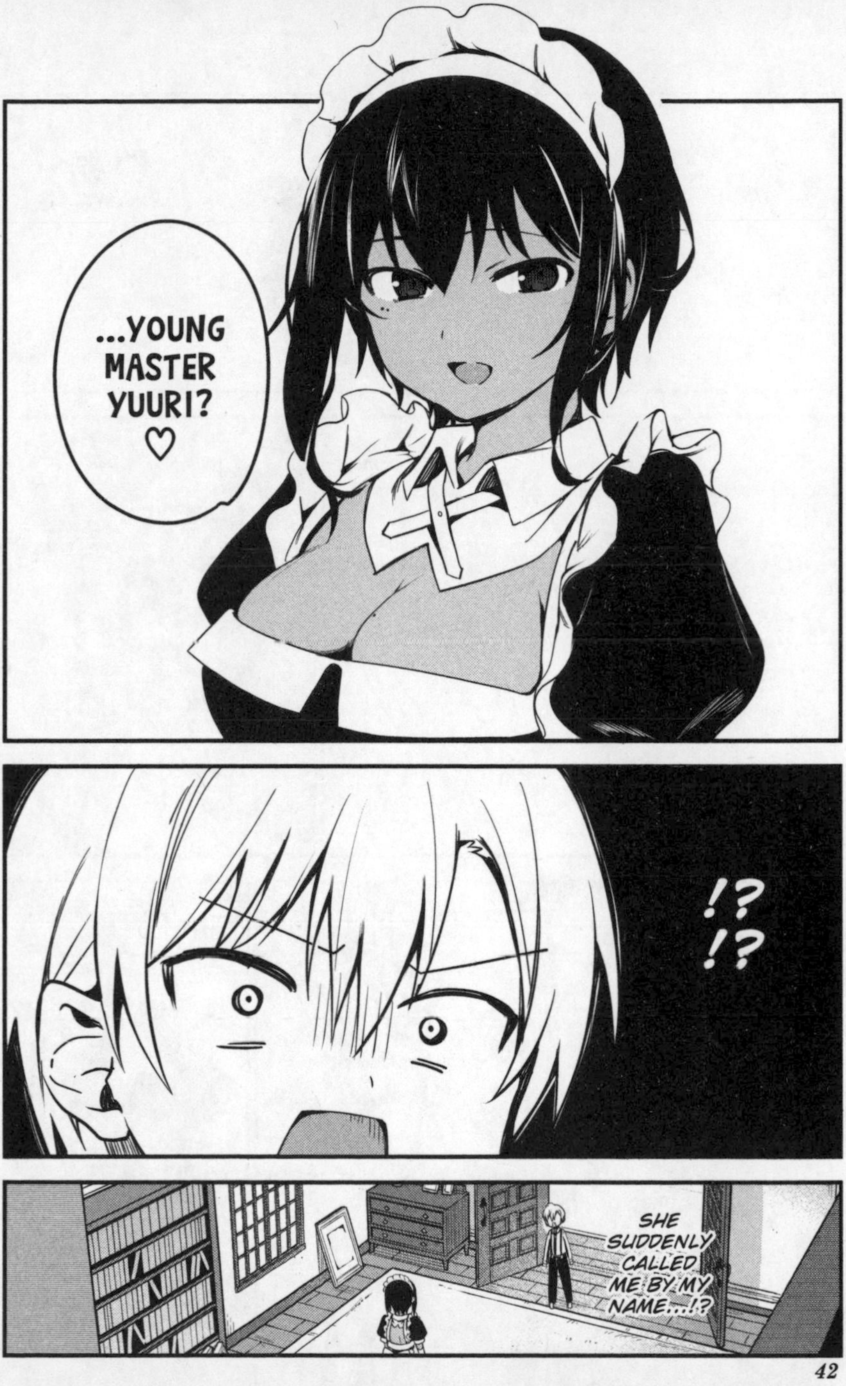
...YOUNG MASTER YUURI? ♡
!? !?
SHE SUDDENLY CALLED ME BY MY NAME...!?

CHAPTER 6

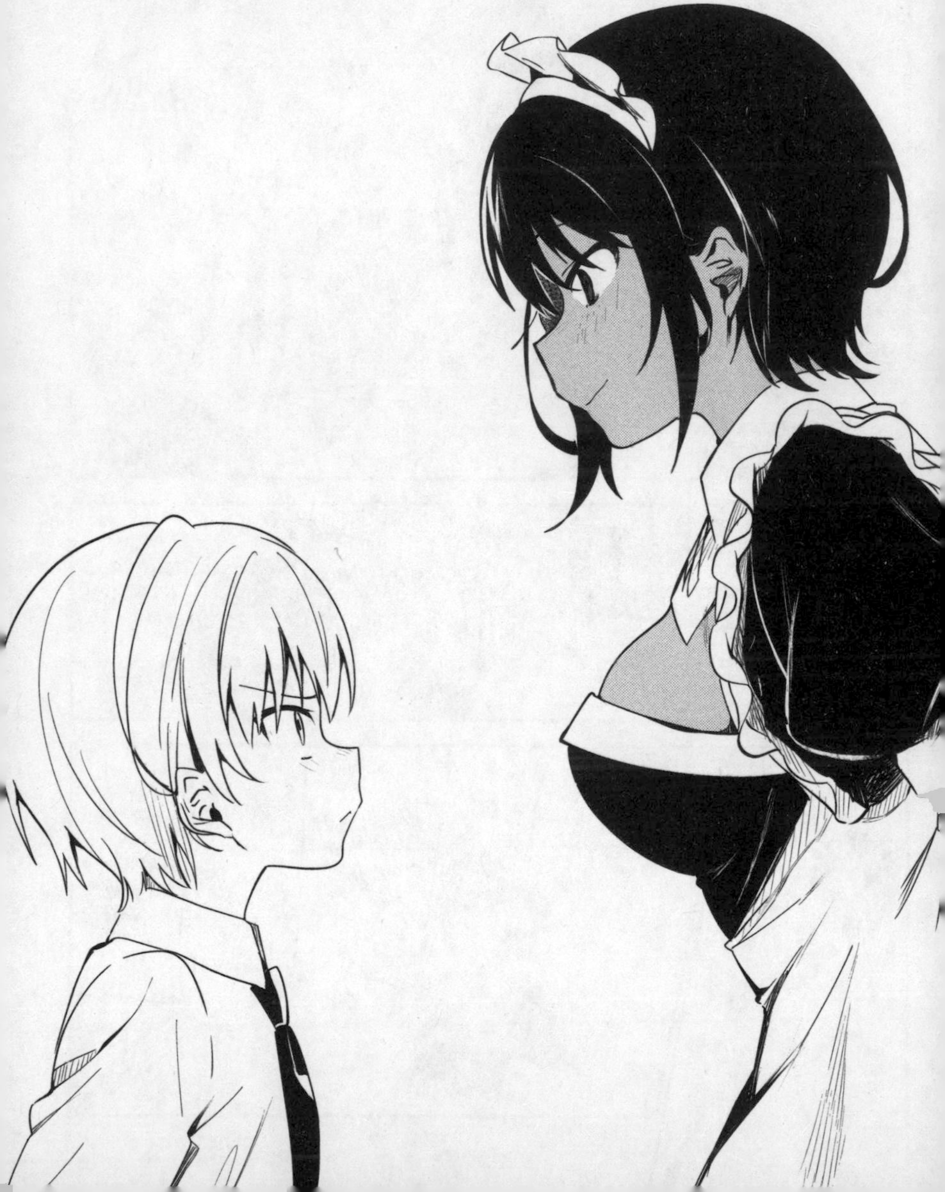

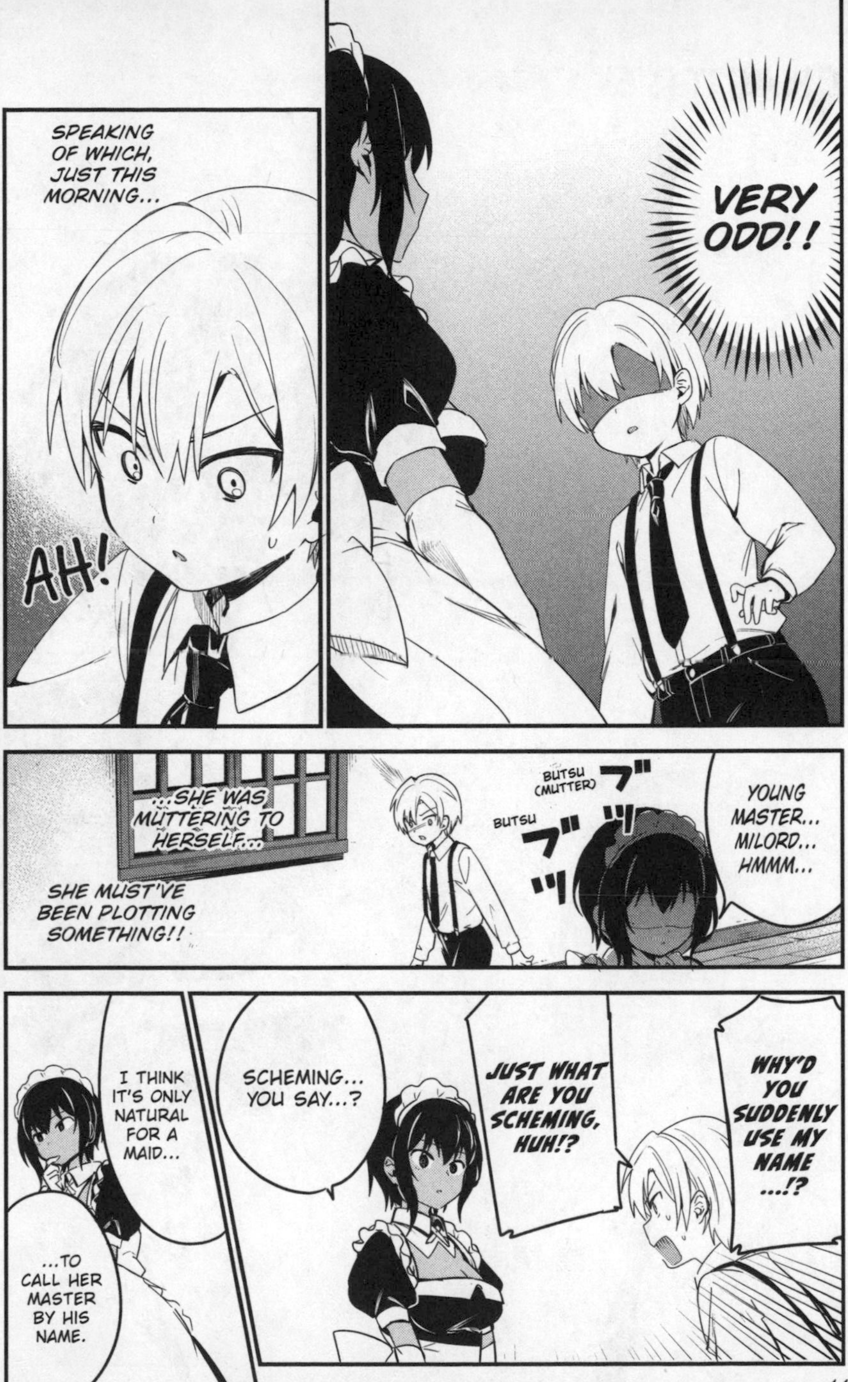
VERY ODD!!
SPEAKING OF WHICH, JUST THIS MORNING...
AH!
YOUNG MASTER... MILORD... HMMM...
BUTSU (MUTTER)
ブツ
BUTSU
ブツ
...SHE WAS MUTTERING TO HERSELF...
SHE MUST'VE BEEN PLOTTING SOMETHING!!
WHY'D YOU SUDDENLY USE MY NAME ...!?
JUST WHAT ARE YOU SCHEMING, HUH!?
SCHEMING... YOU SAY...?
I THINK IT'S ONLY NATURAL FOR A MAID...
...TO CALL HER MASTER BY HIS NAME.

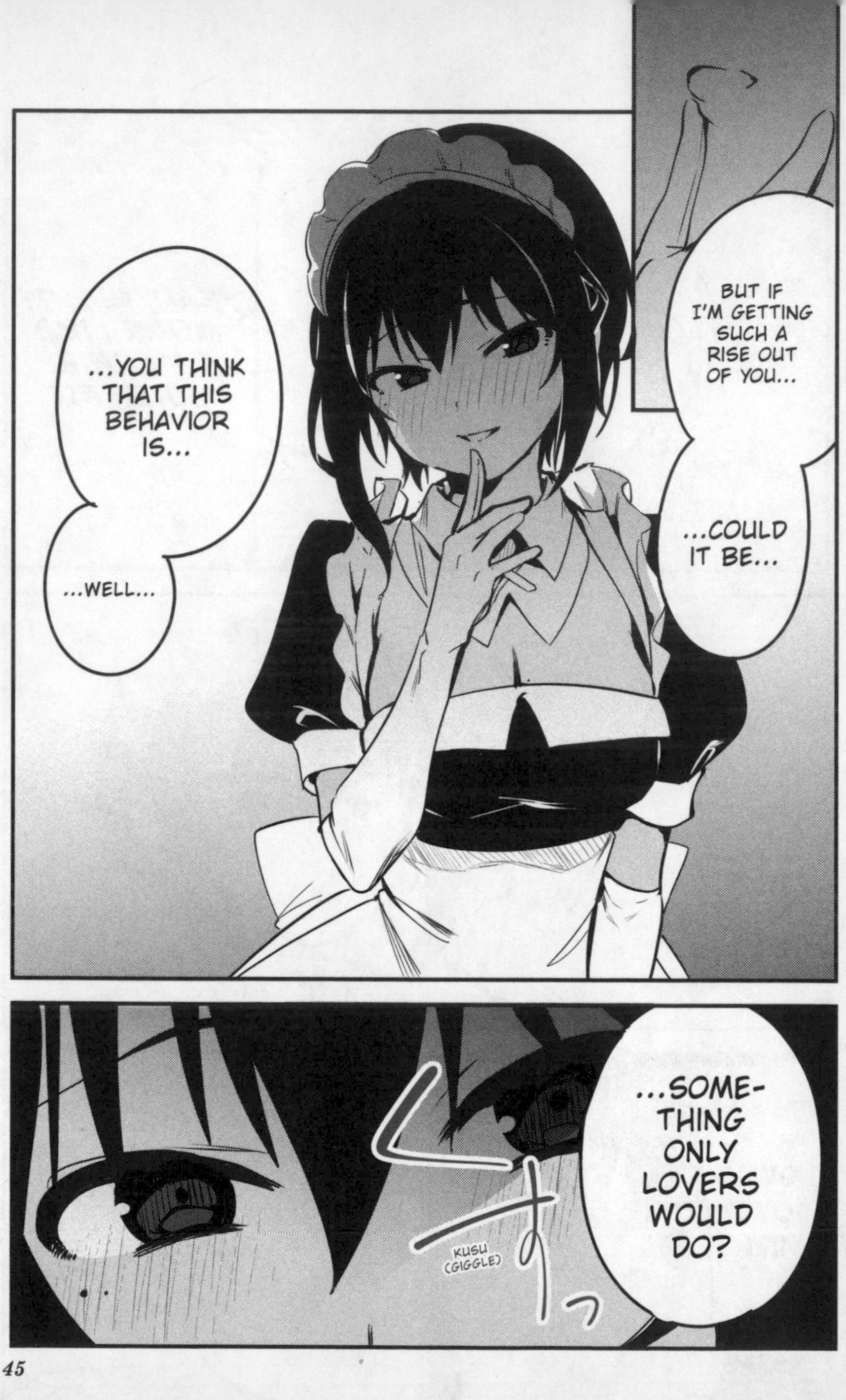
BUT IF I'M GETTING SUCH A RISE OUT OF YOU...
...COULD IT BE...
...YOU THINK THAT THIS BEHAVIOR IS...
...WELL...
...SOME-THING ONLY LOVERS WOULD DO?
KUSU (GIGGLE)

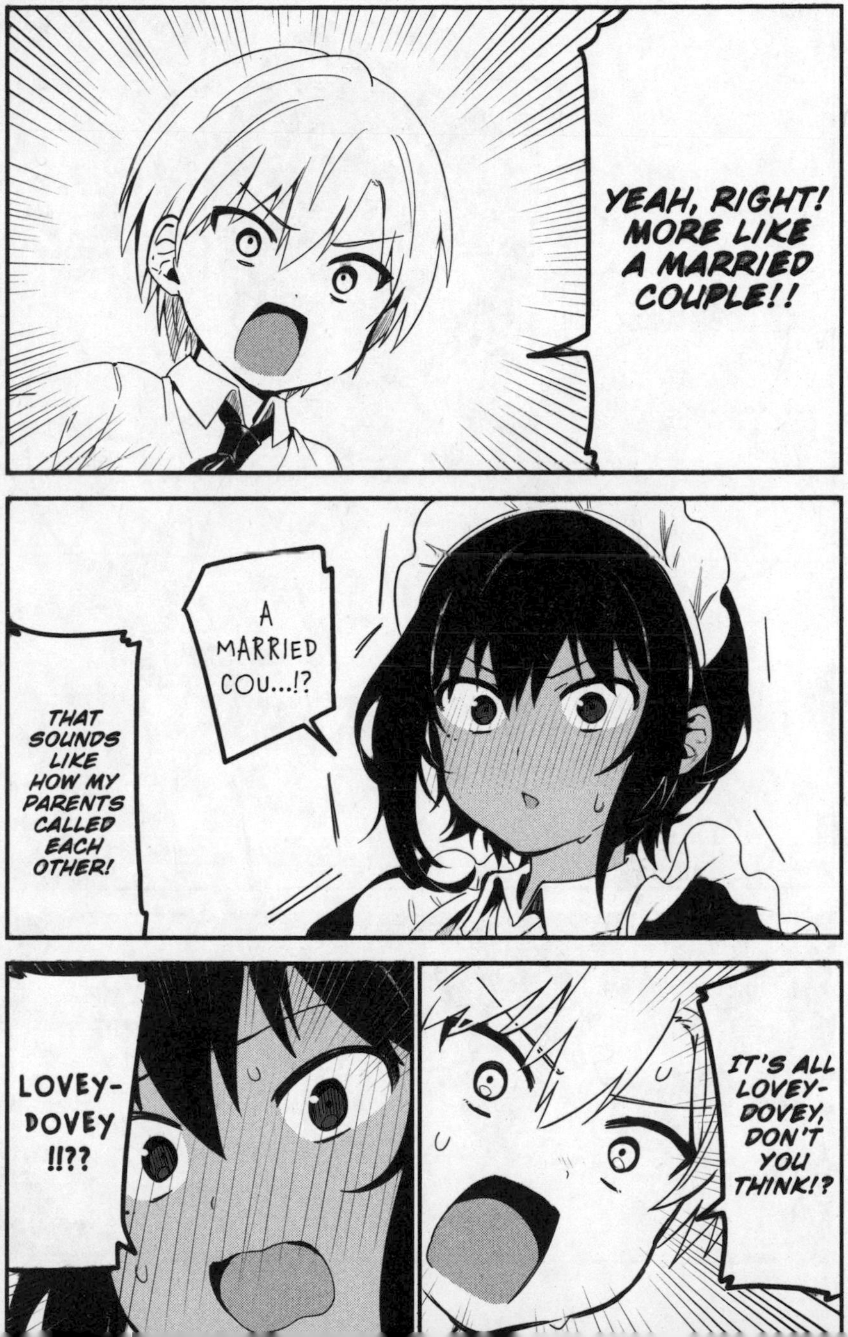

YEAH, RIGHT! MORE LIKE A MARRIED COUPLE!!
A MARRIED COU...!?
THAT SOUNDS LIKE HOW MY PARENTS CALLED EACH OTHER!
IT'S ALL LOVEY-DOVEY, DON'T YOU THINK!?
LOVEY-DOVEY!!??

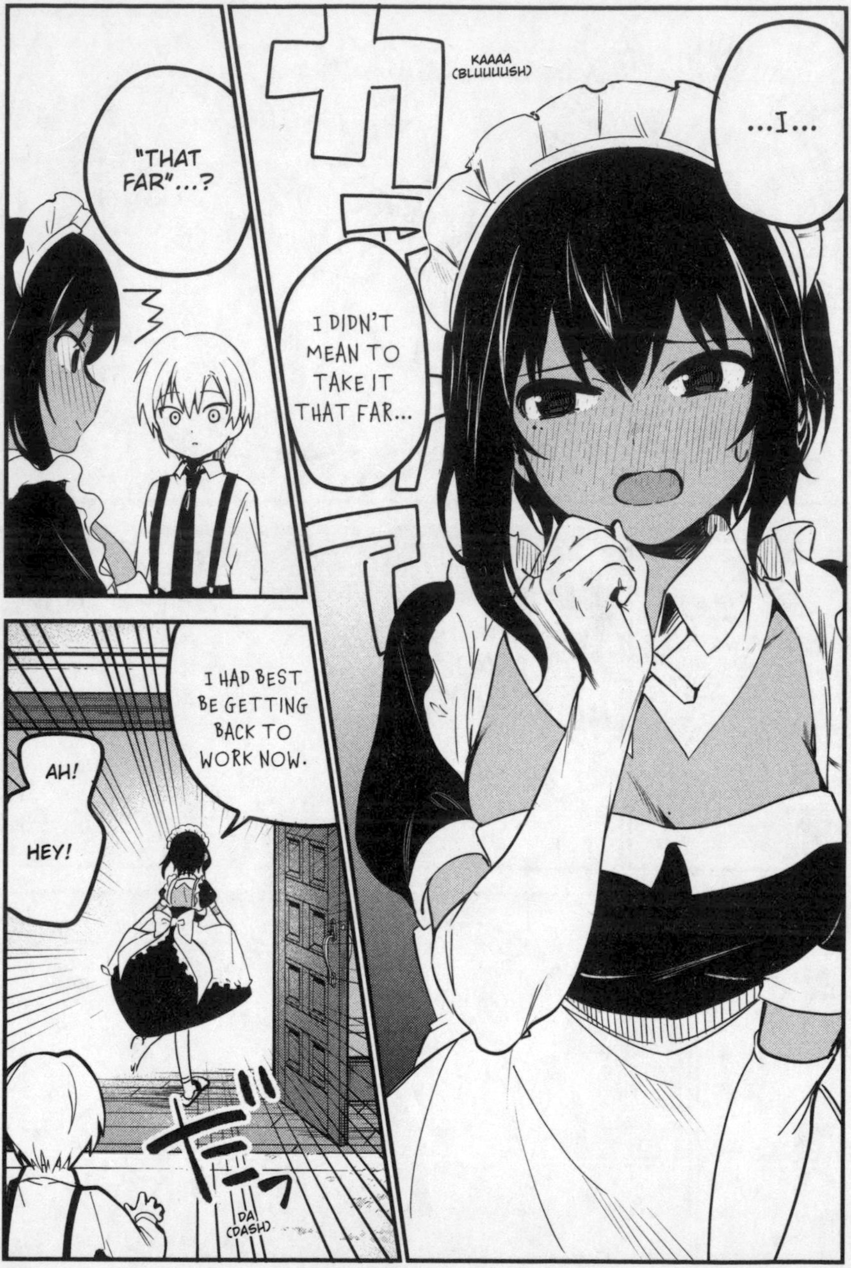
KAAAA (BLUUUUSH)
...I...
I DIDN'T MEAN TO TAKE IT THAT FAR...
"THAT FAR"...?
I HAD BEST BE GETTING BACK TO WORK NOW.
AH!
HEY!
DA (DASH)

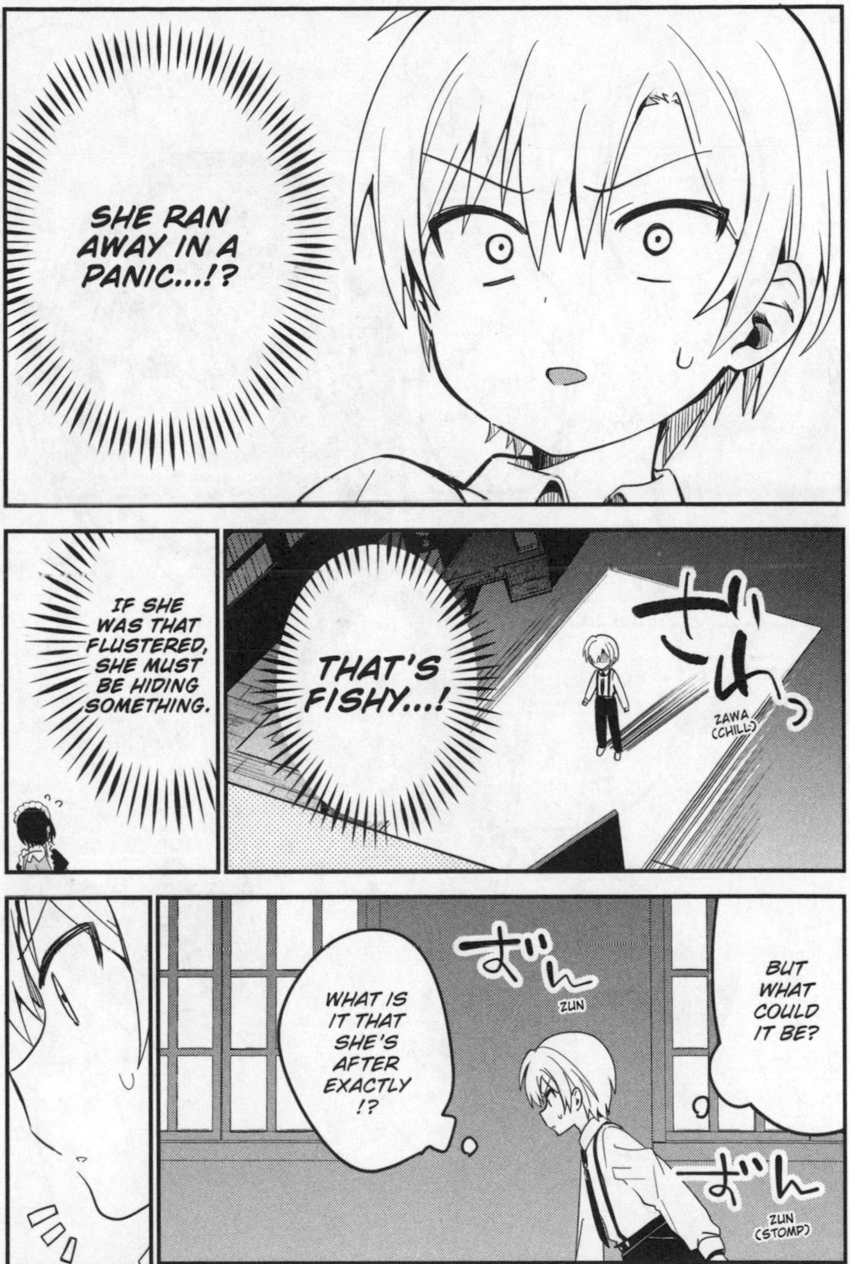
SHE RAN AWAY IN A PANIC...!?
ざわっ
ZAWA (CHILL)
THAT'S FISHY...!
IF SHE WAS THAT FLUSTERED, SHE MUST BE HIDING SOMETHING.
BUT WHAT COULD IT BE?
ずん
ZUN
WHAT IS IT THAT SHE'S AFTER EXACTLY !?
ずん
ZUN (STOMP)

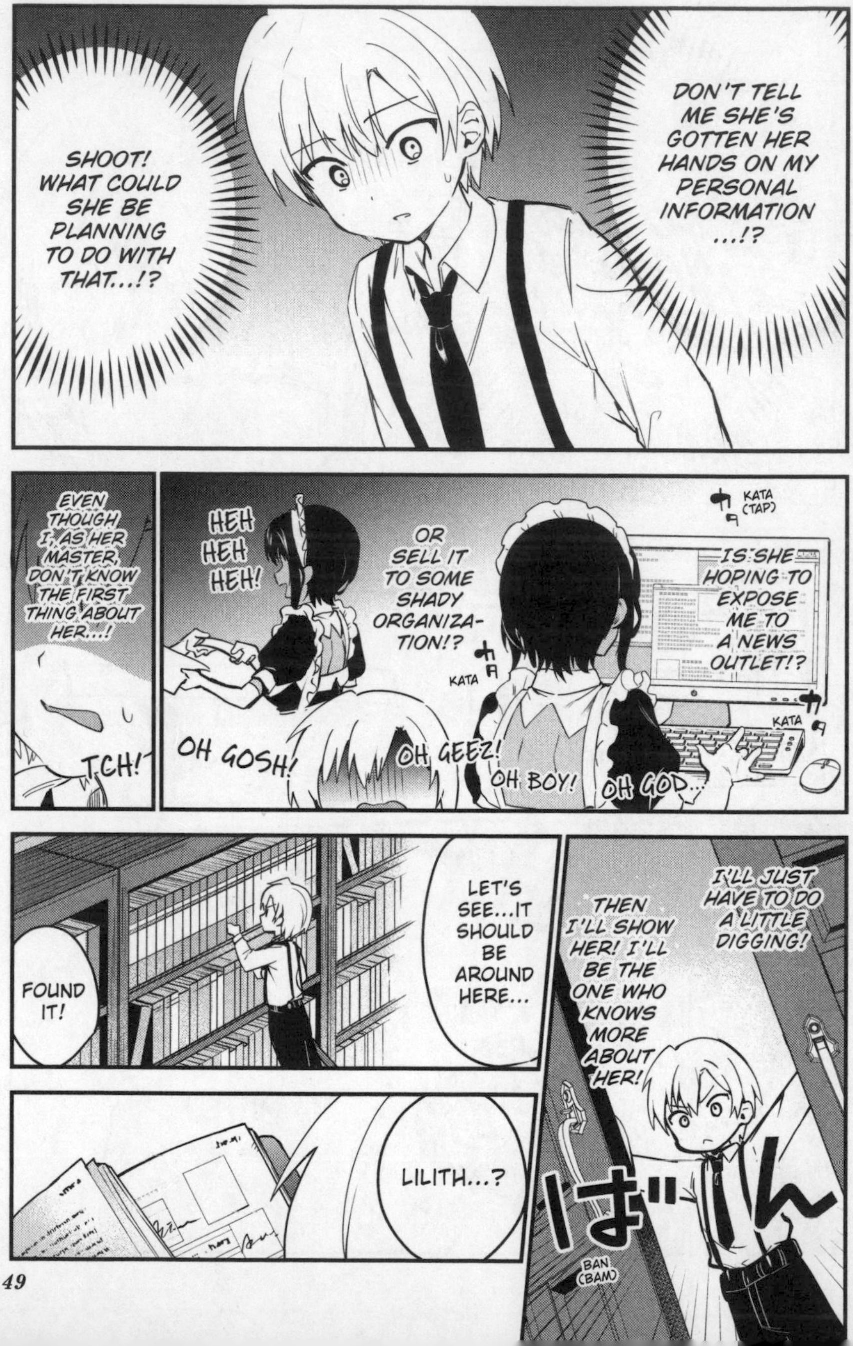
DON'T TELL ME SHE'S GOTTEN HER HANDS ON MY PERSONAL INFORMATION ...!?
SHOOT! WHAT COULD SHE BE PLANNING TO DO WITH THAT...!?
カタ KATA (TAP)
IS SHE HOPING TO EXPOSE ME TO A NEWS OUTLET!?
カタ KATA
OR SELL IT TO SOME SHADY ORGANIZA-TION!?
カタ KATA
HEH HEH HEH!
OH GOD...
OH BOY!
OH GEEZ!
OH GOSH!
EVEN THOUGH I, AS HER MASTER, DON'T KNOW THE FIRST THING ABOUT HER...!
TCH!
I'LL JUST HAVE TO DO A LITTLE DIGGING!
THEN I'LL SHOW HER! I'LL BE THE ONE WHO KNOWS MORE ABOUT HER!
ばーん
BAN (BAM)
LET'S SEE...IT SHOULD BE AROUND HERE...
FOUND IT!
LILITH...?

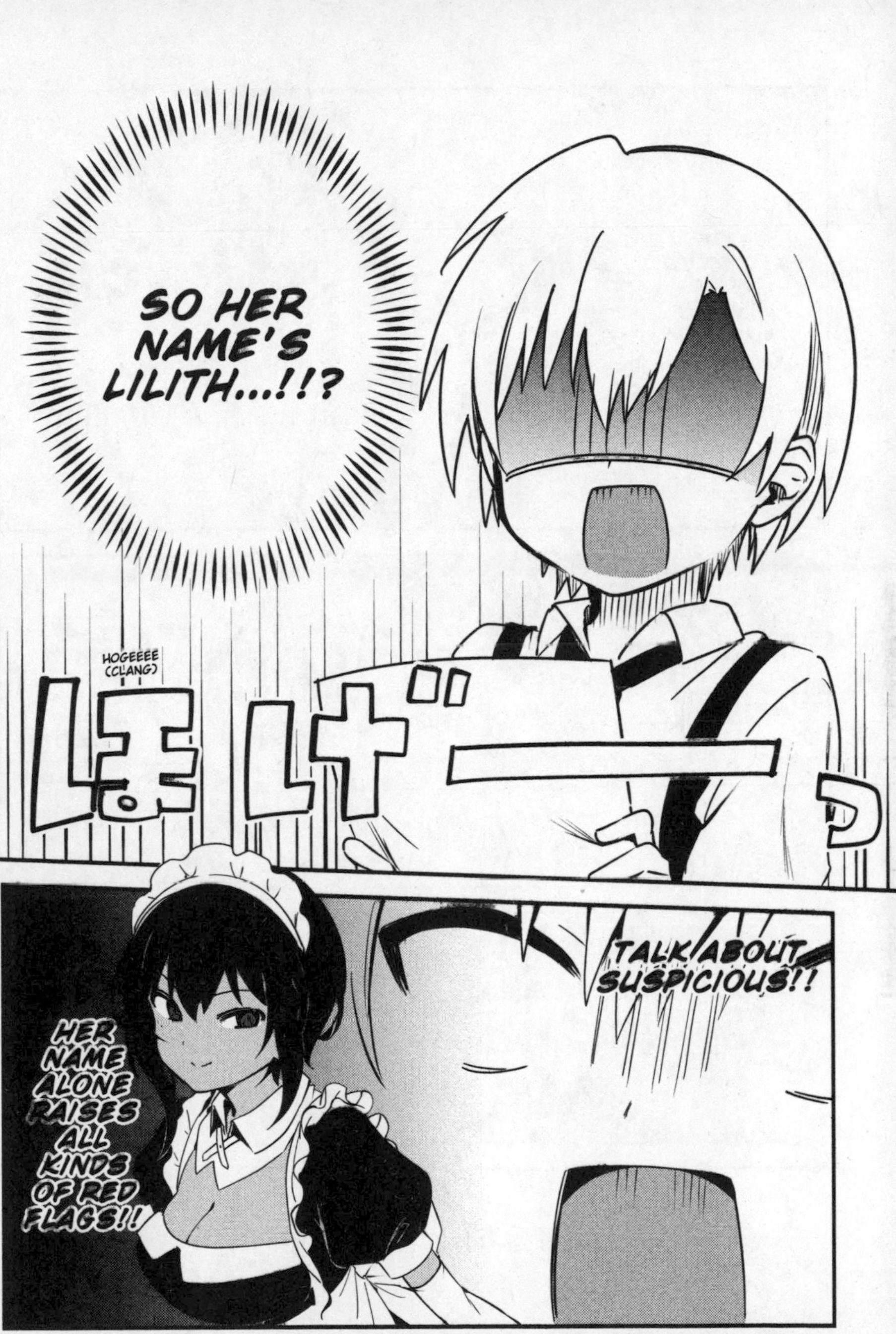
SO HER NAME'S LILITH...!!?
HOGEEEE (CLANG)
ほげーっ
TALK ABOUT SUSPICIOUS!!
HER NAME ALONE RAISES ALL KINDS OF RED FLAGS!!

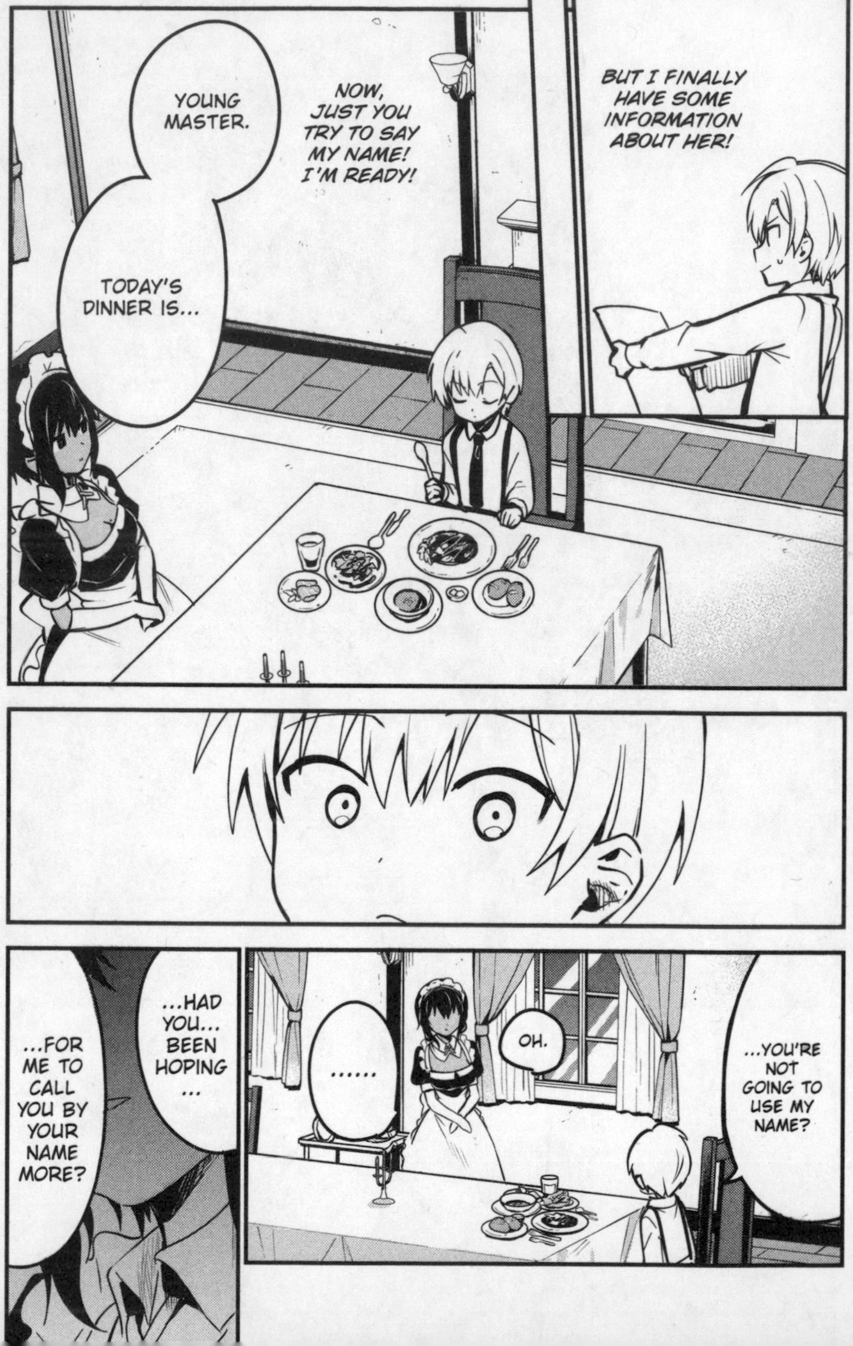
BUT I FINALLY HAVE SOME INFORMATION ABOUT HER!
NOW, JUST YOU TRY TO SAY MY NAME! I'M READY!
YOUNG MASTER.
TODAY'S DINNER IS...
...YOU'RE NOT GOING TO USE MY NAME?
OH.
......
...HAD YOU... BEEN HOPING ...
...FOR ME TO CALL YOU BY YOUR NAME MORE?

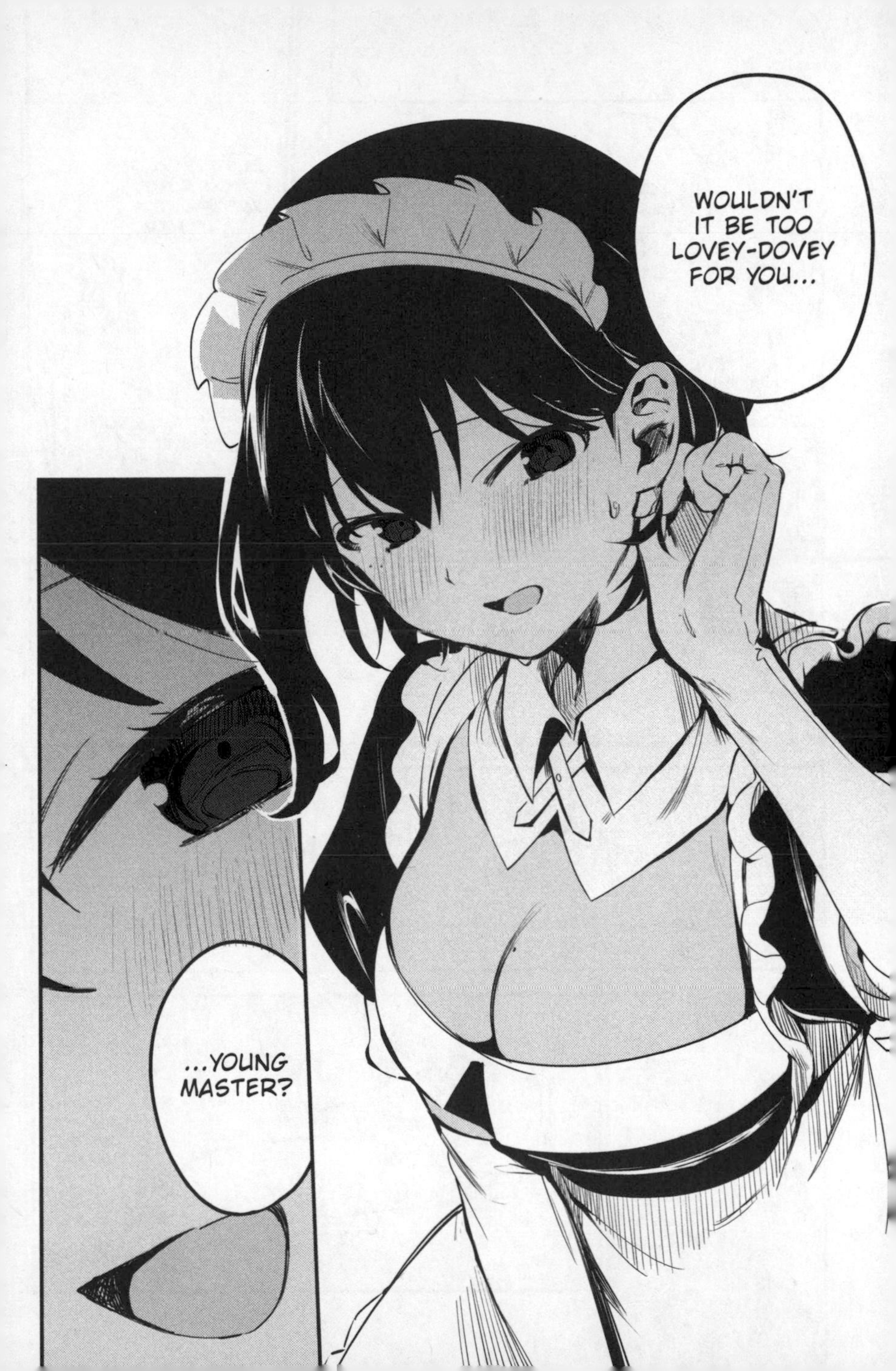
WOULDN'T IT BE TOO LOVEY-DOVEY FOR YOU...
...YOUNG MASTER?

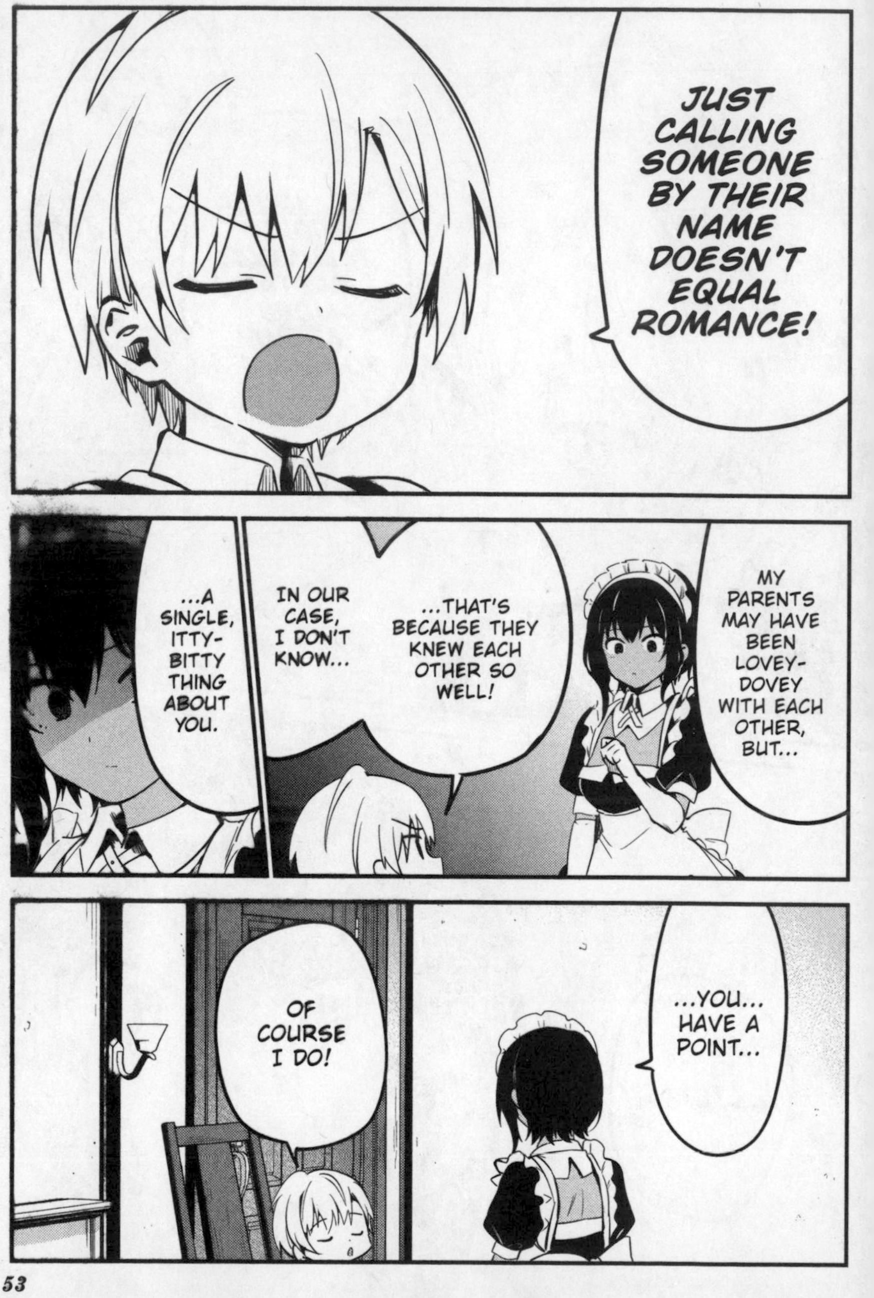
JUST CALLING SOMEONE BY THEIR NAME DOESN'T EQUAL ROMANCE!
MY PARENTS MAY HAVE BEEN LOVEY-DOVEY WITH EACH OTHER, BUT...
...THAT'S BECAUSE THEY KNEW EACH OTHER SO WELL!
IN OUR CASE, I DON'T KNOW...
...A SINGLE, ITTY-BITTY THING ABOUT YOU.
...YOU... HAVE A POINT...
OF COURSE I DO!

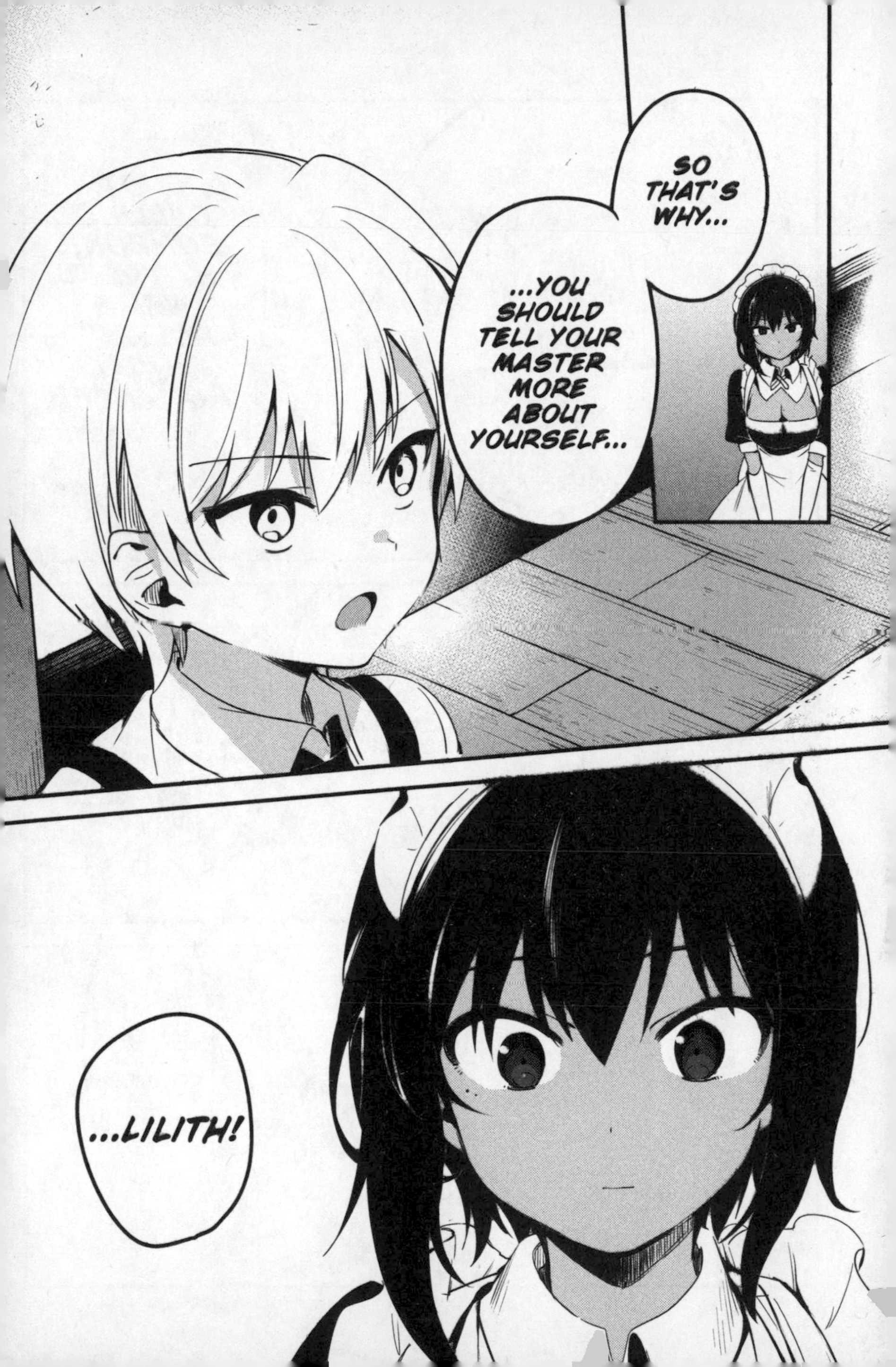
SO THAT'S WHY...
...YOU SHOULD TELL YOUR MASTER MORE ABOUT YOURSELF...
...LILITH!

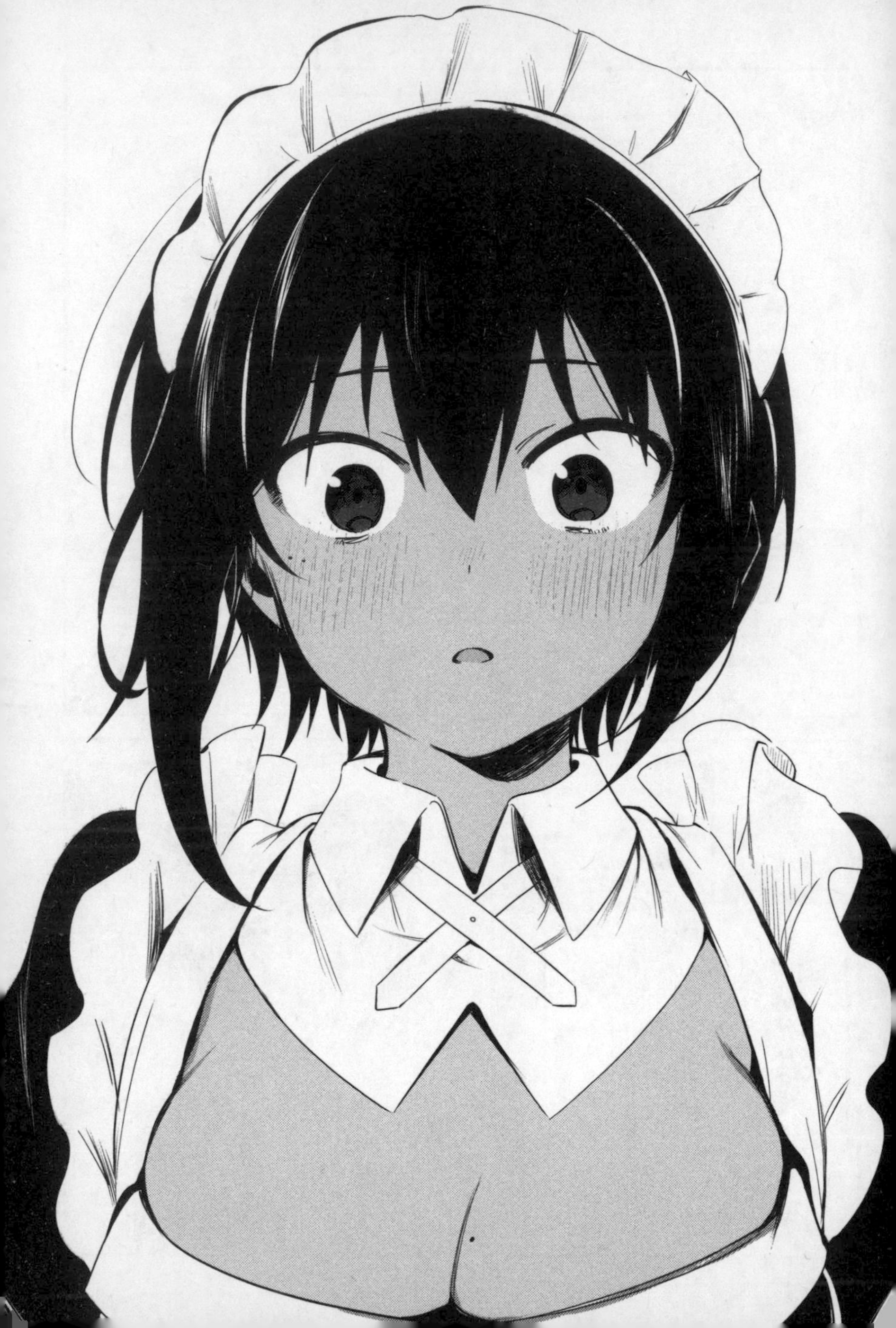

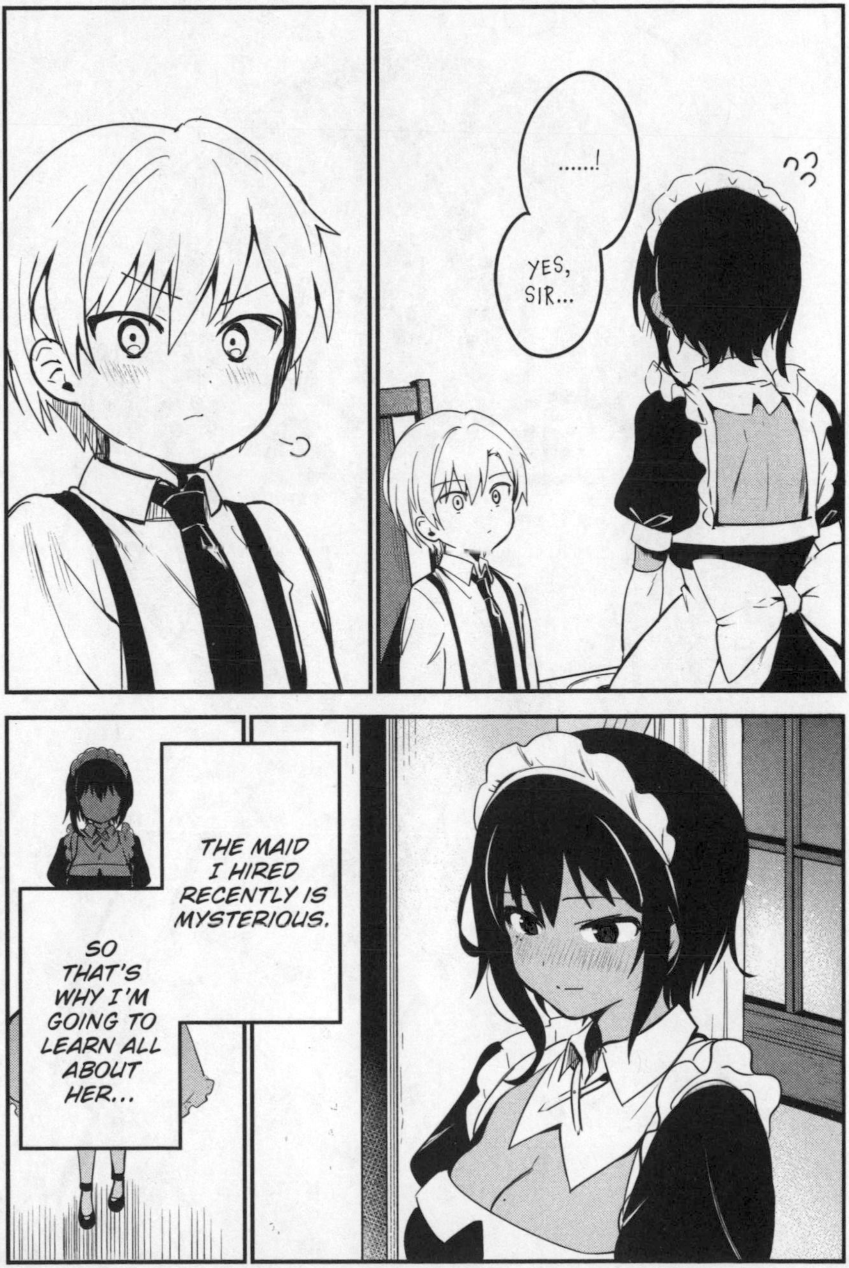
......!
YES, SIR...
THE MAID I HIRED RECENTLY IS MYSTERIOUS.
SO THAT'S WHY I'M GOING TO LEARN ALL ABOUT HER...

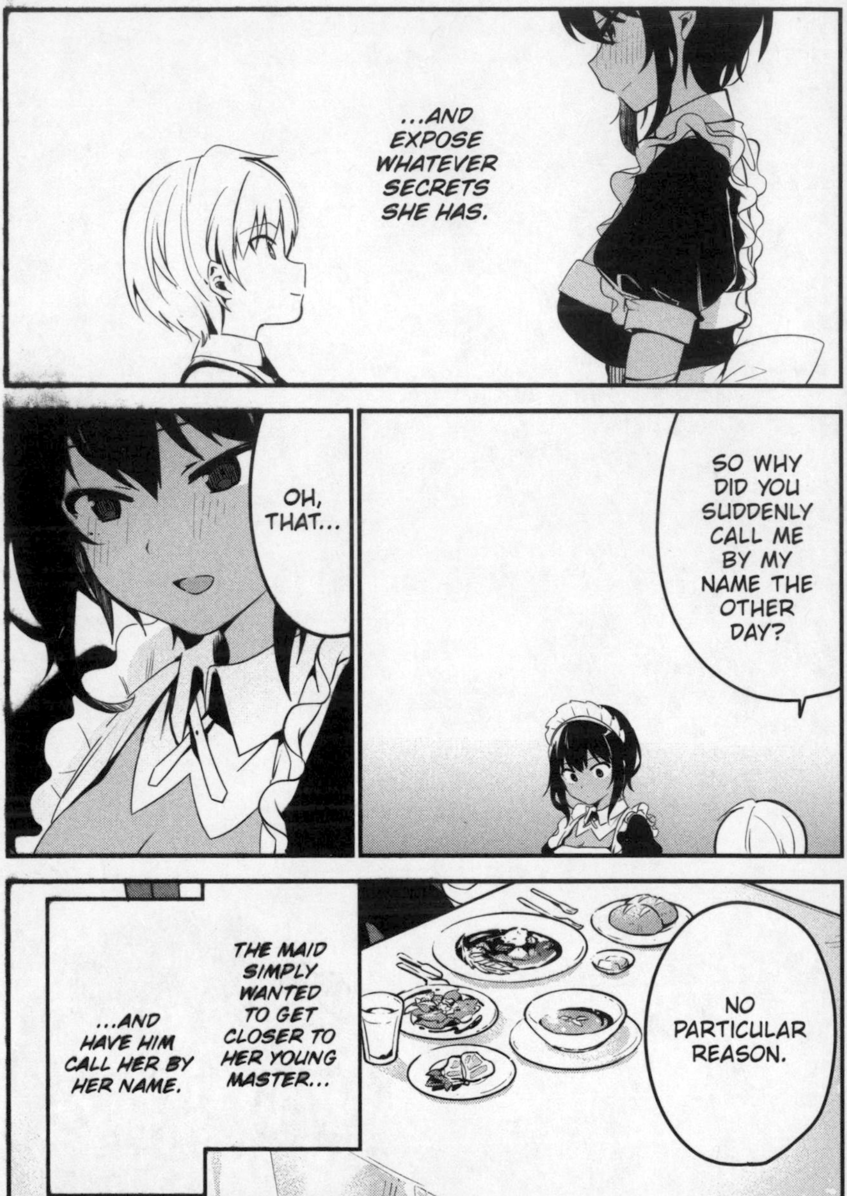
...AND EXPOSE WHATEVER SECRETS SHE HAS.
SO WHY DID YOU SUDDENLY CALL ME BY MY NAME THE OTHER DAY?
OH, THAT...
NO PARTICULAR REASON.
THE MAID SIMPLY WANTED TO GET CLOSER TO HER YOUNG MASTER...
...AND HAVE HIM CALL HER BY HER NAME.

The Maid I Hired Recently Is Mysterious

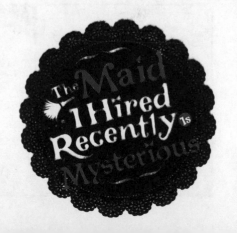

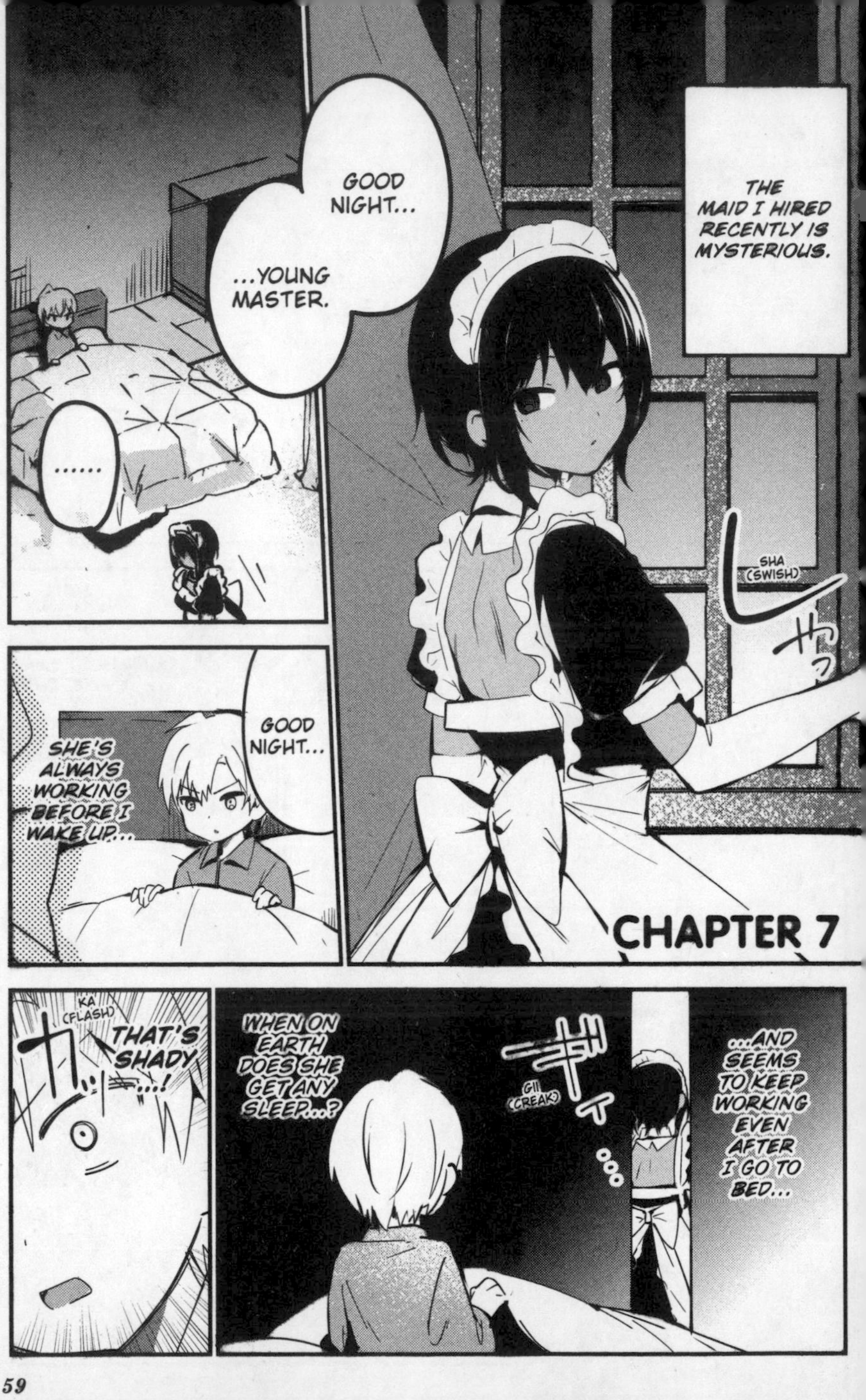
THE MAID I HIRED RECENTLY IS MYSTERIOUS.
SHA (SWISH)
CHAPTER 7
GOOD NIGHT...
...YOUNG MASTER.
......
GOOD NIGHT...
SHE'S ALWAYS WORKING BEFORE I WAKE UP...
...AND SEEMS TO KEEP WORKING EVEN AFTER I GO TO BED...
GII (CREAK)
WHEN ON EARTH DOES SHE GET ANY SLEEP...?
KA (FLASH)
THAT'S SHADY...!

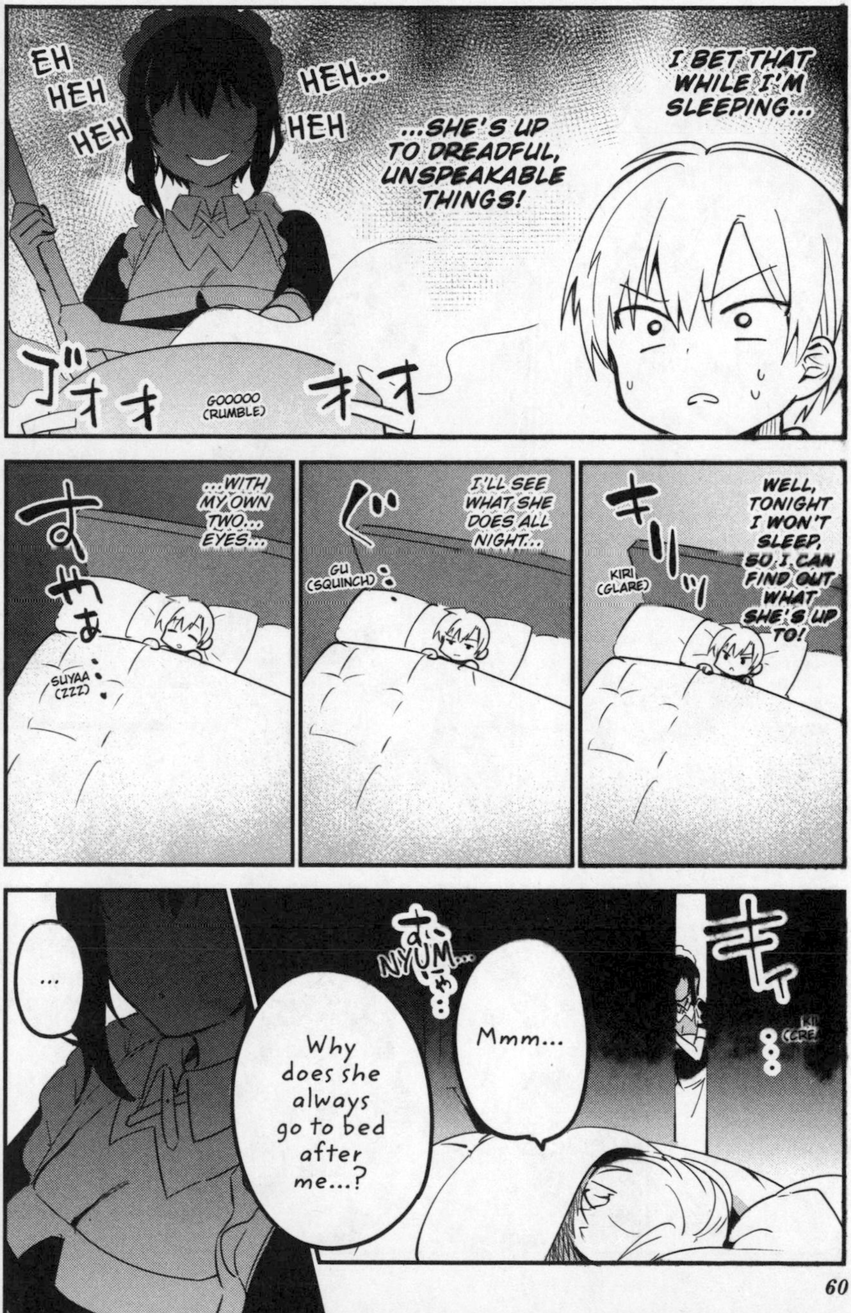
I BET THAT WHILE I'M SLEEPING...
...SHE'S UP TO DREADFUL, UNSPEAKABLE THINGS!
HEH... HEH
EH HEH HEH
GOOOOO (RUMBLE)
WELL, TONIGHT I WON'T SLEEP, SO I CAN FIND OUT WHAT SHE'S UP TO!
KIRI (GLARE)
I'LL SEE WHAT SHE DOES ALL NIGHT...
GU (SQUINCH)
...WITH MY OWN TWO... EYES...
SUYAA (ZZZ)
Mmm...
NYUM...
Why does she always go to bed after me...?
...

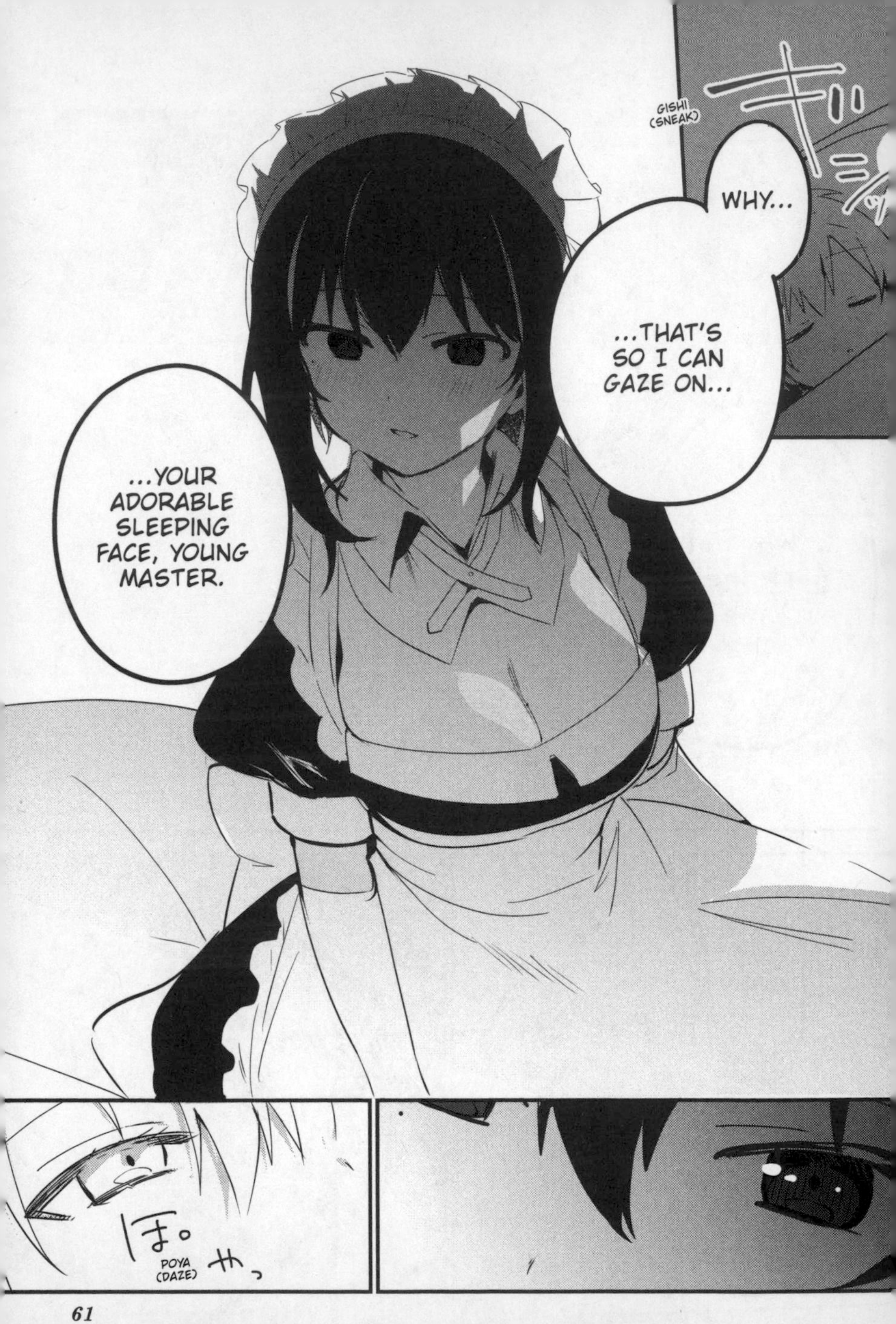
GISHI (SNEAK)
WHY...
...THAT'S SO I CAN GAZE ON...
...YOUR ADORABLE SLEEPING FACE, YOUNG MASTER.
POYA (DAZE)

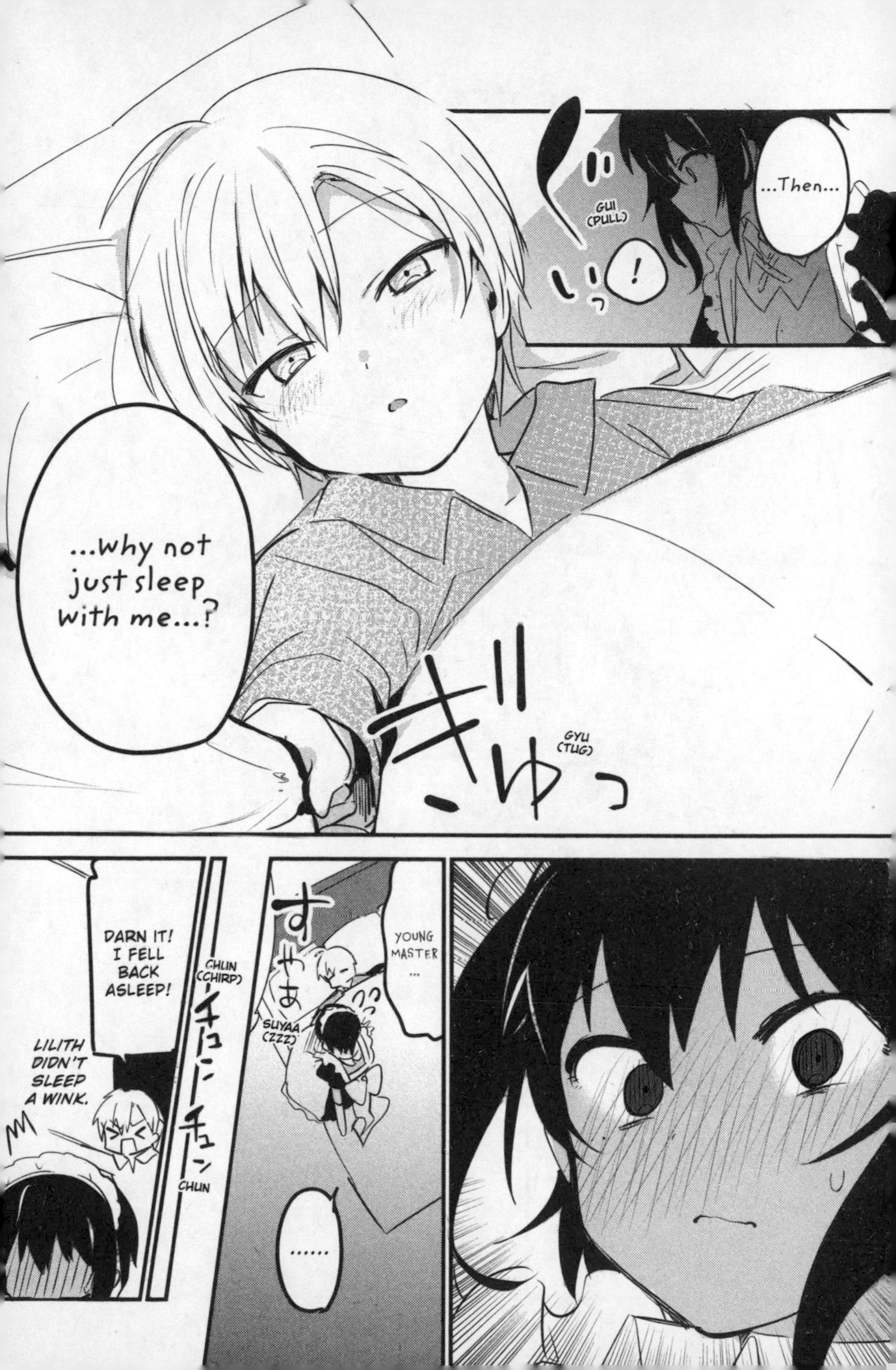
...Then...
!
GUI (PULL)
...why not just sleep with me...?
GYU (TUG)
YOUNG MASTER ...
SUYAA (ZZZ)
......
DARN IT! I FELL BACK ASLEEP!
CHUN (CHIRP)
CHUN
LILITH DIDN'T SLEEP A WINK.

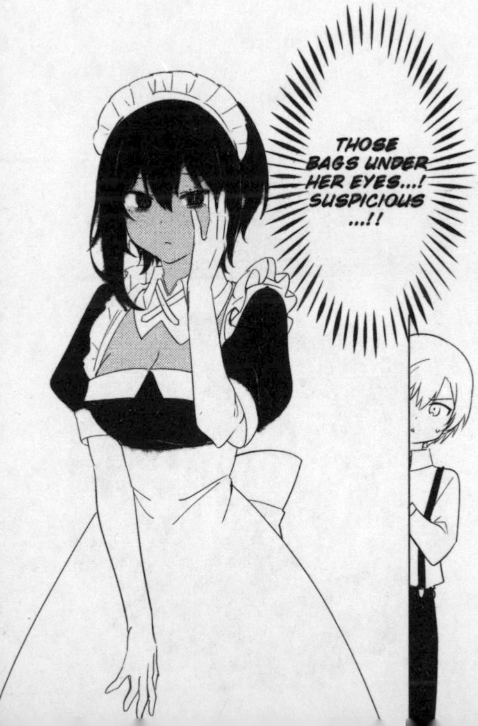
THOSE BAGS UNDER HER EYES...! SUSPICIOUS ...!!

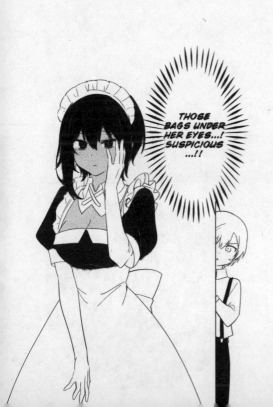

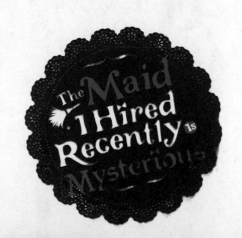

The Maid I Hired Recently is Mysterious

CHAPTER 8

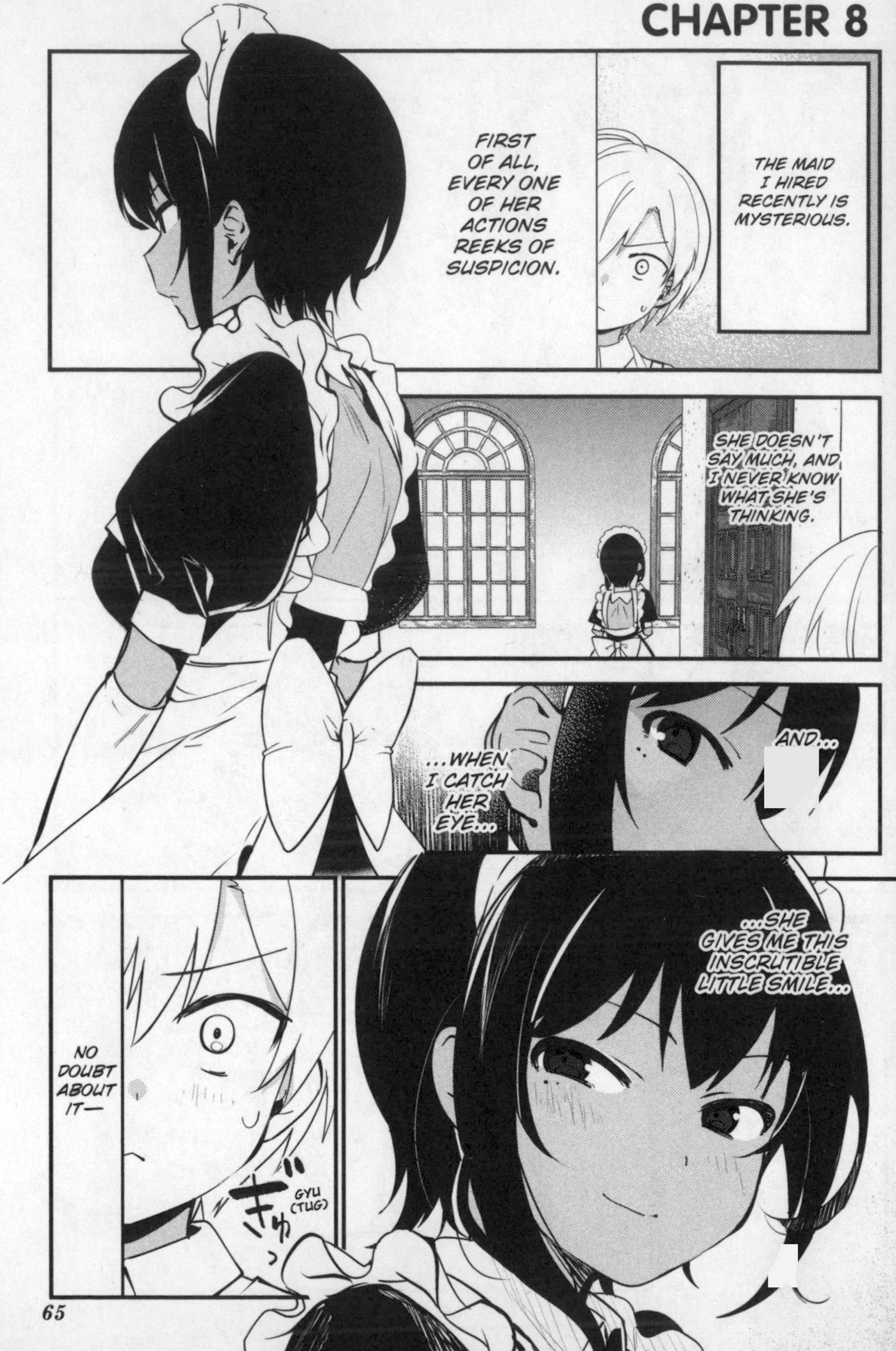
THE MAID I HIRED RECENTLY IS MYSTERIOUS.
FIRST OF ALL, EVERY ONE OF HER ACTIONS REEKS OF SUSPICION.
SHE DOESN'T SAY MUCH, AND I NEVER KNOW WHAT SHE'S THINKING.
AND...
...WHEN I CATCH HER EYE...
...SHE GIVES ME THIS INSCRUTIBLE LITTLE SMILE...
NO DOUBT ABOUT IT—
GYU (TUG)

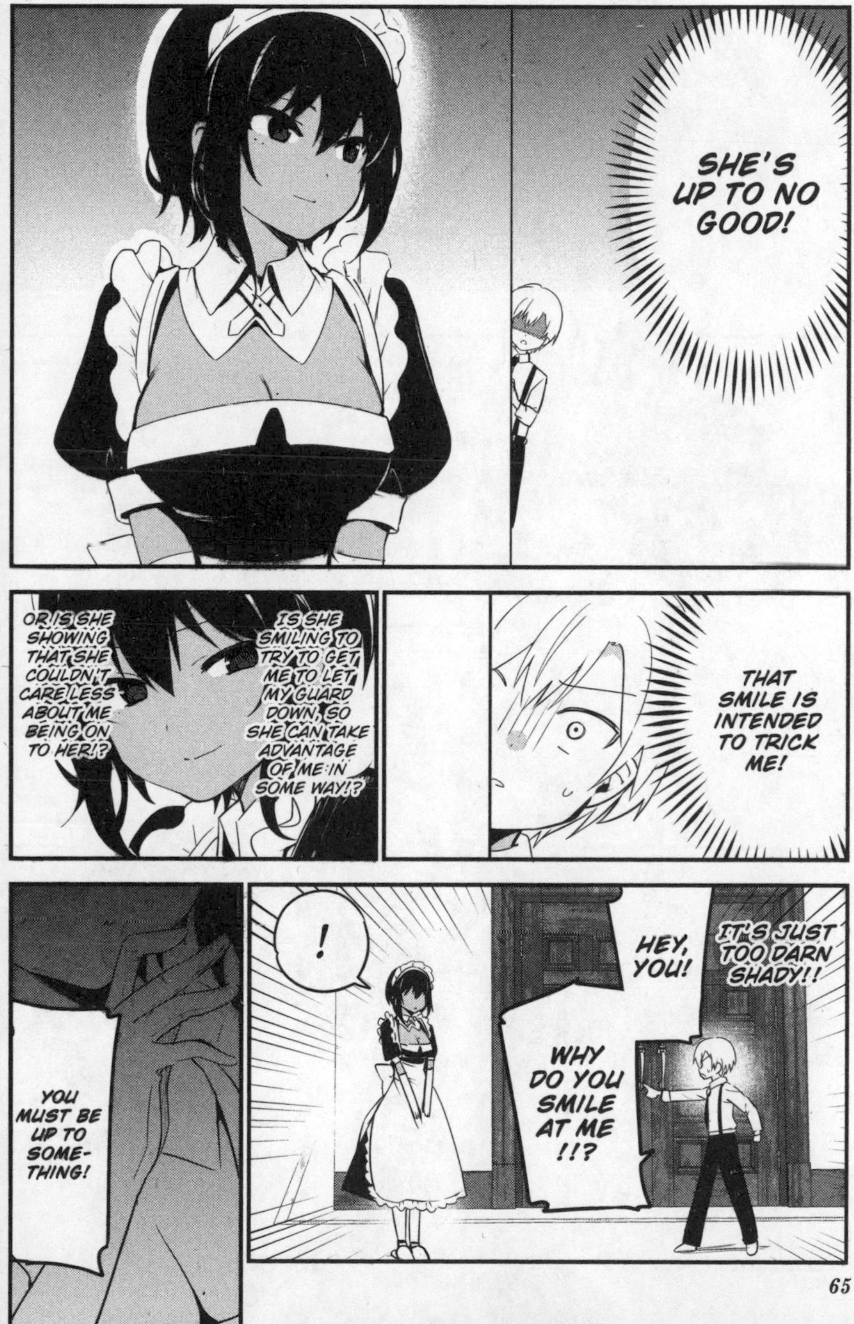
SHE'S UP TO NO GOOD!
THAT SMILE IS INTENDED TO TRICK ME!
IS SHE SMILING TO TRY TO GET ME TO LET MY GUARD DOWN, SO SHE CAN TAKE ADVANTAGE OF ME IN SOME WAY!?
OR IS SHE SHOWING THAT SHE COULDN'T CARE LESS ABOUT ME BEING ON TO HER!?
IT'S JUST TOO DARN SHADY!!
HEY, YOU!
WHY DO YOU SMILE AT ME !!?
!
YOU MUST BE UP TO SOME-THING!

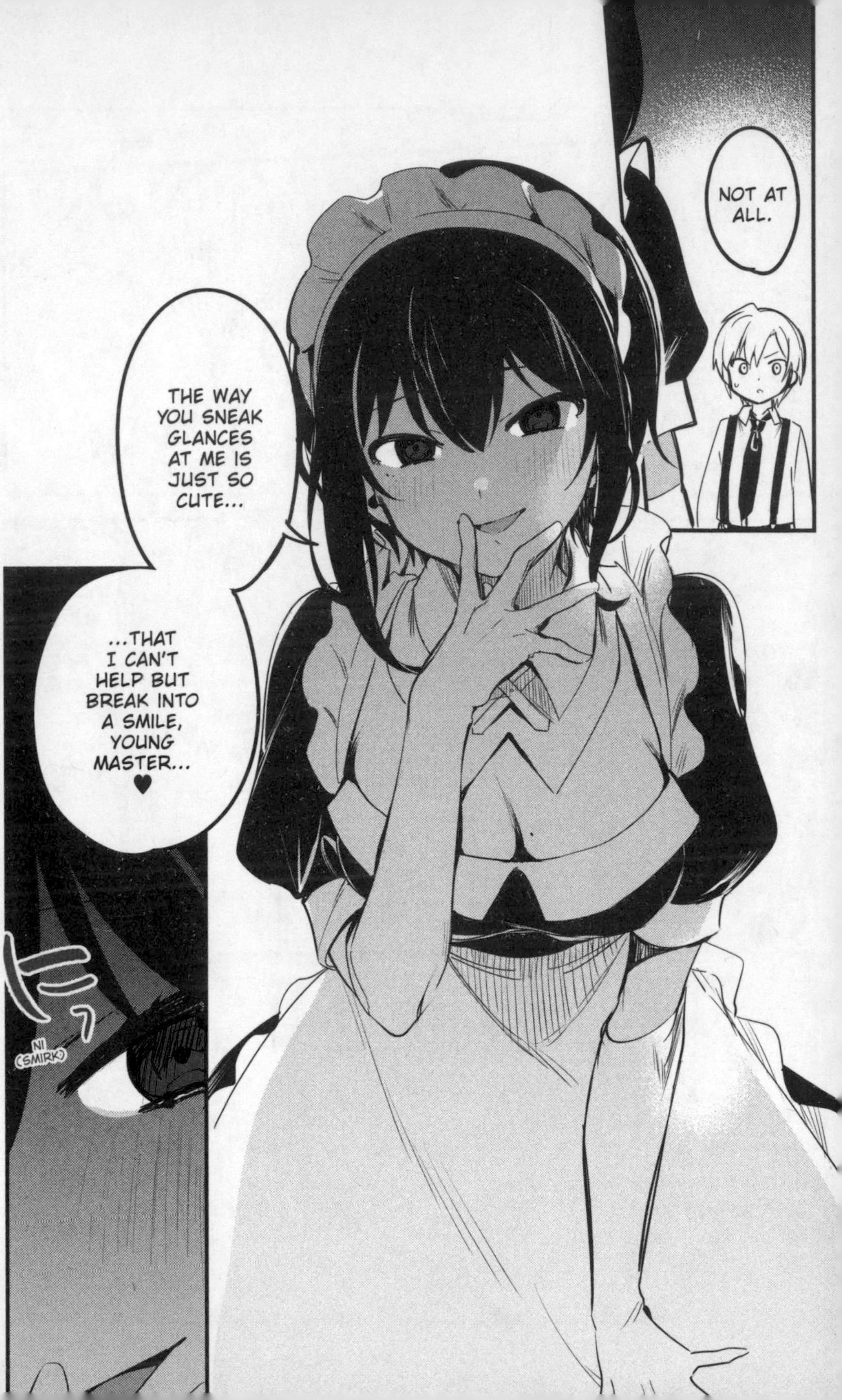
NOT AT ALL.
THE WAY YOU SNEAK GLANCES AT ME IS JUST SO CUTE...
...THAT I CAN'T HELP BUT BREAK INTO A SMILE, YOUNG MASTER... ♥
NI (SMIRK)

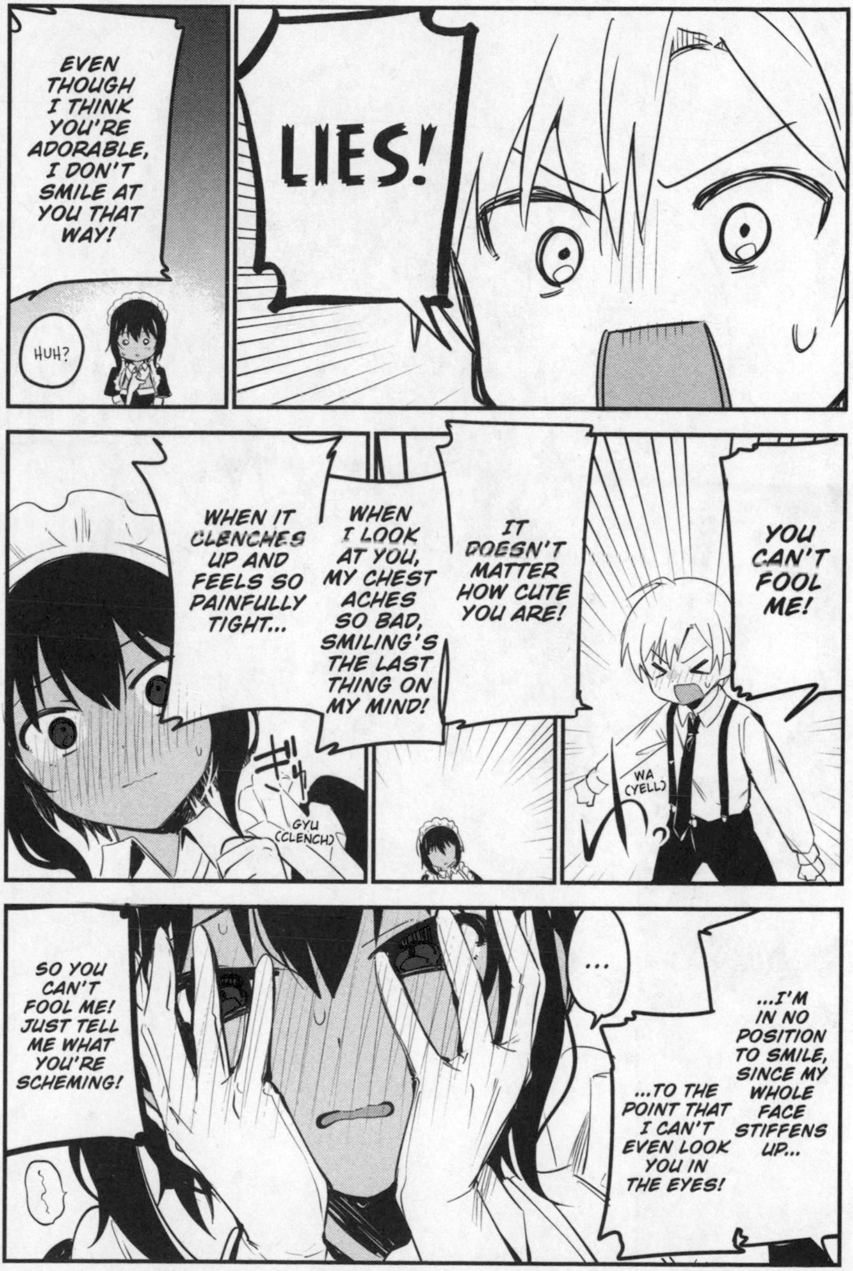
LIES!
EVEN THOUGH I THINK YOU'RE ADORABLE, I DON'T SMILE AT YOU THAT WAY!
HUH?
YOU CAN'T FOOL ME!
WA (YELL)
IT DOESN'T MATTER HOW CUTE YOU ARE!
WHEN I LOOK AT YOU, MY CHEST ACHES SO BAD, SMILING'S THE LAST THING ON MY MIND!
WHEN IT CLENCHES UP AND FEELS SO PAINFULLY TIGHT...
GYU (CLENCH)
...
...I'M IN NO POSITION TO SMILE, SINCE MY WHOLE FACE STIFFENS UP...
...TO THE POINT THAT I CAN'T EVEN LOOK YOU IN THE EYES!
SO YOU CAN'T FOOL ME! JUST TELL ME WHAT YOU'RE SCHEMING!

CHAPTER 9

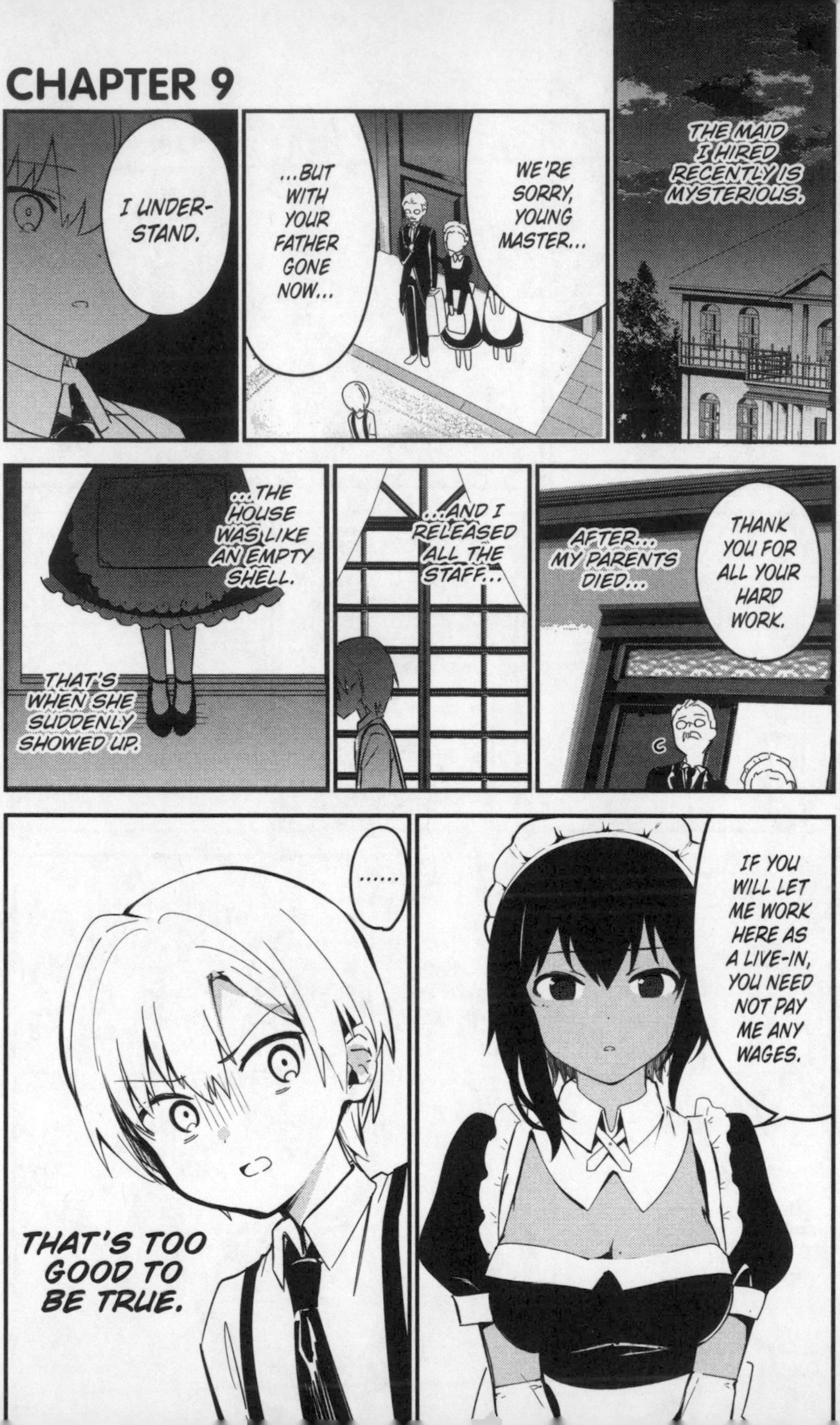
THE MAID I HIRED RECENTLY IS MYSTERIOUS.
WE'RE SORRY, YOUNG MASTER...
...BUT WITH YOUR FATHER GONE NOW...
I UNDER-STAND.
THANK YOU FOR ALL YOUR HARD WORK.
AFTER... MY PARENTS DIED...
...AND I RELEASED ALL THE STAFF...
...THE HOUSE WAS LIKE AN EMPTY SHELL.
THAT'S WHEN SHE SUDDENLY SHOWED UP.
IF YOU WILL LET ME WORK HERE AS A LIVE-IN, YOU NEED NOT PAY ME ANY WAGES.
......
THAT'S TOO GOOD TO BE TRUE.

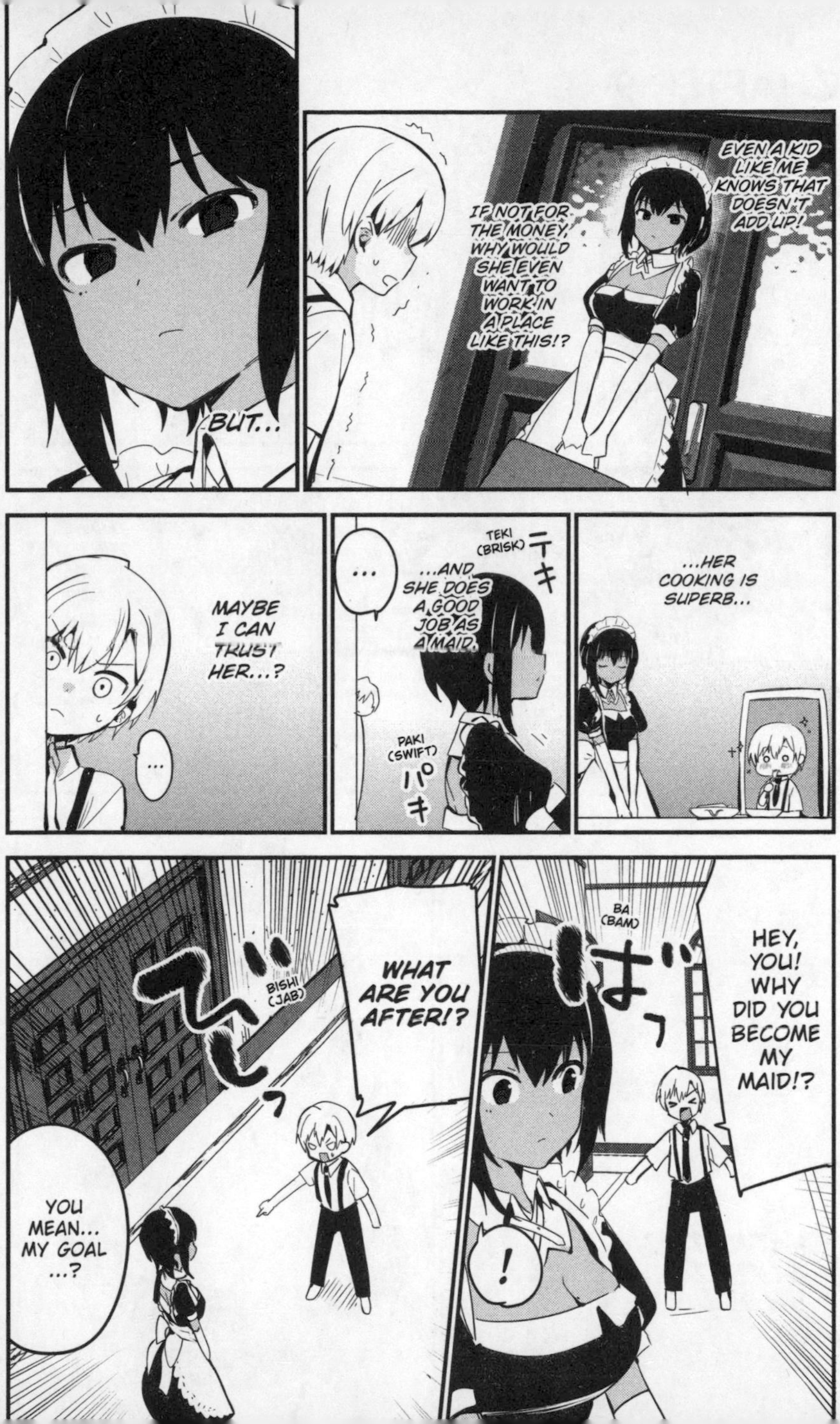
EVEN A KID LIKE ME KNOWS THAT DOESN'T ADD UP!
IF NOT FOR THE MONEY, WHY WOULD SHE EVEN WANT TO WORK IN A PLACE LIKE THIS!?
BUT...
...HER COOKING IS SUPERB...
TEKI (BRISK)
テキ
...AND SHE DOES A GOOD JOB AS A MAID.
...
PAKI (SWIFT)
パキ
MAYBE I CAN TRUST HER...?
...
HEY, YOU! WHY DID YOU BECOME MY MAID!?
BA (BAM)
ばっ
!
WHAT ARE YOU AFTER!?
BISHI (JAB)
びしっ
YOU MEAN... MY GOAL ...?

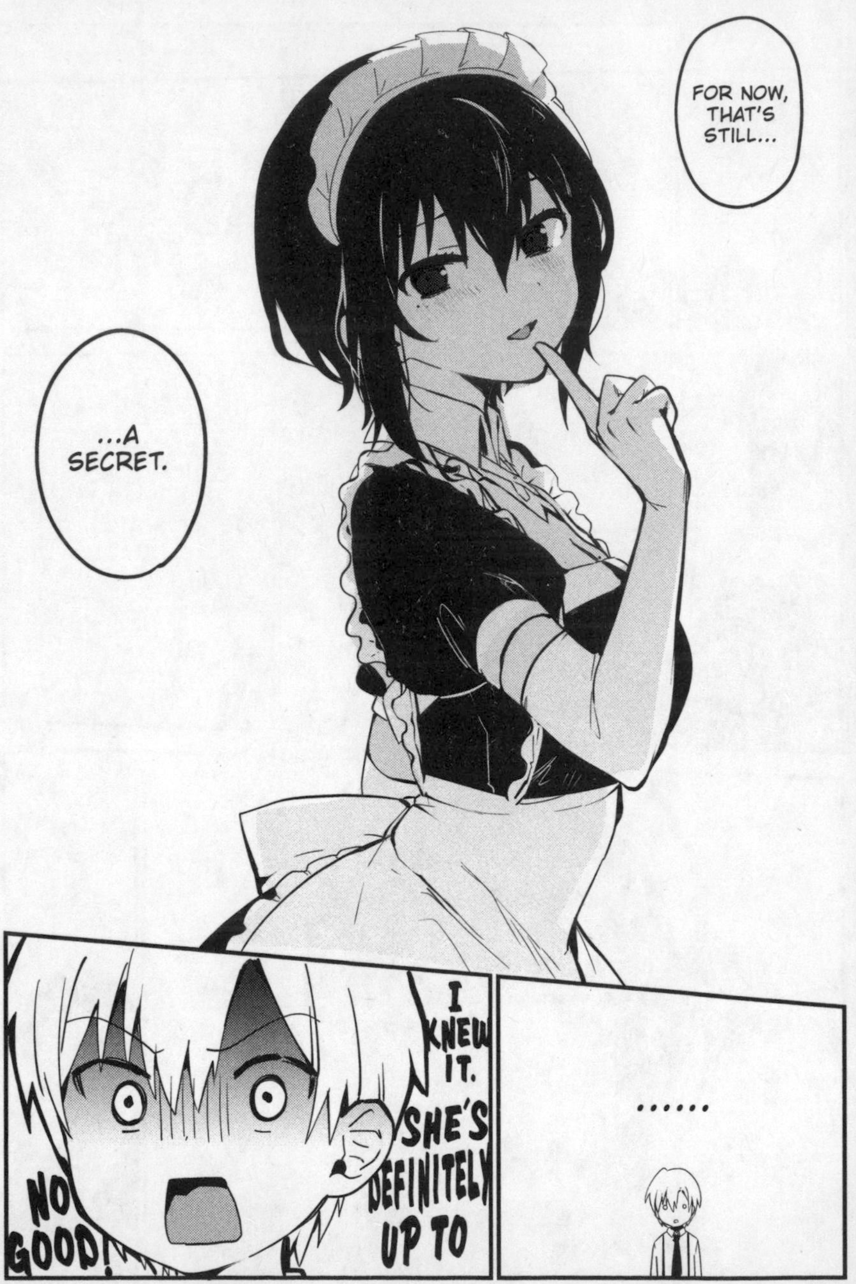

FOR NOW, THAT'S STILL...
...A SECRET.
......
I KNEW IT.
SHE'S DEFINITELY UP TO
NO GOOD!

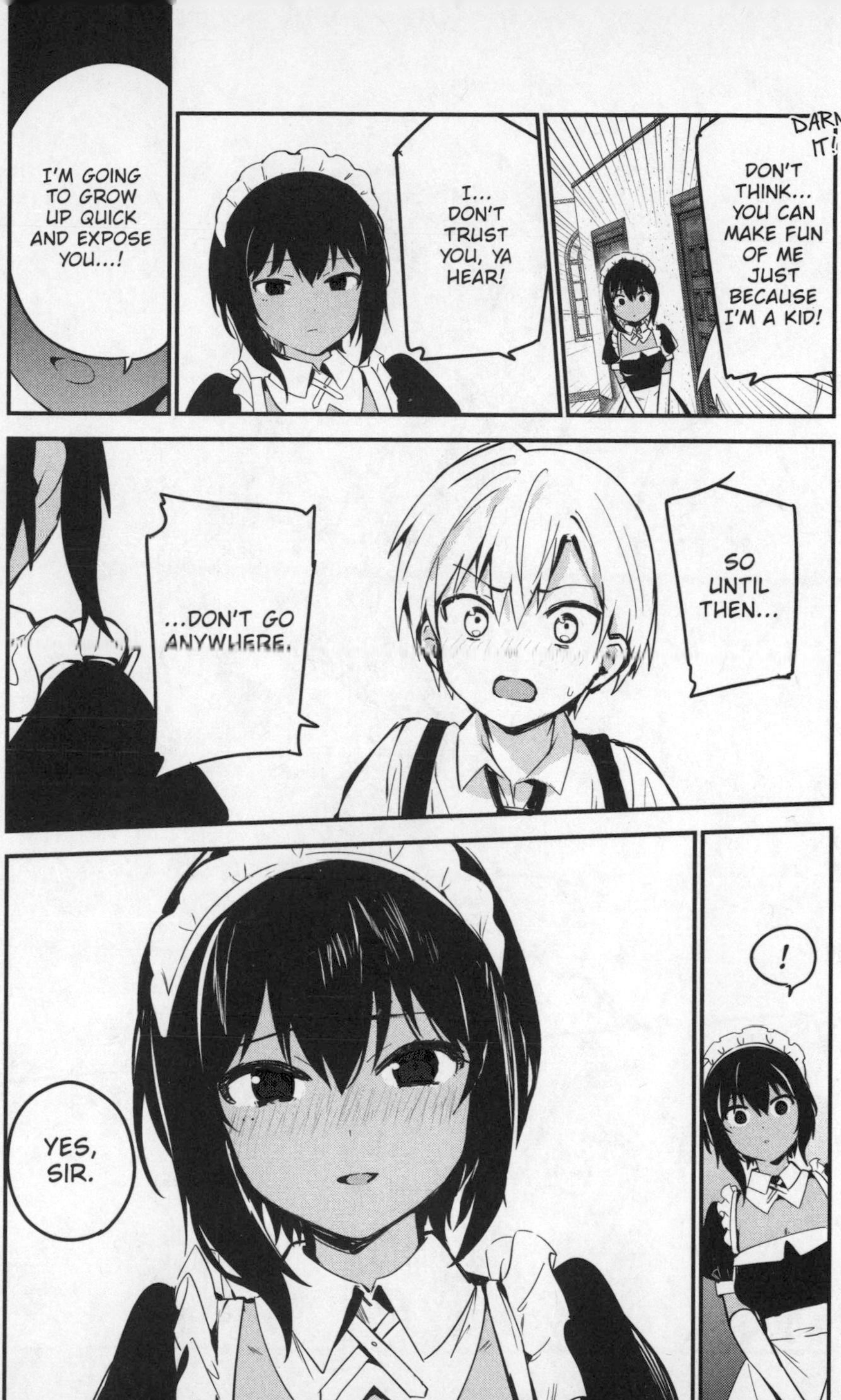
DARN IT!
DON'T THINK... YOU CAN MAKE FUN OF ME JUST BECAUSE I'M A KID!
I... DON'T TRUST YOU, YA HEAR!
I'M GOING TO GROW UP QUICK AND EXPOSE YOU...!
SO UNTIL THEN...
...DON'T GO ANYWHERE.
!
YES, SIR.

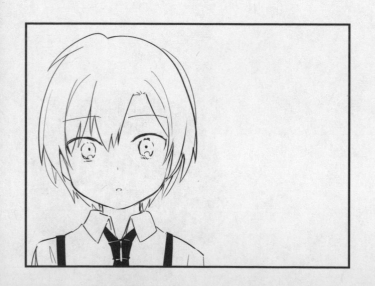

The Maid I Hired Recently Is Mysterious

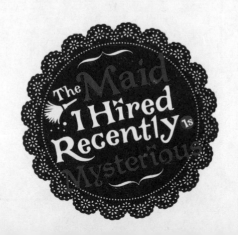

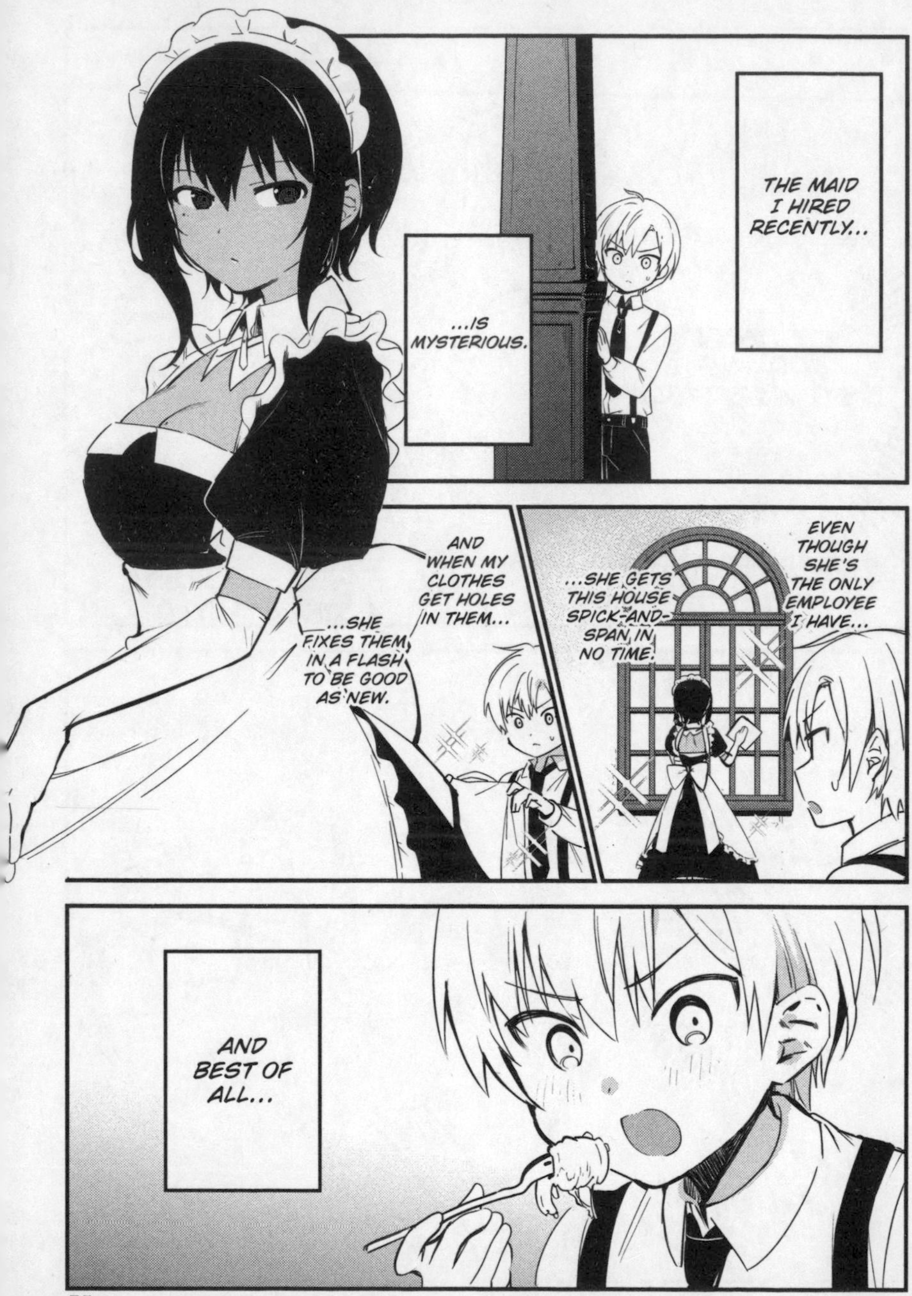

THE MAID I HIRED RECENTLY...
...IS MYSTERIOUS.
EVEN THOUGH SHE'S THE ONLY EMPLOYEE I HAVE...
...SHE GETS THIS HOUSE SPICK-AND-SPAN IN NO TIME.
AND WHEN MY CLOTHES GET HOLES IN THEM...
...SHE FIXES THEM IN A FLASH TO BE GOOD AS NEW.
AND BEST OF ALL...

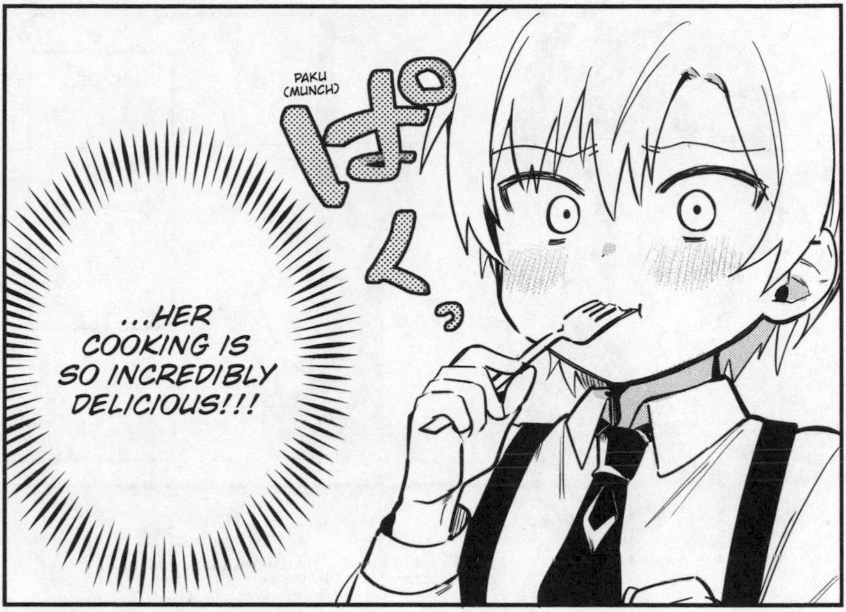
ぱくっ
PAKU (MUNCH)
...HER COOKING IS SO INCREDIBLY DELICIOUS!!!
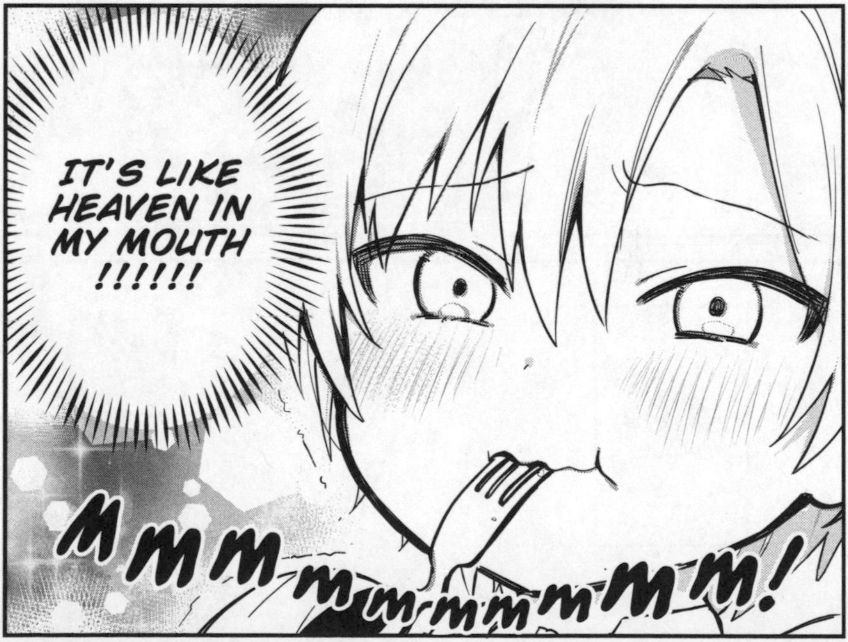
IT'S LIKE HEAVEN IN MY MOUTH !!!!!!
MMMMmmmmmmMMM!

CHAPTER 10

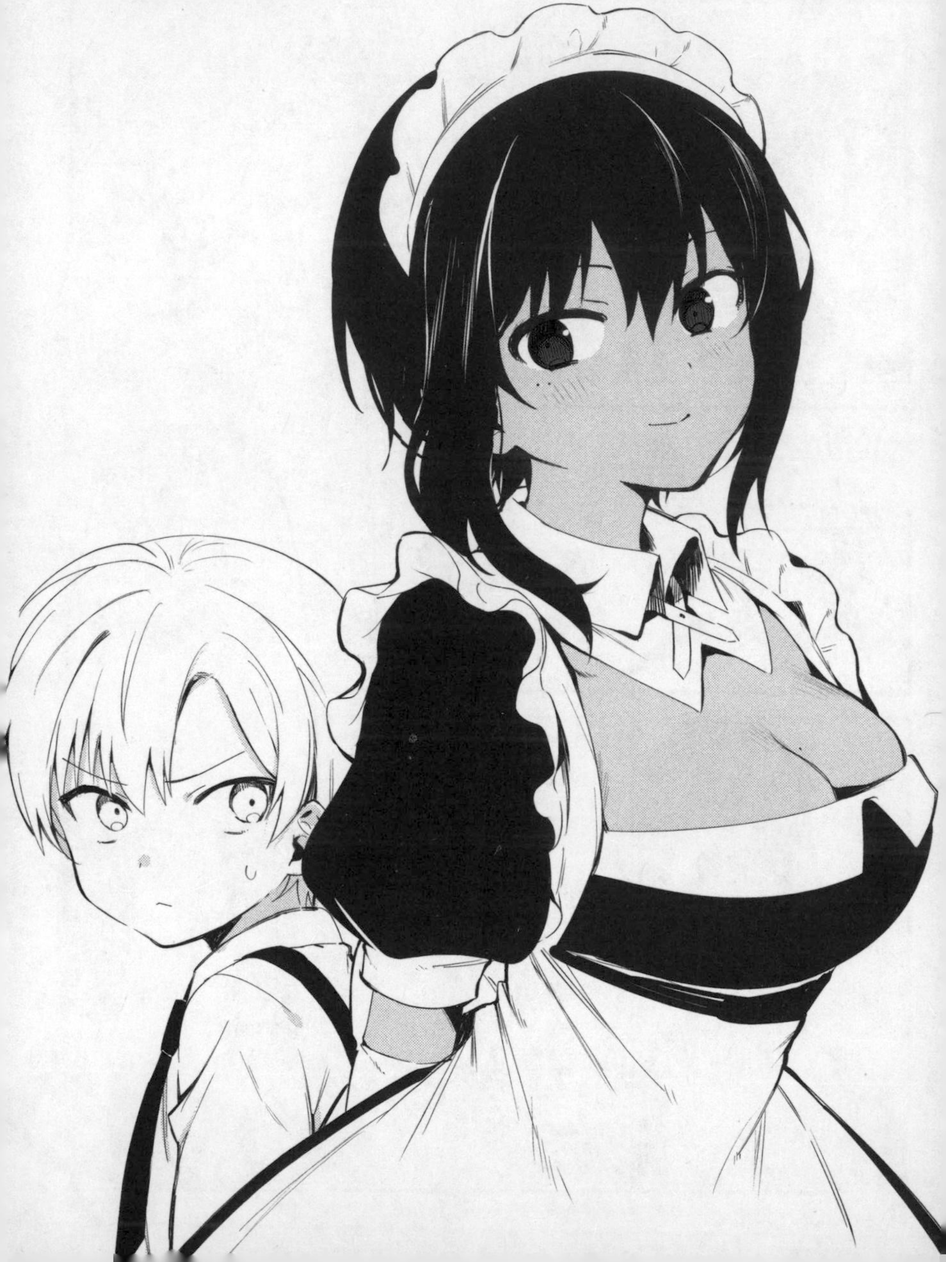

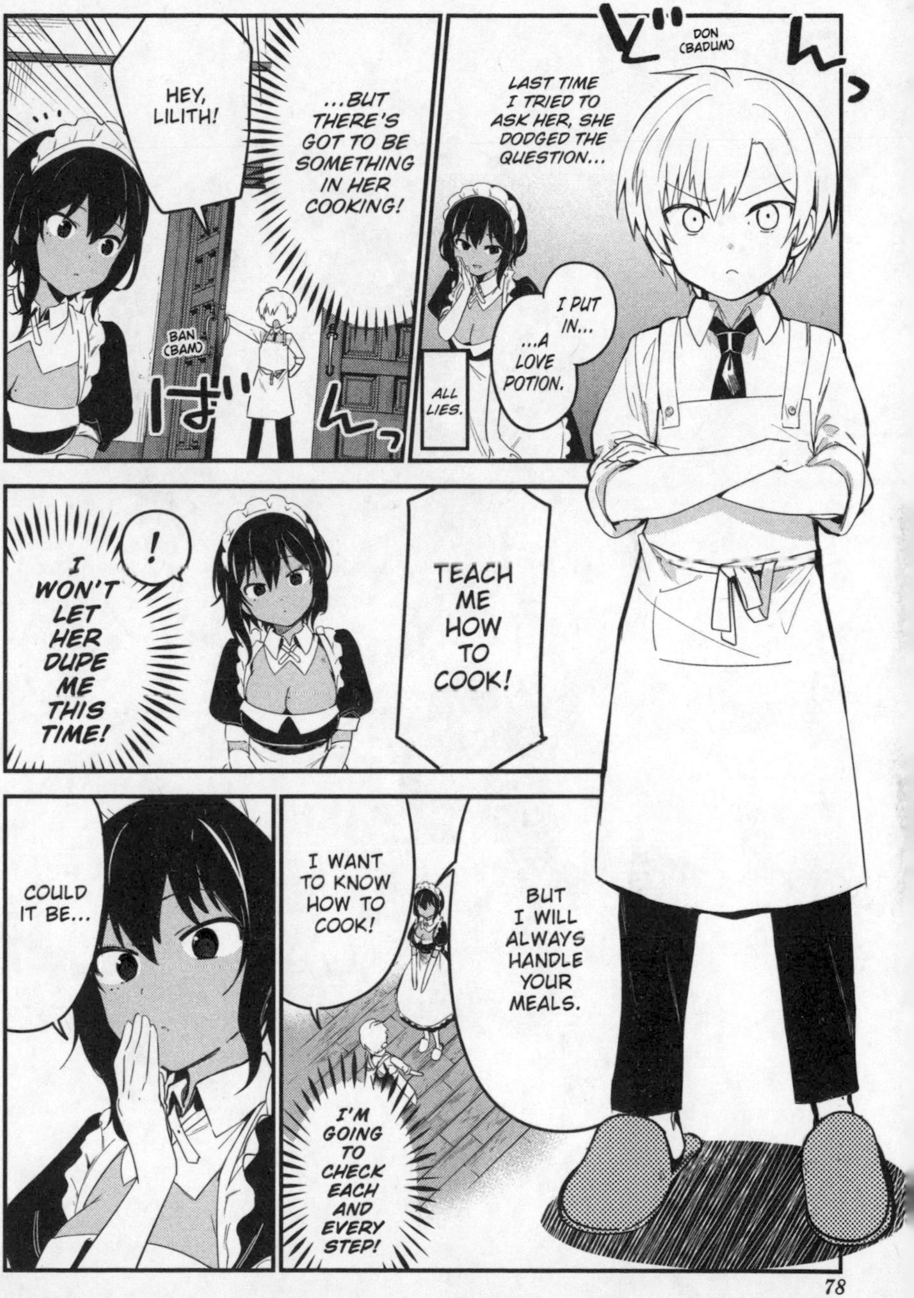
DON (BADUM)
LAST TIME I TRIED TO ASK HER, SHE DODGED THE QUESTION...
I PUT IN...
...A LOVE POTION.
ALL LIES.
...BUT THERE'S GOT TO BE SOMETHING IN HER COOKING!
HEY, LILITH!
...
BAN (BAM)
TEACH ME HOW TO COOK!
!
I WON'T LET HER DUPE ME THIS TIME!
BUT I WILL ALWAYS HANDLE YOUR MEALS.
I WANT TO KNOW HOW TO COOK!
I'M GOING TO CHECK EACH AND EVERY STEP!
COULD IT BE...

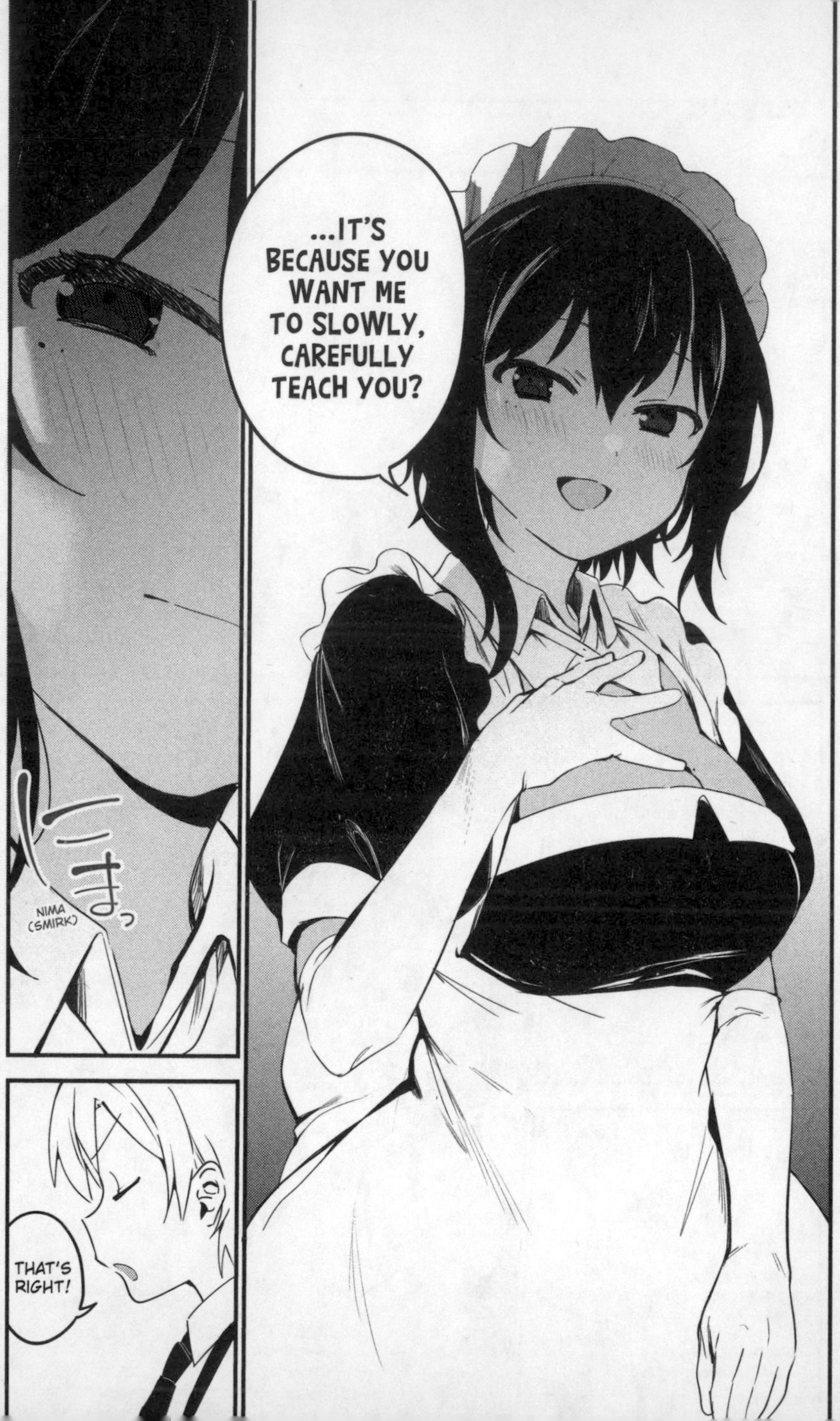
...IT'S BECAUSE YOU WANT ME TO SLOWLY, CAREFULLY TEACH YOU?
にまっ
NIMA (SMIRK)
THAT'S RIGHT!

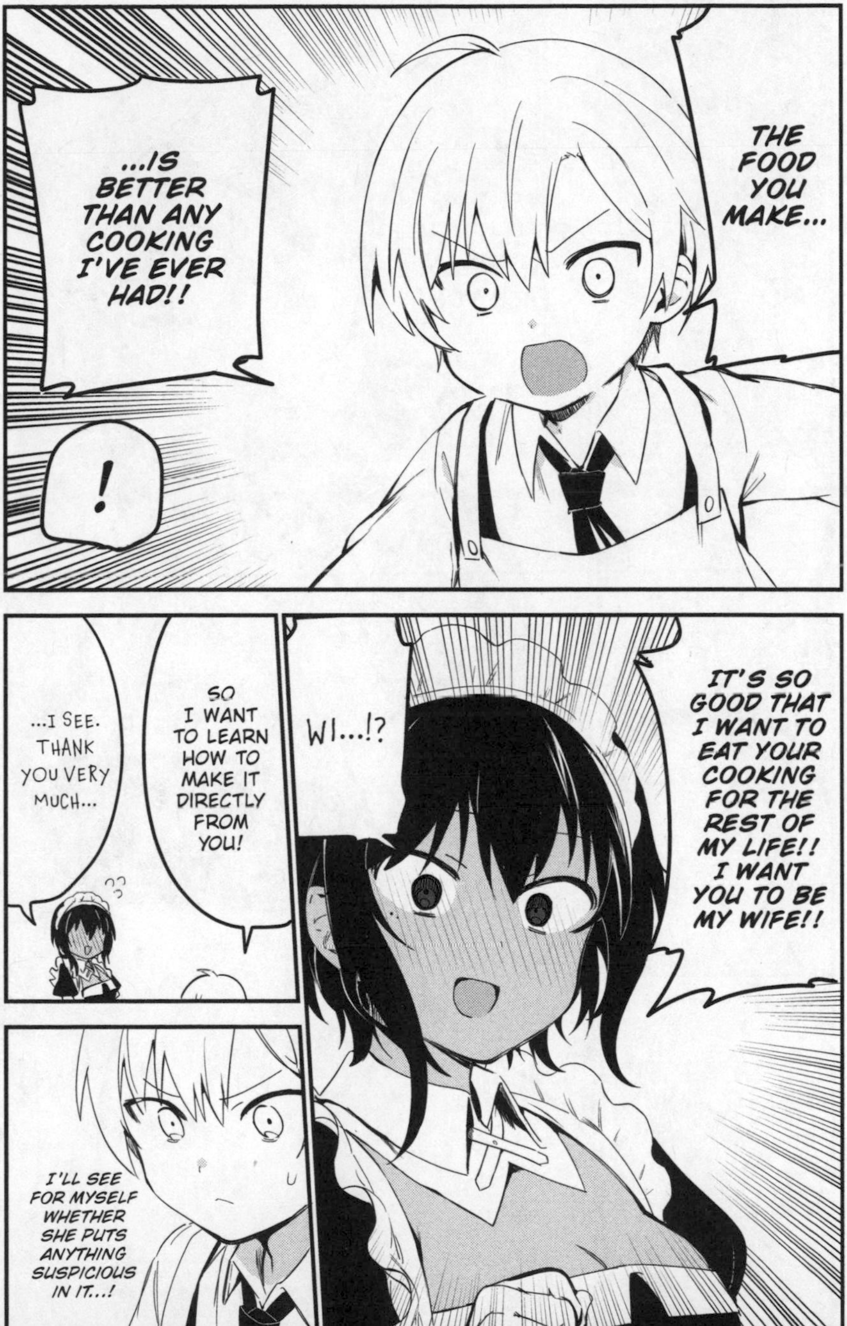
THE FOOD YOU MAKE...
...IS BETTER THAN ANY COOKING I'VE EVER HAD!!
!
IT'S SO GOOD THAT I WANT TO EAT YOUR COOKING FOR THE REST OF MY LIFE!! I WANT YOU TO BE MY WIFE!!
WI...!?
SO I WANT TO LEARN HOW TO MAKE IT DIRECTLY FROM YOU!
...I SEE. THANK YOU VERY MUCH...
I'LL SEE FOR MYSELF WHETHER SHE PUTS ANYTHING SUSPICIOUS IN IT...!

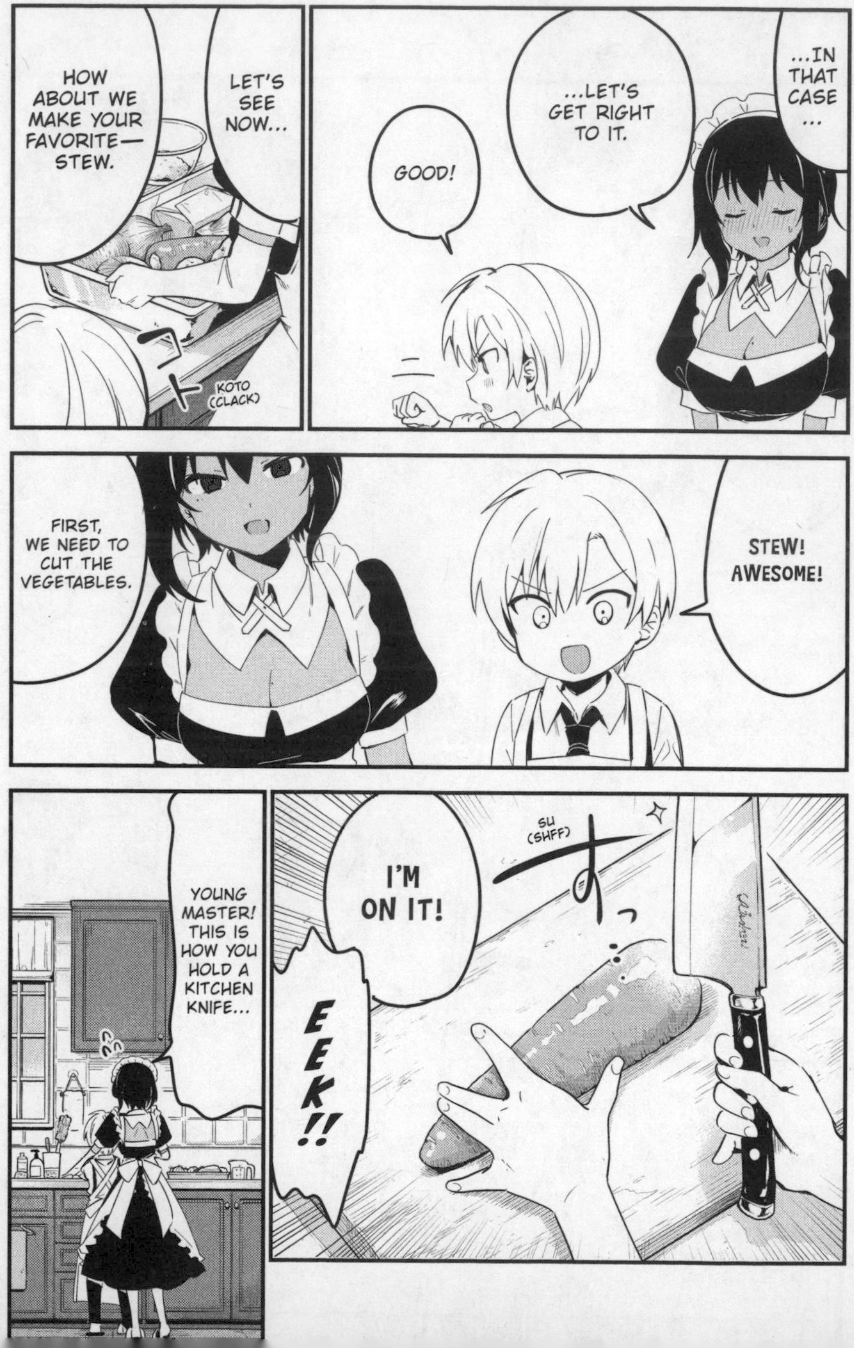

...IN THAT CASE ...
...LET'S GET RIGHT TO IT.
GOOD!
LET'S SEE NOW...
HOW ABOUT WE MAKE YOUR FAVORITE— STEW.
KOTO (CLACK)
STEW! AWESOME!
FIRST, WE NEED TO CUT THE VEGETABLES.
SU (SHFF)
I'M ON IT!
EEK!!
YOUNG MASTER! THIS IS HOW YOU HOLD A KITCHEN KNIFE...

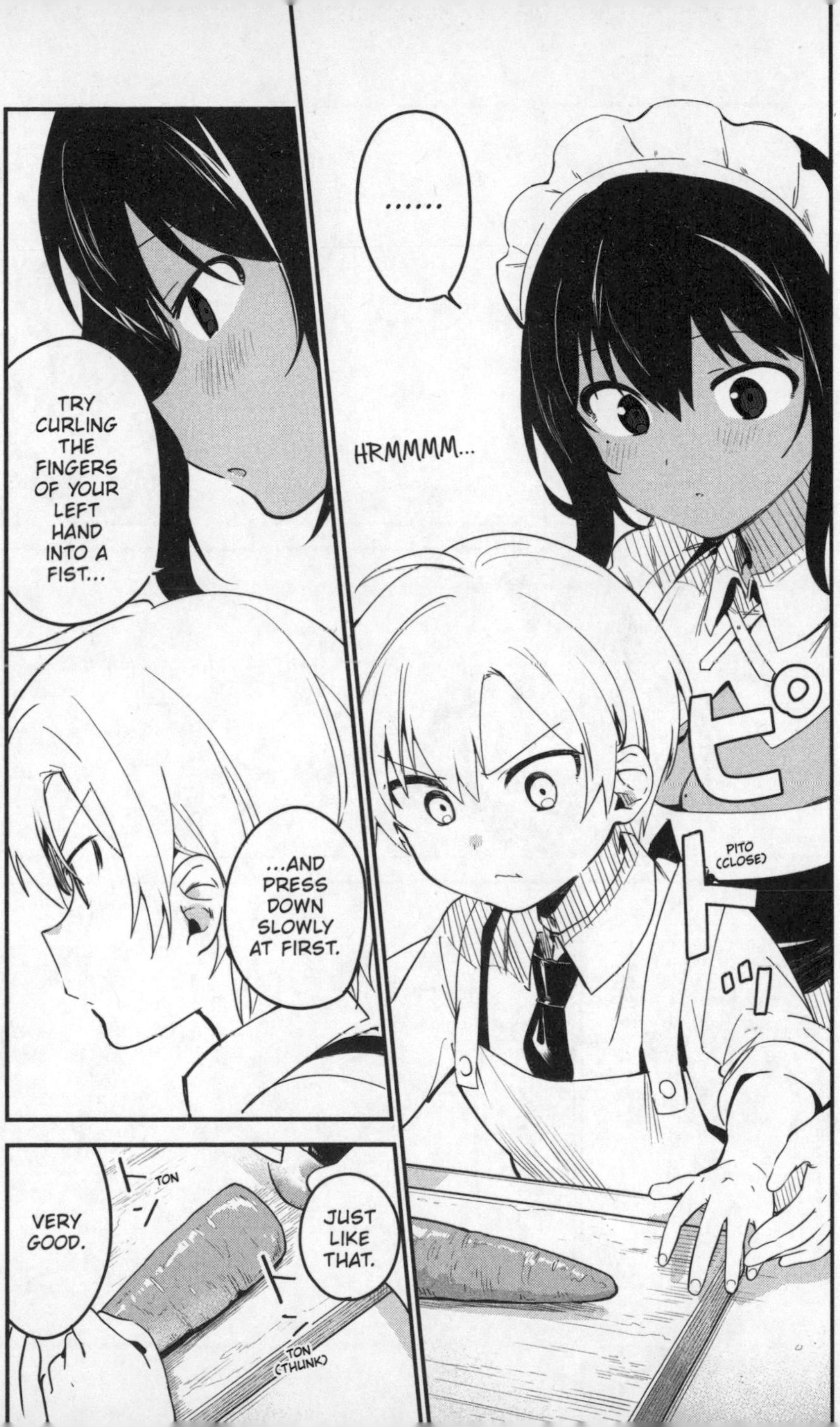
......
HRMMMM...
PITO (CLOSE)
TRY CURLING THE FINGERS OF YOUR LEFT HAND INTO A FIST...
...AND PRESS DOWN SLOWLY AT FIRST.
TON
JUST LIKE THAT.
VERY GOOD.
TON (THUNK)

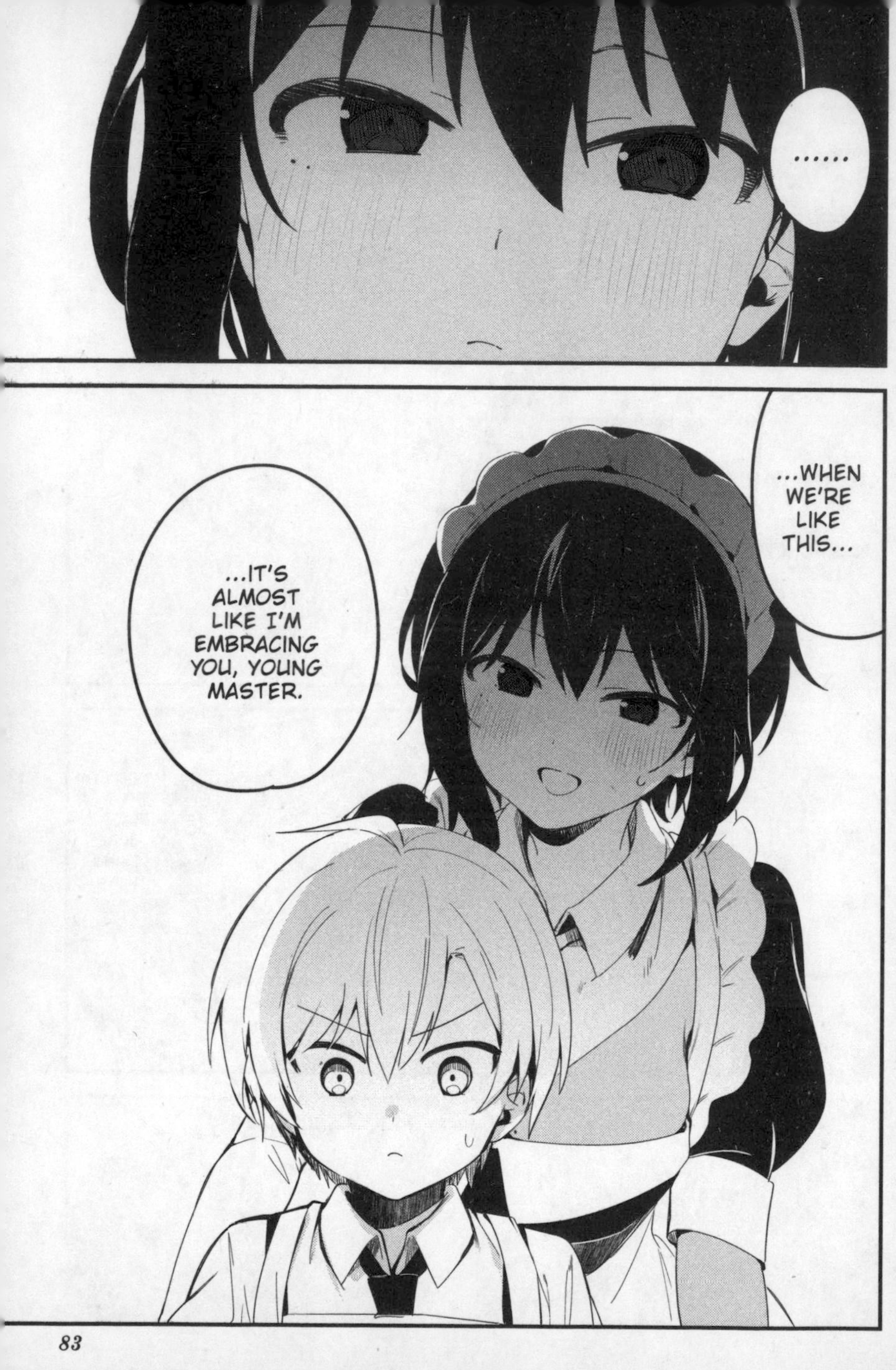
......
...WHEN WE'RE LIKE THIS...
...IT'S ALMOST LIKE I'M EMBRACING YOU, YOUNG MASTER.

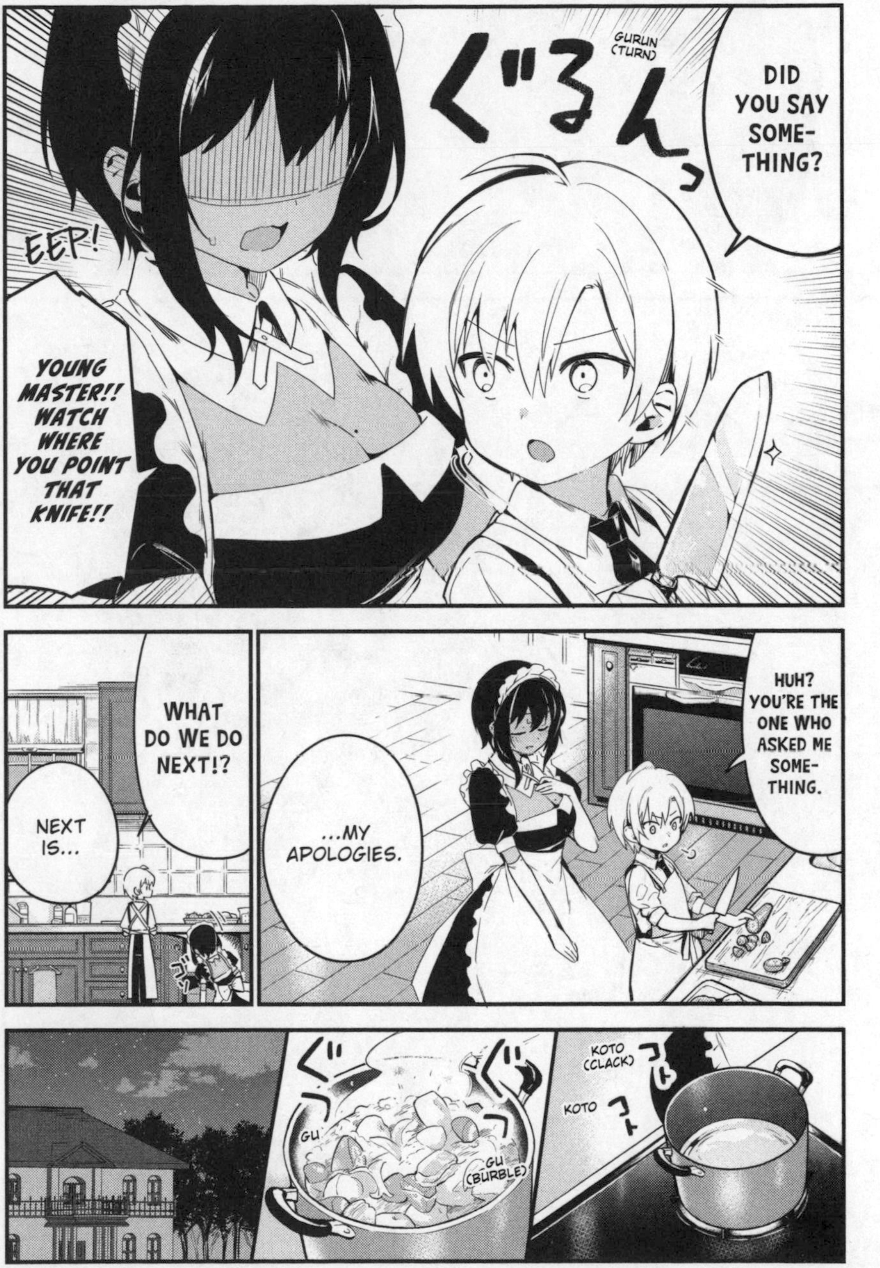
GURUN (TURN)
ぐるんっ
DID YOU SAY SOME-THING?
EEP!
YOUNG MASTER!! WATCH WHERE YOU POINT THAT KNIFE!!
HUH? YOU'RE THE ONE WHO ASKED ME SOME-THING.
...MY APOLOGIES.
WHAT DO WE DO NEXT!?
NEXT IS...
KOTO (CLACK)
コト
KOTO
コト
ぐつ
ぐつ
GU
GU (BURBLE)

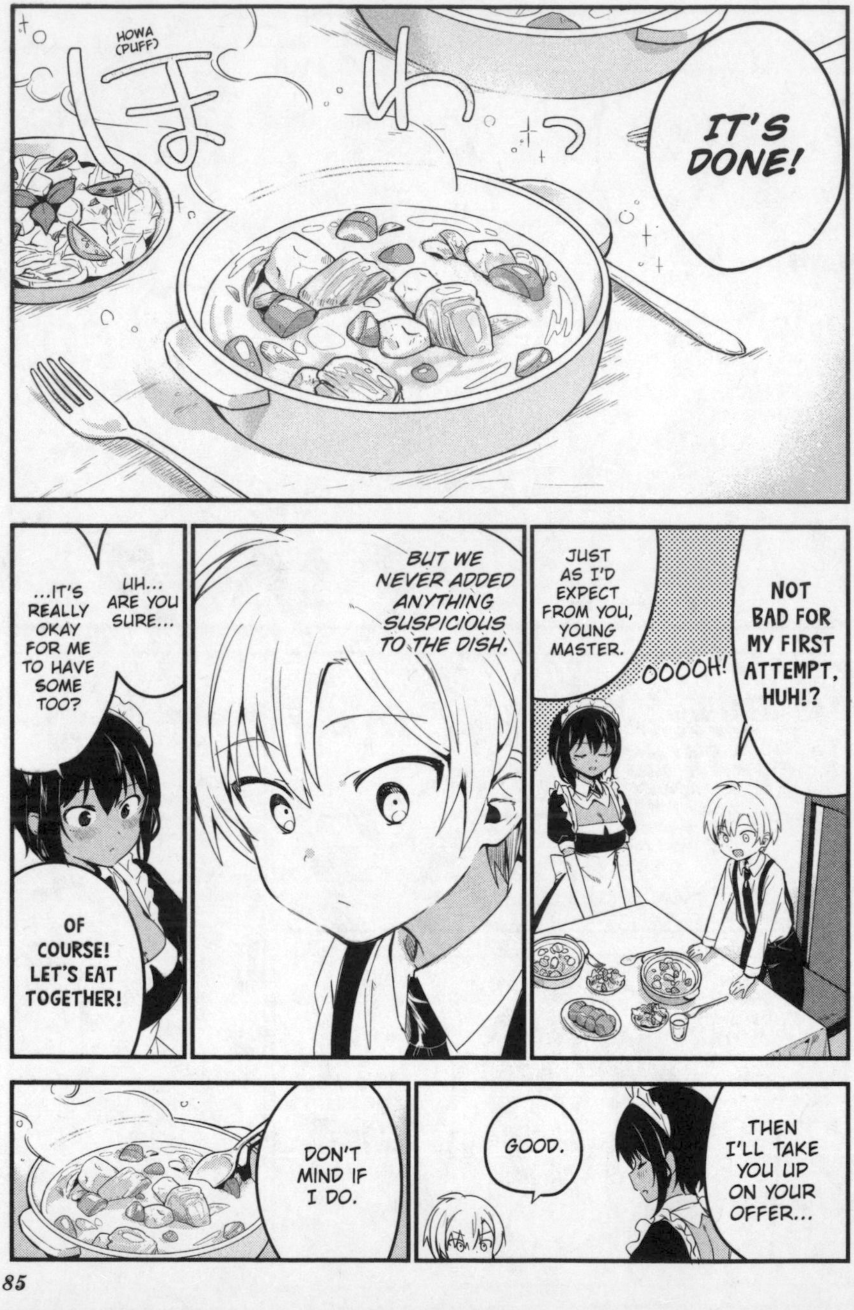
IT'S DONE!
HOWA (PUFF)
NOT BAD FOR MY FIRST ATTEMPT, HUH!?
OOOOH!
JUST AS I'D EXPECT FROM YOU, YOUNG MASTER.
BUT WE NEVER ADDED ANYTHING SUSPICIOUS TO THE DISH.
UH... ARE YOU SURE...
...IT'S REALLY OKAY FOR ME TO HAVE SOME TOO?
OF COURSE! LET'S EAT TOGETHER!
THEN I'LL TAKE YOU UP ON YOUR OFFER...
GOOD.
DON'T MIND IF I DO.

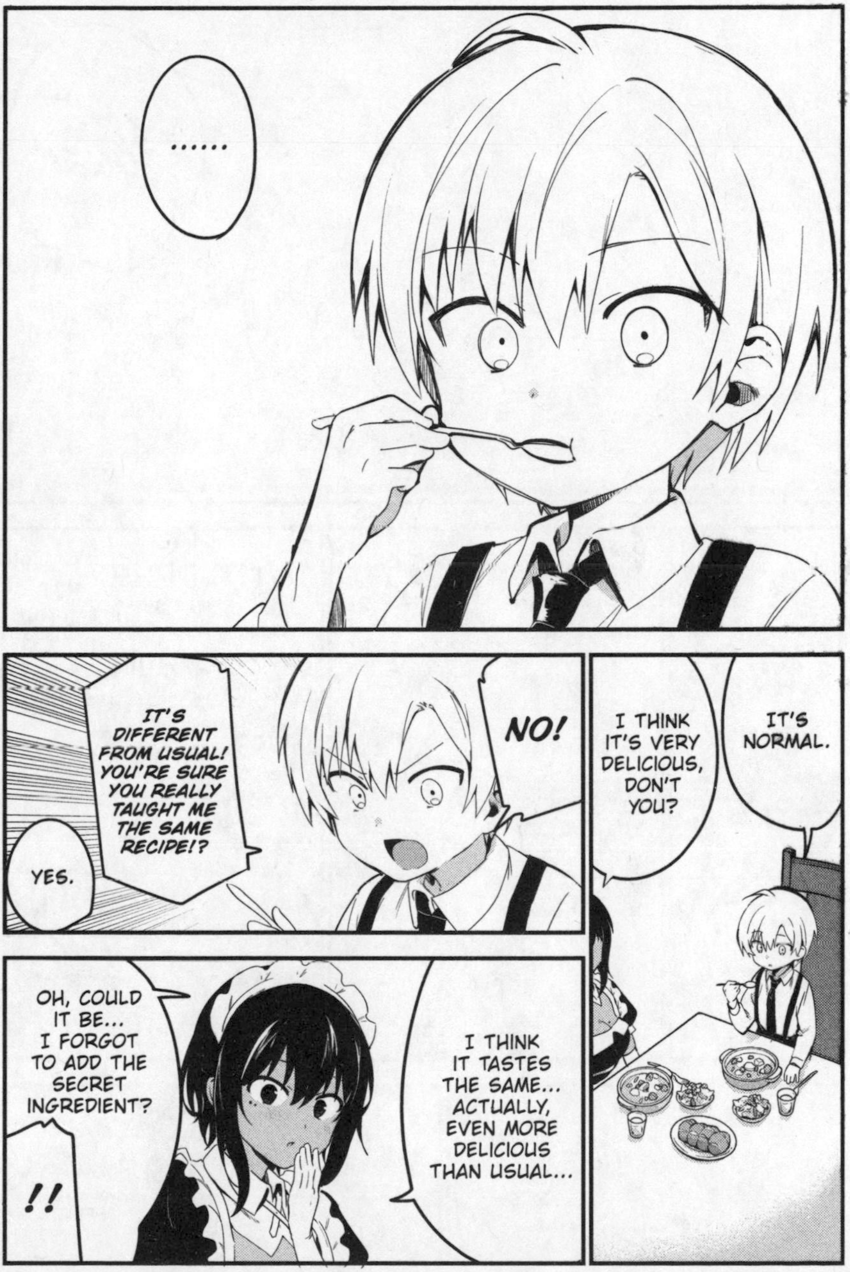
......
IT'S NORMAL.
I THINK IT'S VERY DELICIOUS, DON'T YOU?
NO!
IT'S DIFFERENT FROM USUAL! YOU'RE SURE YOU REALLY TAUGHT ME THE SAME RECIPE!?
YES.
I THINK IT TASTES THE SAME... ACTUALLY, EVEN MORE DELICIOUS THAN USUAL...
OH, COULD IT BE... I FORGOT TO ADD THE SECRET INGREDIENT?
!!

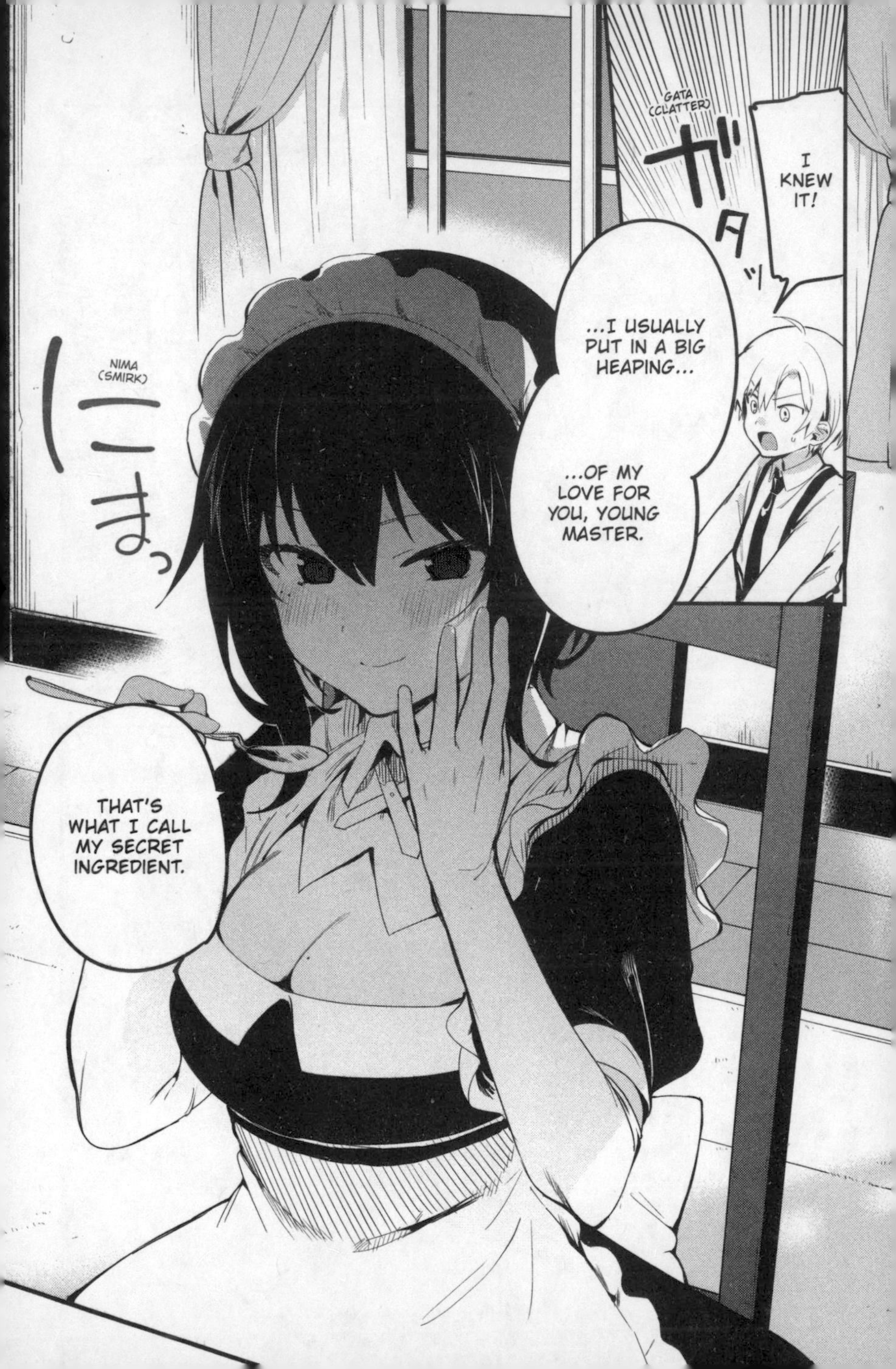
GATA (CLATTER)
ガタッ
I KNEW IT!
...I USUALLY PUT IN A BIG HEAPING...
...OF MY LOVE FOR YOU, YOUNG MASTER.
NIMA (SMIRK)
にまっ
THAT'S WHAT I CALL MY SECRET INGREDIENT.

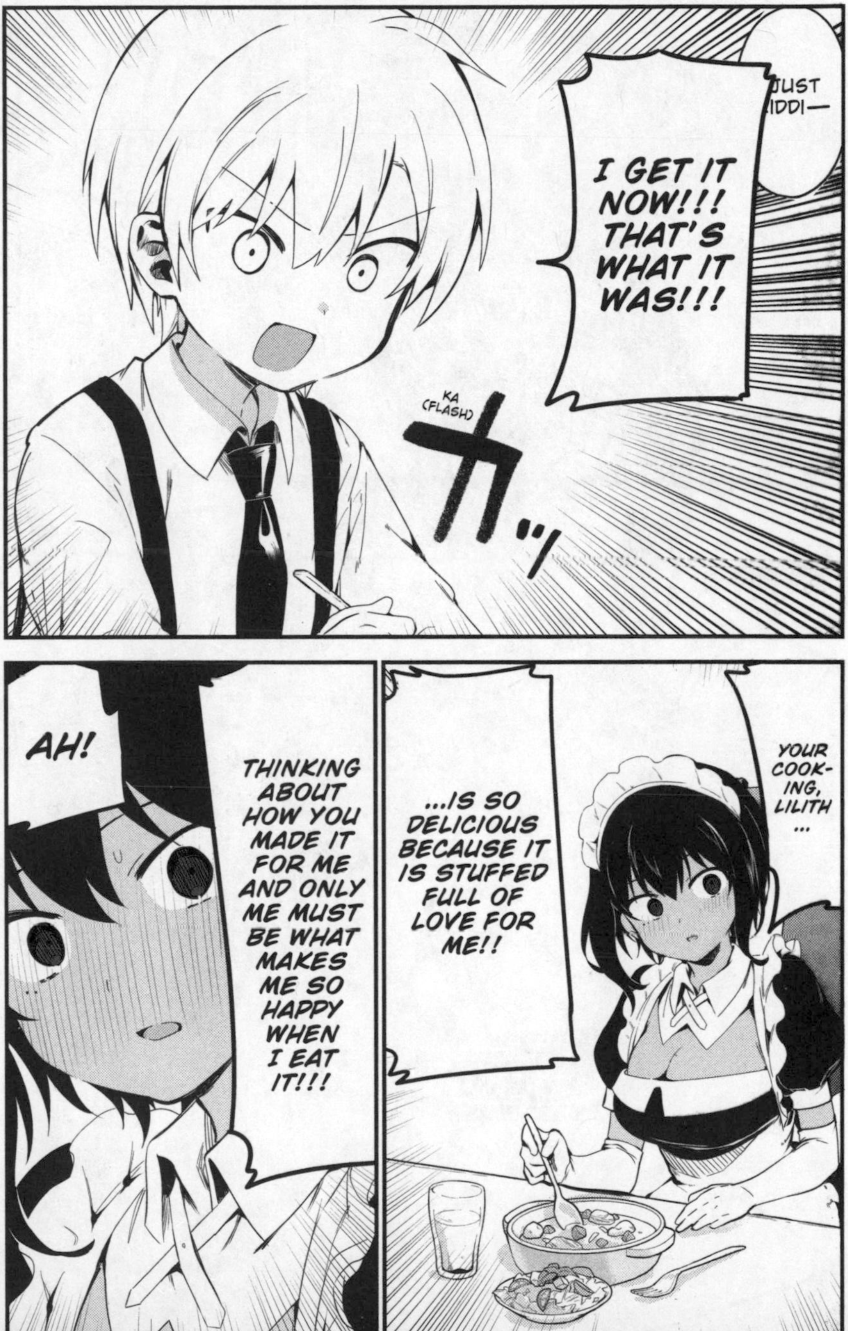
JUST IDDI—
I GET IT NOW!!! THAT'S WHAT IT WAS!!!
KA (FLASH)
YOUR COOKING, LILITH...
...IS SO DELICIOUS BECAUSE IT IS STUFFED FULL OF LOVE FOR ME!!
THINKING ABOUT HOW YOU MADE IT FOR ME AND ONLY ME MUST BE WHAT MAKES ME SO HAPPY WHEN I EAT IT!!!
AH!

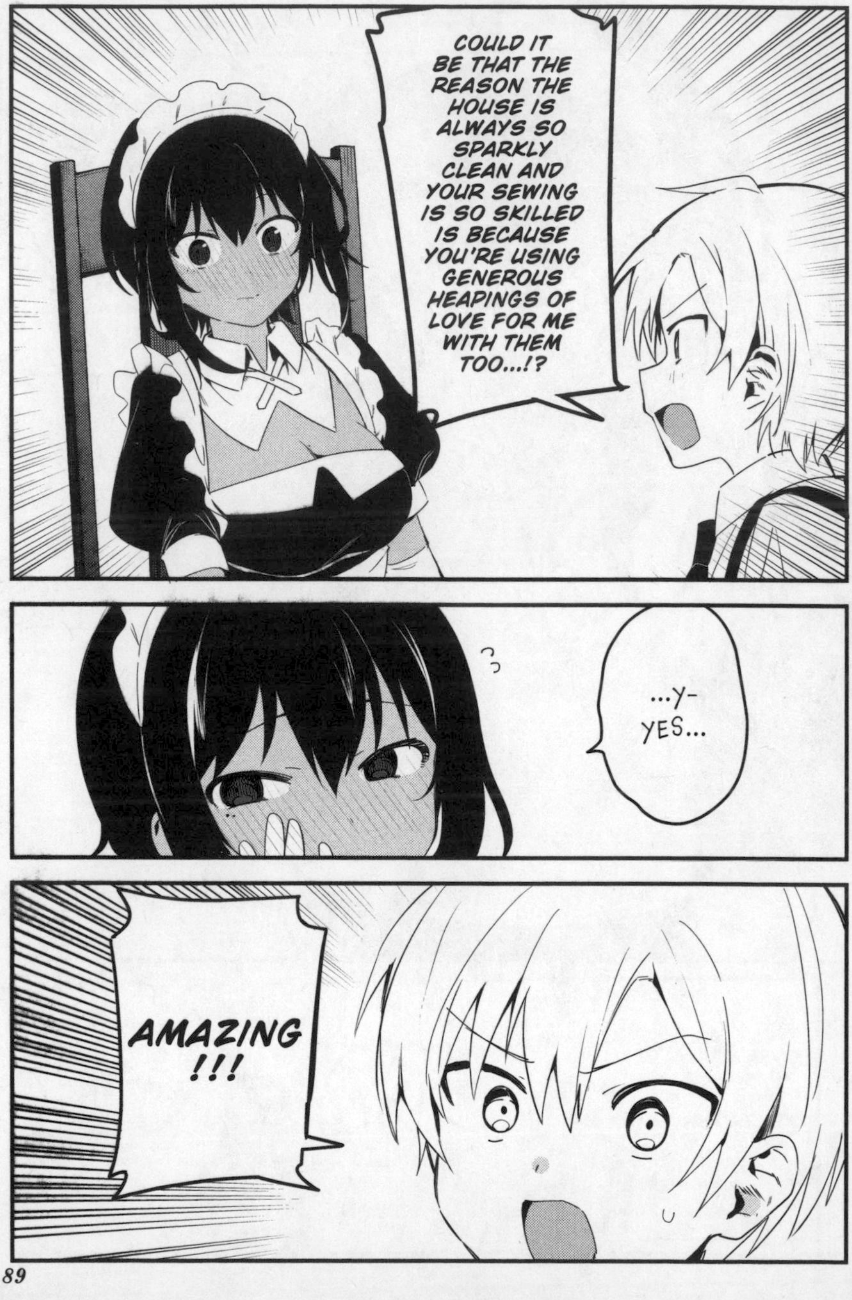
COULD IT BE THAT THE REASON THE HOUSE IS ALWAYS SO SPARKLY CLEAN AND YOUR SEWING IS SO SKILLED IS BECAUSE YOU'RE USING GENEROUS HEAPINGS OF LOVE FOR ME WITH THEM TOO...!?
...Y-YES...
AMAZING!!!

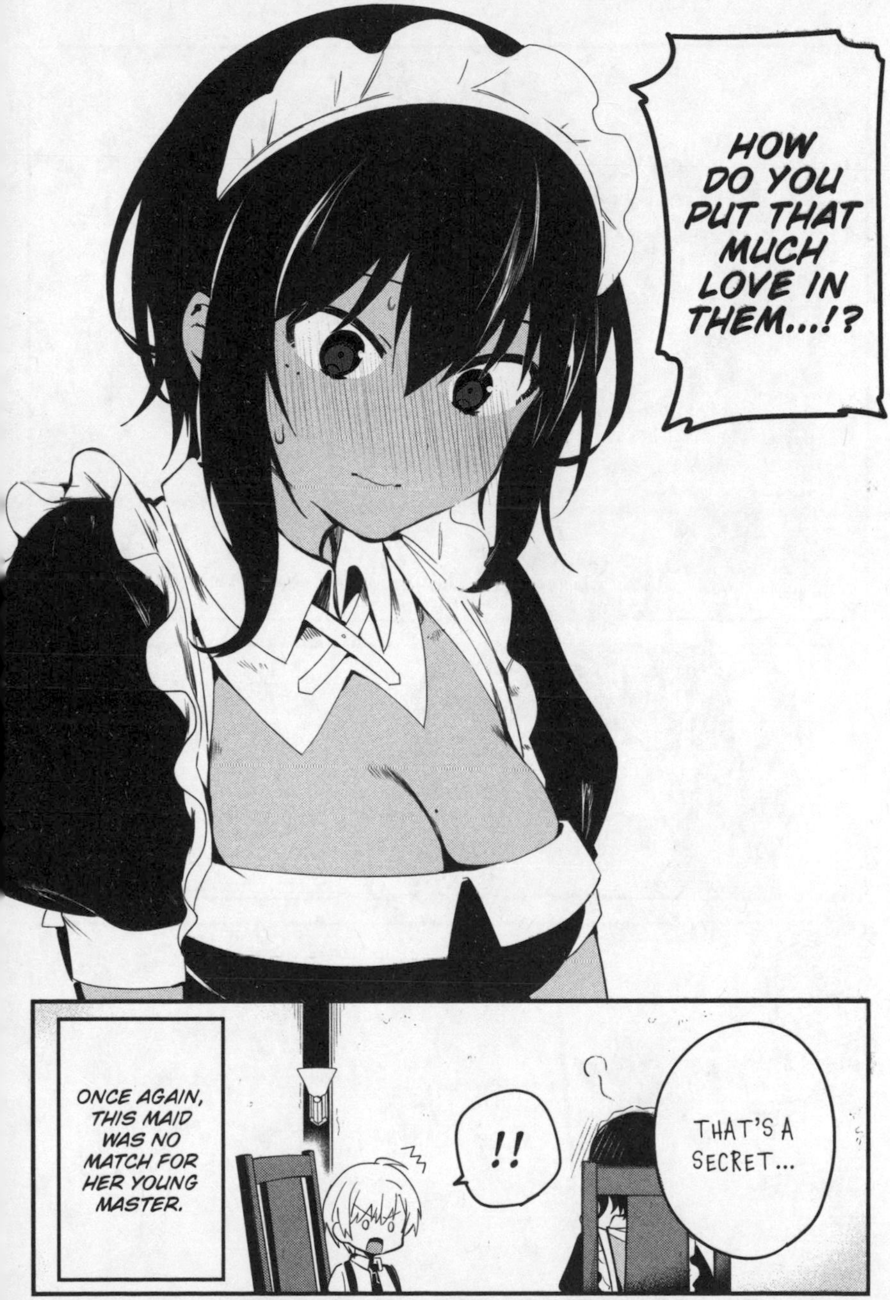
HOW DO YOU PUT THAT MUCH LOVE IN THEM...!?
THAT'S A SECRET...
!!
ONCE AGAIN, THIS MAID WAS NO MATCH FOR HER YOUNG MASTER.

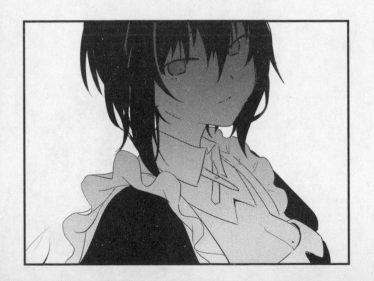

The Maid I Hired Recently Is Mysterious

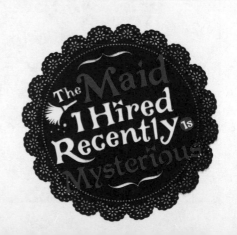

CHAPTER 11

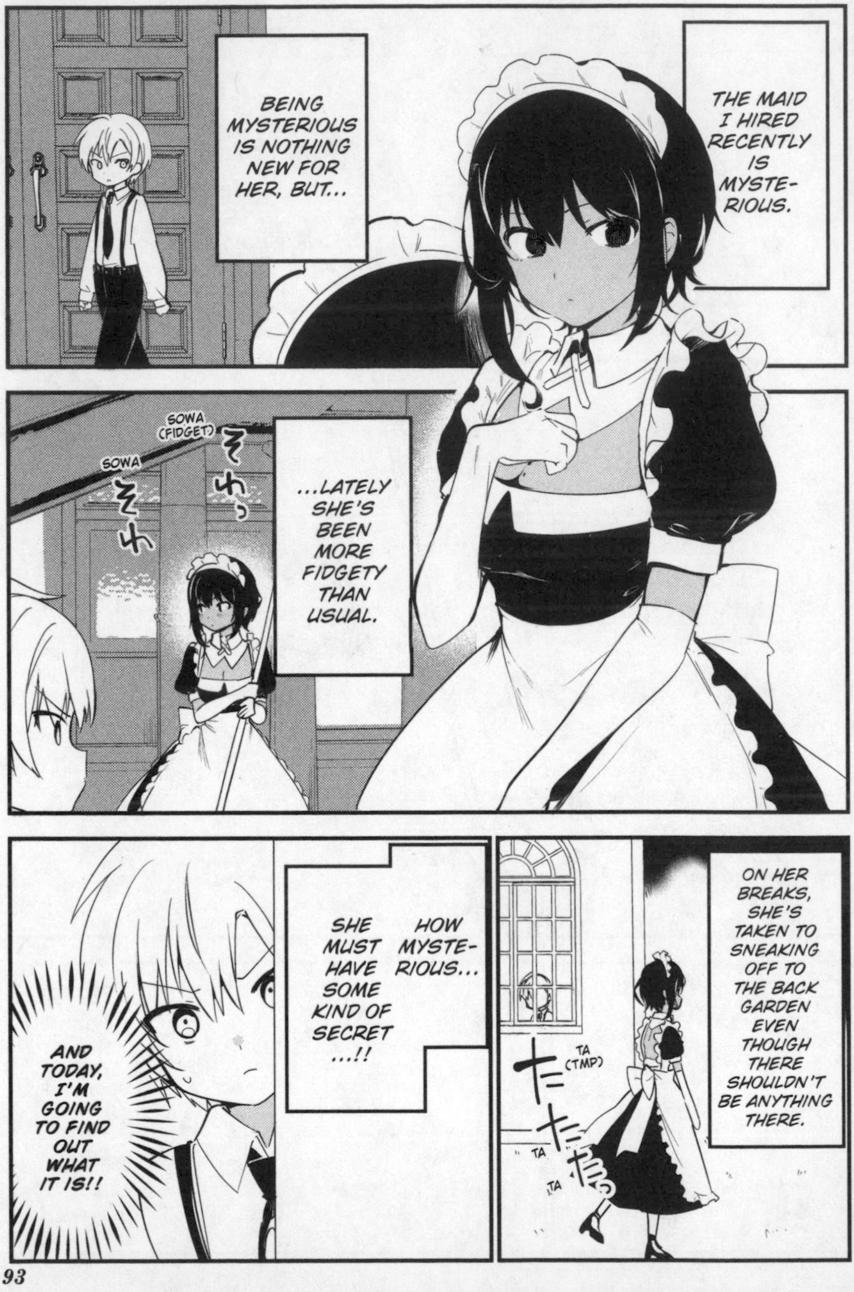
THE MAID I HIRED RECENTLY IS MYSTERIOUS.
BEING MYSTERIOUS IS NOTHING NEW FOR HER, BUT...
...LATELY SHE'S BEEN MORE FIDGETY THAN USUAL.
SOWA (FIDGET)
SOWA
ON HER BREAKS, SHE'S TAKEN TO SNEAKING OFF TO THE BACK GARDEN EVEN THOUGH THERE SHOULDN'T BE ANYTHING THERE.
TA (TMP)
TA
TA
HOW MYSTERIOUS...
SHE MUST HAVE SOME KIND OF SECRET...!!
AND TODAY, I'M GOING TO FIND OUT WHAT IT IS!!

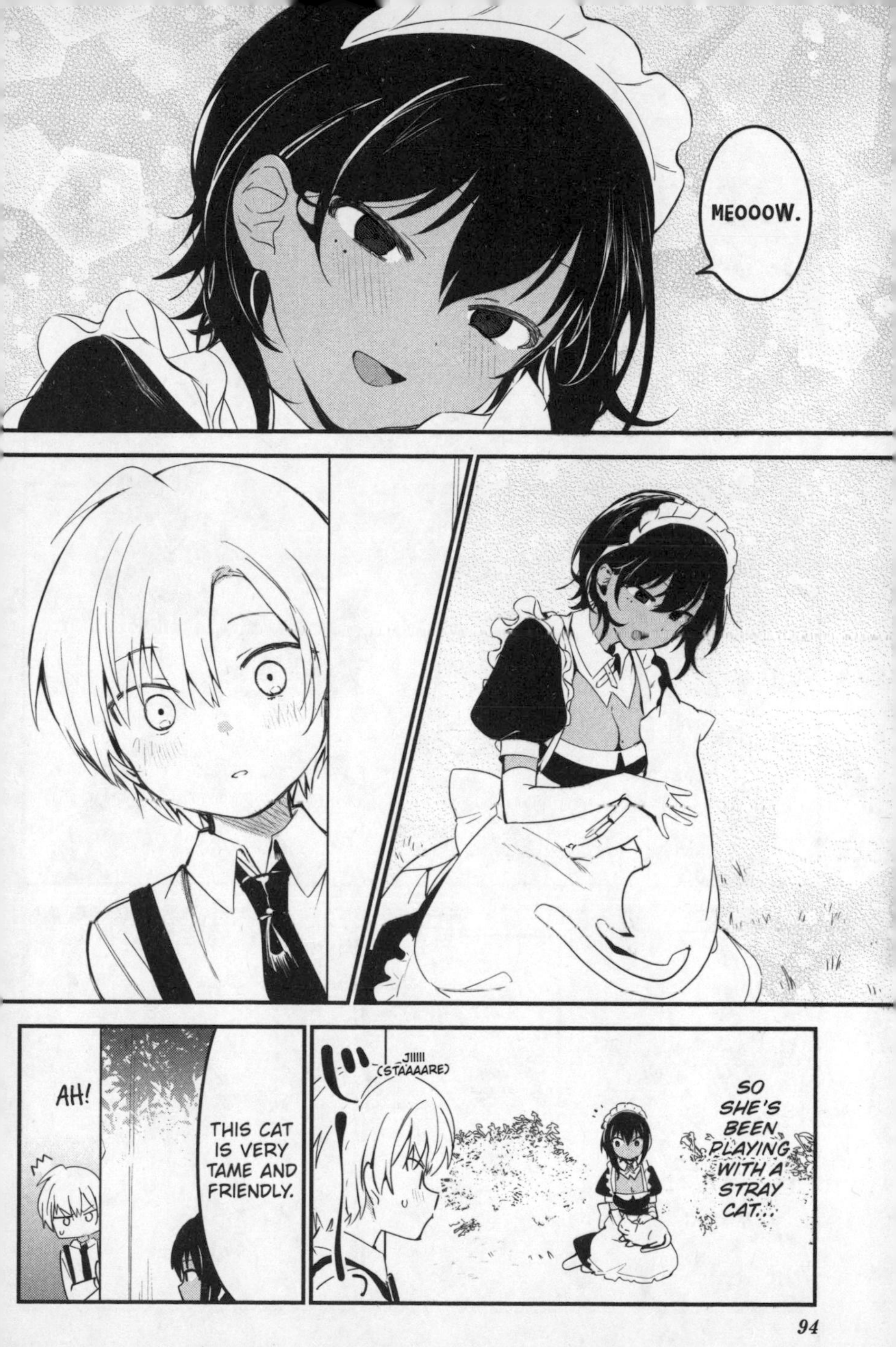
MEOOOW.
SO SHE'S BEEN PLAYING WITH A STRAY CAT...
JIIIII (STAAAARE)
THIS CAT IS VERY TAME AND FRIENDLY.
AH!

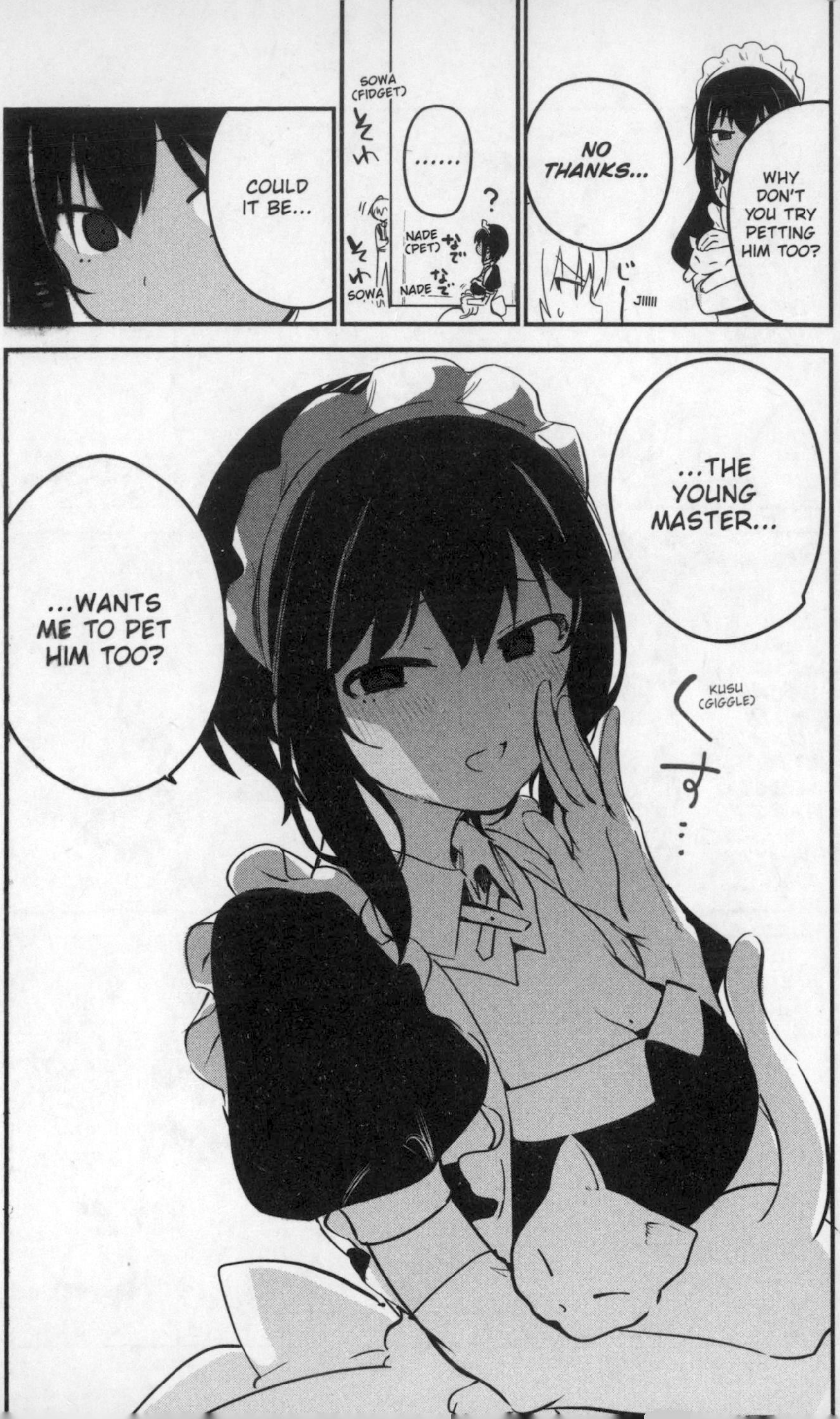
WHY DON'T YOU TRY PETTING HIM TOO?
じー
JIIIII
NO THANKS...
SOWA (FIDGET)
そわ
そわ
SOWA
......
?
NADE (PET)
なで
なで
NADE
COULD IT BE...
...THE YOUNG MASTER...
KUSU (GIGGLE)
くす...
...WANTS ME TO PET HIM TOO?

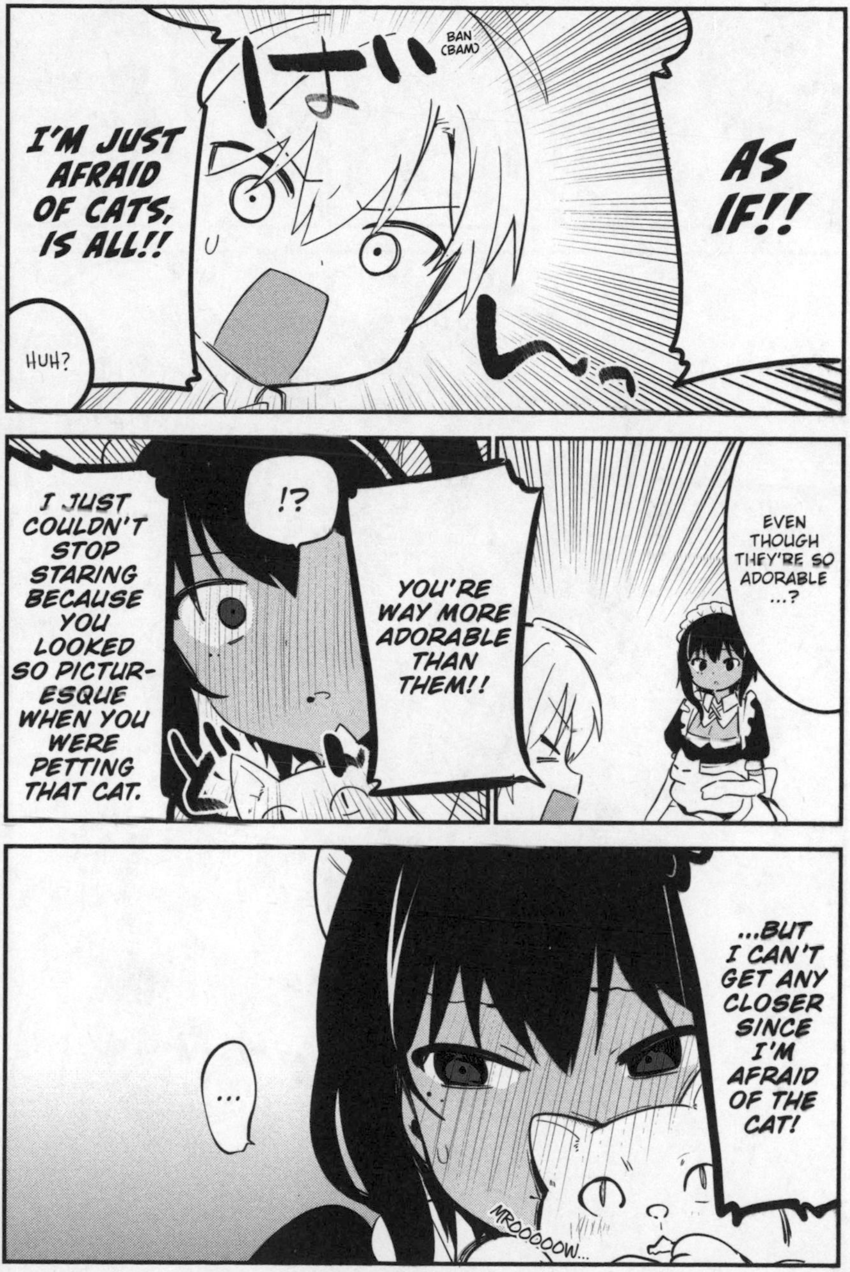
AS IF!!
BAN (BAM)
I'M JUST AFRAID OF CATS, IS ALL!!
HUH?
EVEN THOUGH THEY'RE SO ADORABLE ...?
YOU'RE WAY MORE ADORABLE THAN THEM!!
!?
I JUST COULDN'T STOP STARING BECAUSE YOU LOOKED SO PICTUR-ESQUE WHEN YOU WERE PETTING THAT CAT.
...BUT I CAN'T GET ANY CLOSER SINCE I'M AFRAID OF THE CAT!
...
MROOOOOW...

CHAPTER 12

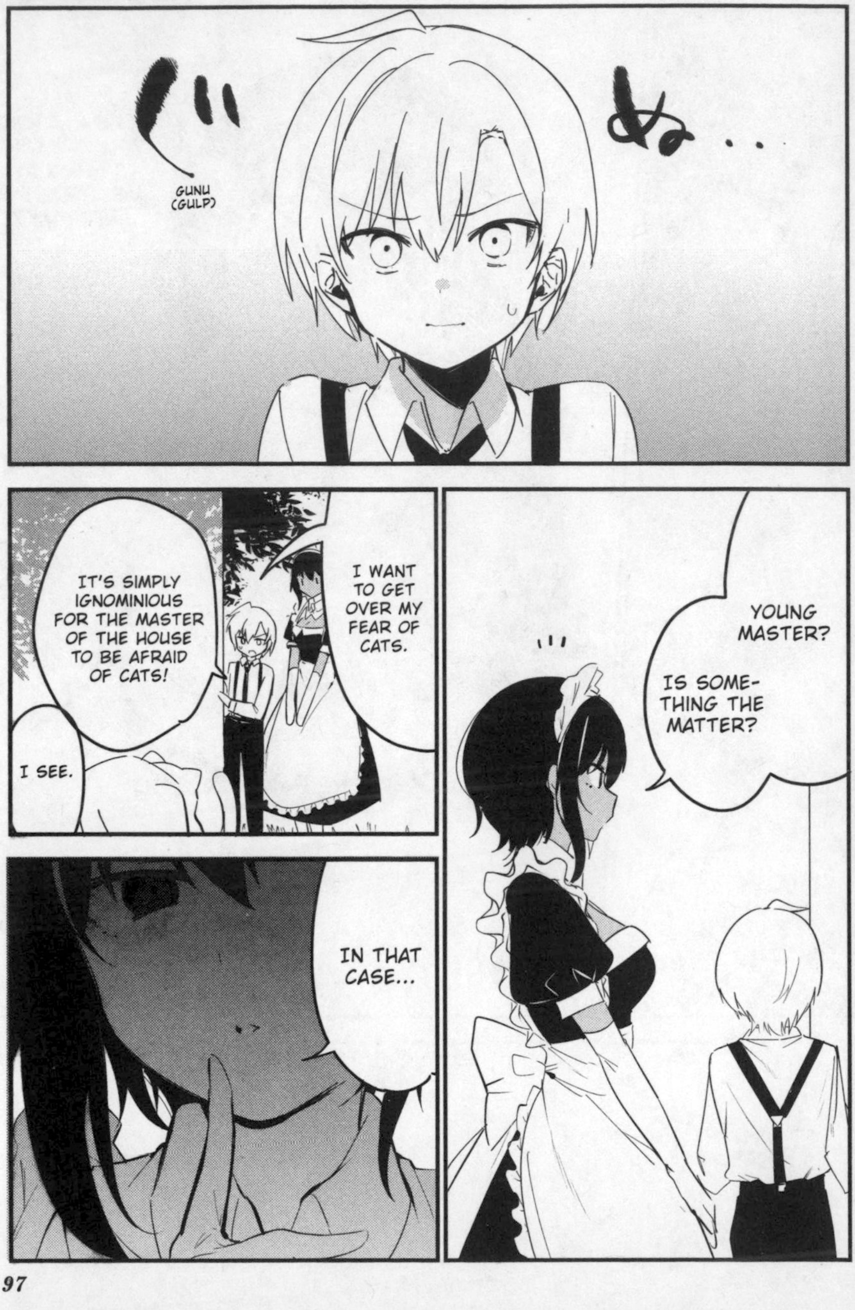
ぐぬ...
GUNU (GULP)
YOUNG MASTER?
IS SOME-THING THE MATTER?
I WANT TO GET OVER MY FEAR OF CATS.
IT'S SIMPLY IGNOMINIOUS FOR THE MASTER OF THE HOUSE TO BE AFRAID OF CATS!
I SEE.
IN THAT CASE...

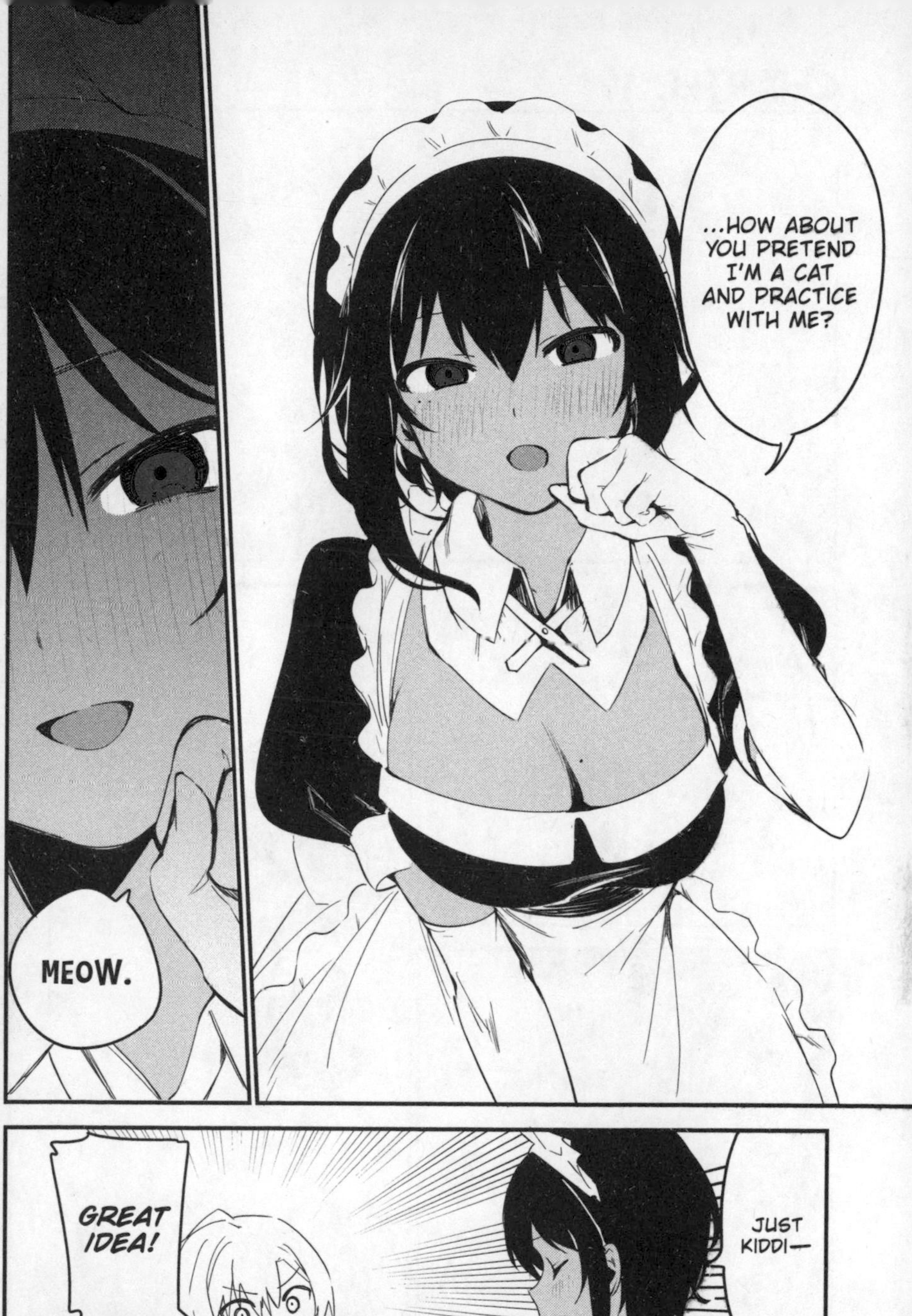
...HOW ABOUT YOU PRETEND I'M A CAT AND PRACTICE WITH ME?
MEOW.
JUST KIDDI—
GREAT IDEA!

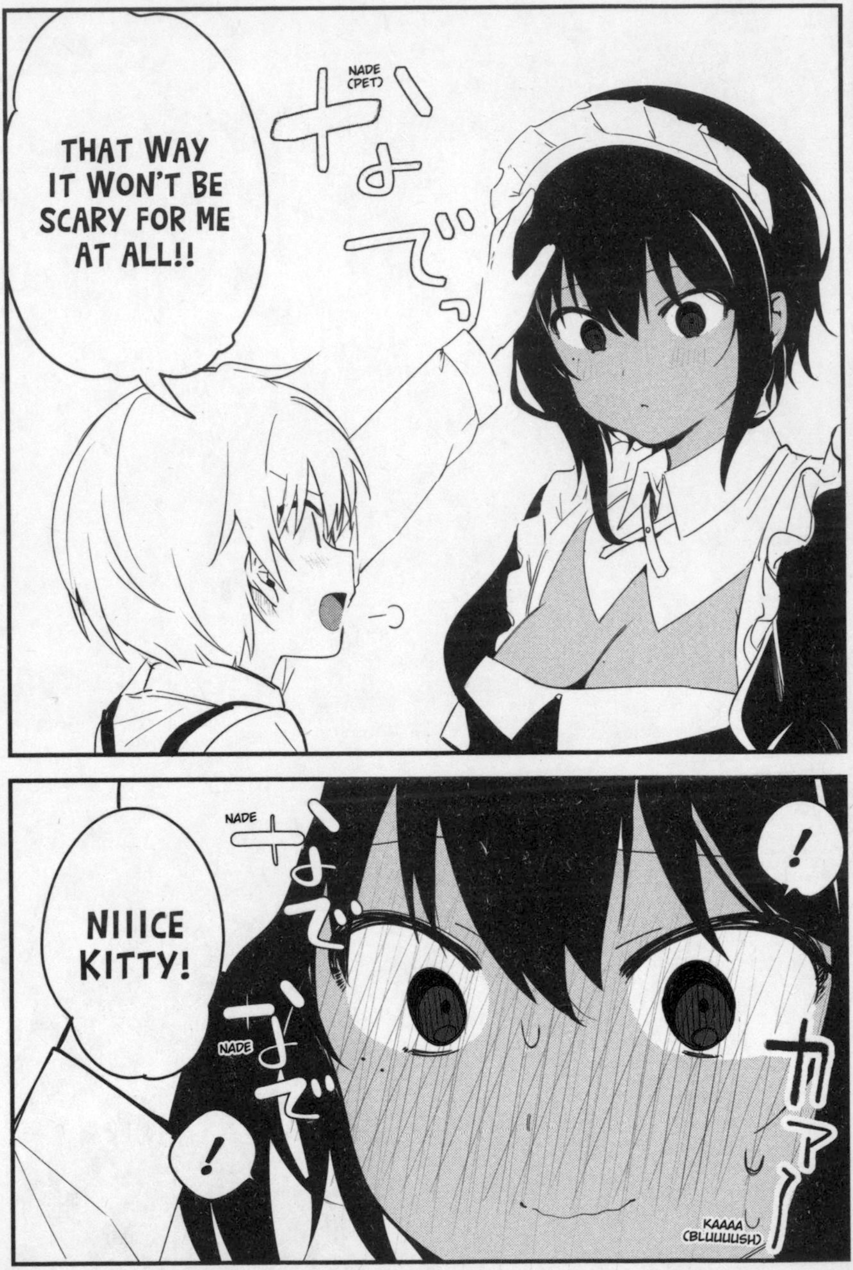
NADE (PET)
THAT WAY IT WON'T BE SCARY FOR ME AT ALL!!
!
NADE
NIIICE KITTY!
NADE
KAAAA (BLUUUUSH)
!

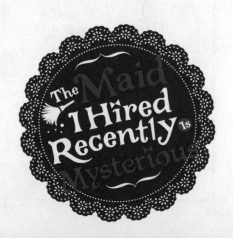

The Maid I Hired Recently is Mysterious

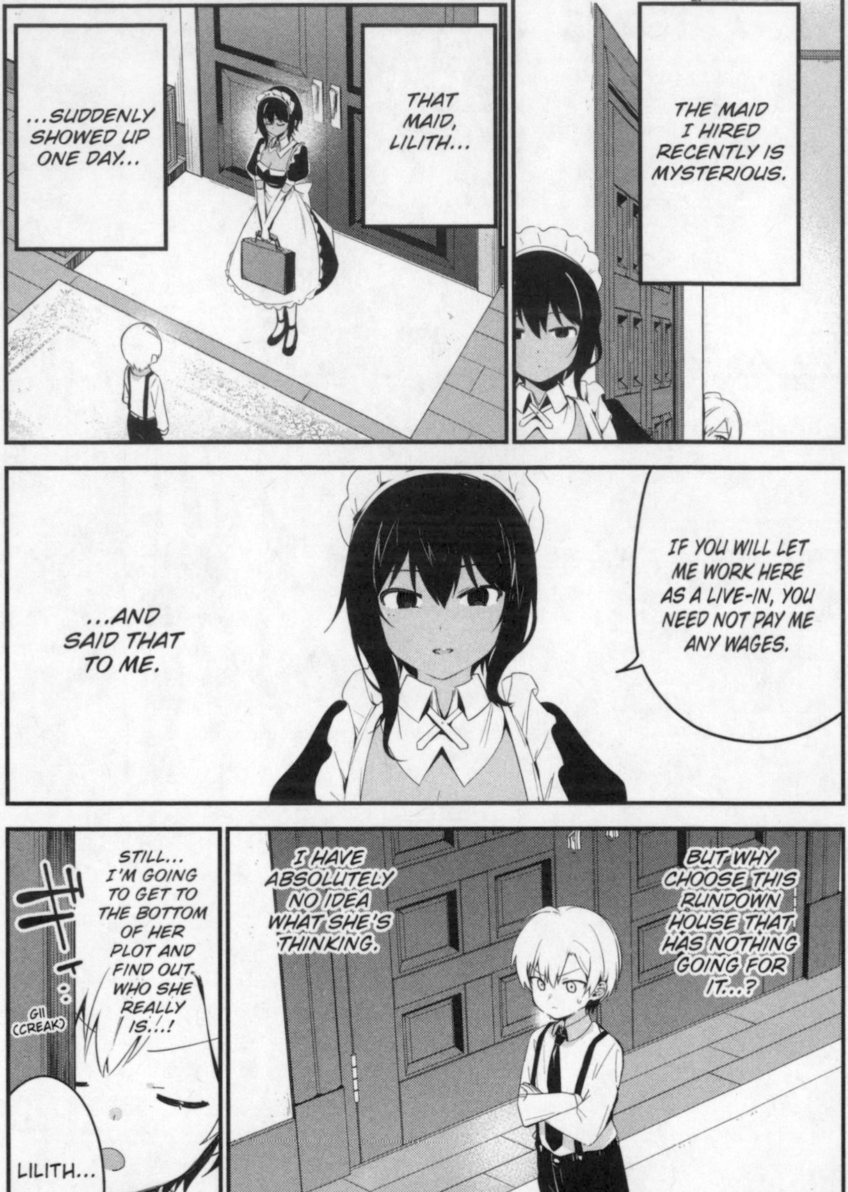
THE MAID I HIRED RECENTLY IS MYSTERIOUS.
THAT MAID, LILITH...
...SUDDENLY SHOWED UP ONE DAY...
IF YOU WILL LET ME WORK HERE AS A LIVE-IN, YOU NEED NOT PAY ME ANY WAGES.
...AND SAID THAT TO ME.
BUT WHY CHOOSE THIS RUNDOWN HOUSE THAT HAS NOTHING GOING FOR IT...?
I HAVE ABSOLUTELY NO IDEA WHAT SHE'S THINKING.
STILL... I'M GOING TO GET TO THE BOTTOM OF HER PLOT AND FIND OUT WHO SHE REALLY IS...!
ギィッ
GII (CREAK)
LILITH...

CHAPTER 13

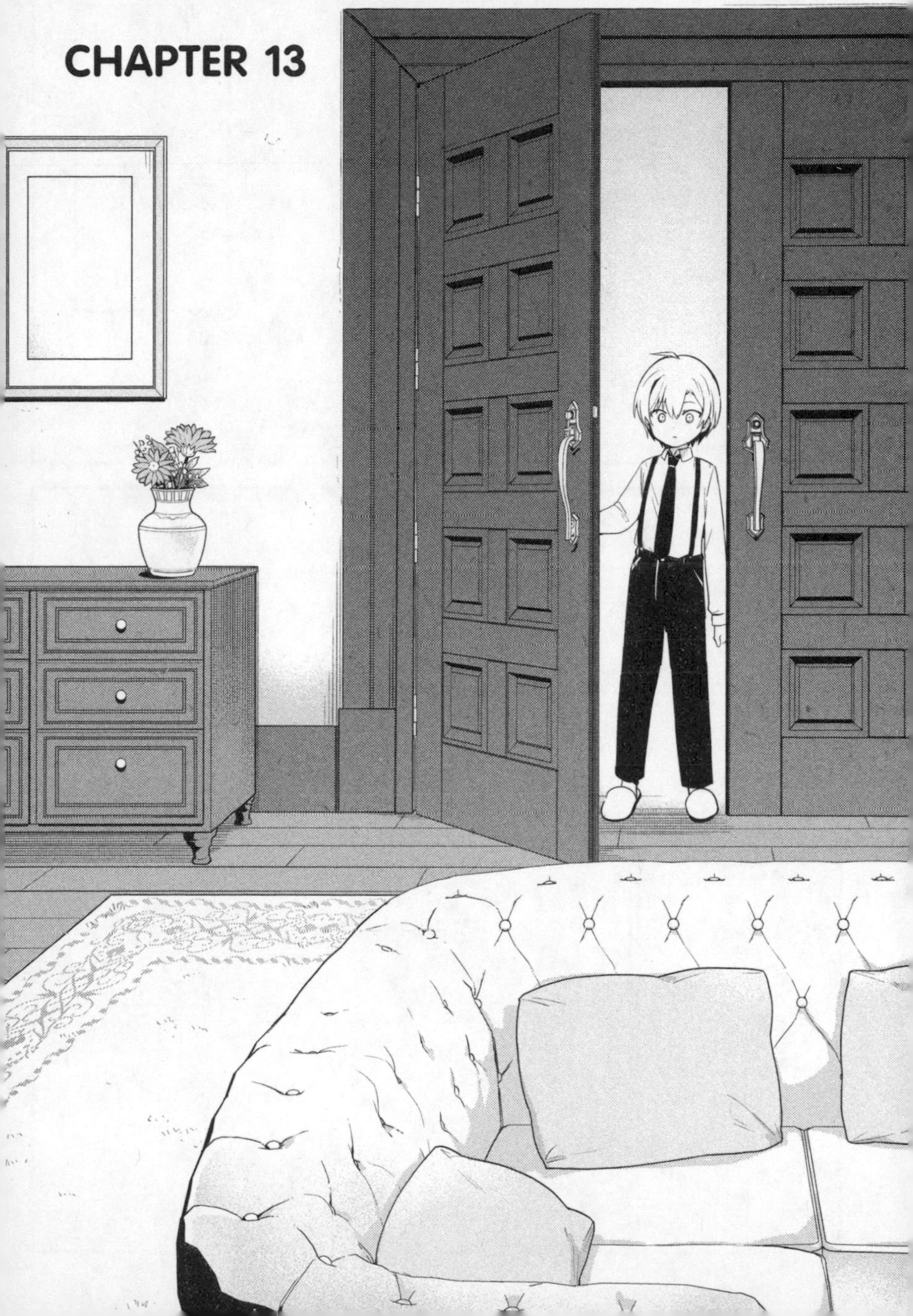

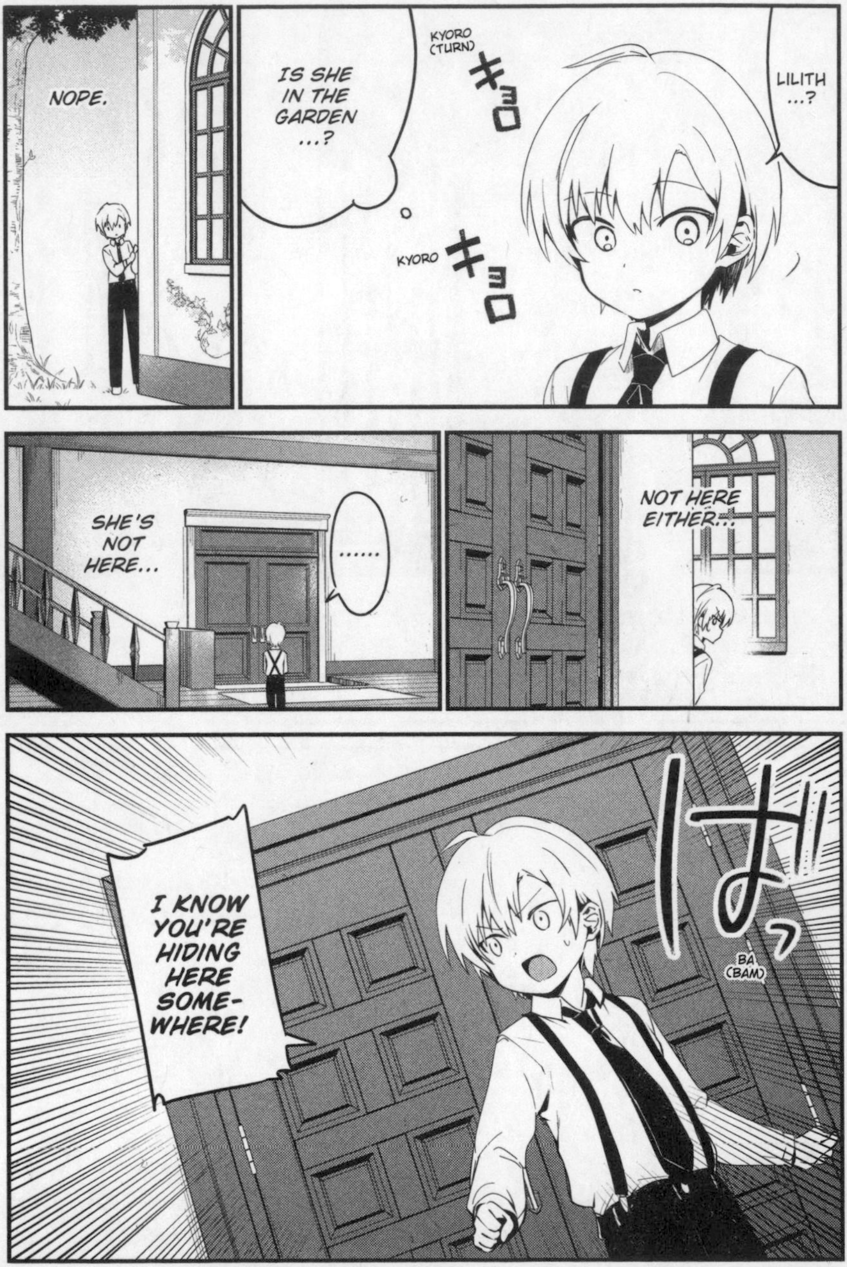
LILITH ...?
KYORO (TURN)
キョロ
IS SHE IN THE GARDEN ...?
KYORO
キョロ
NOPE.
NOT HERE EITHER...
......
SHE'S NOT HERE...
はっ
BA (BAM)
I KNOW YOU'RE HIDING HERE SOME-WHERE!

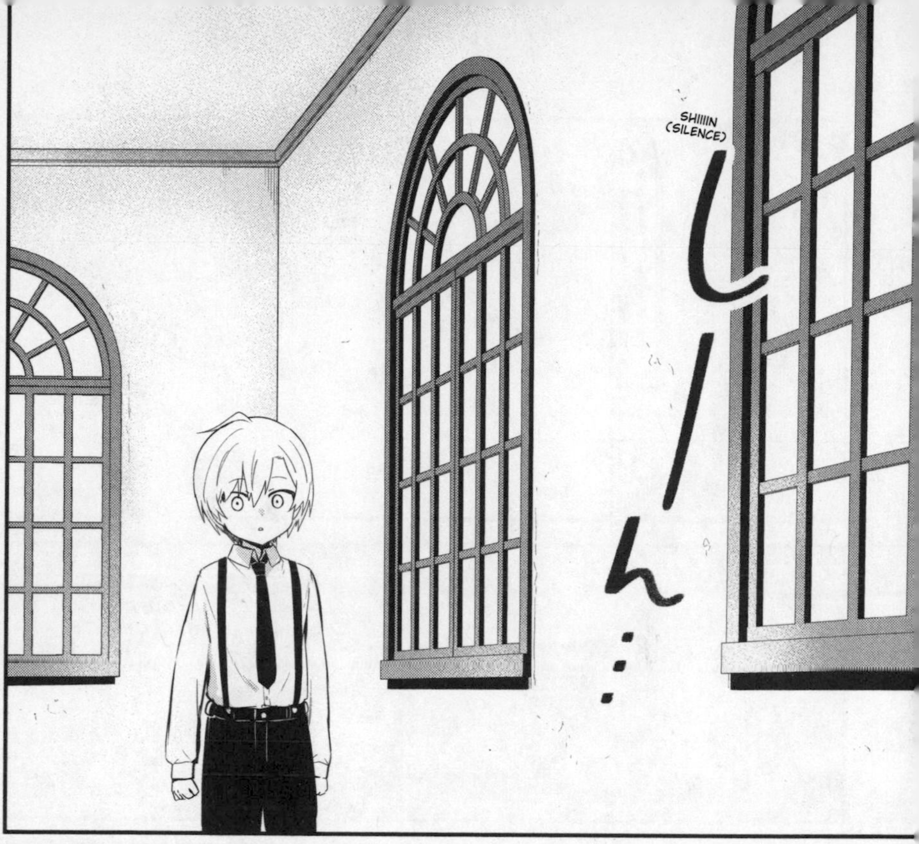
SHIIIIN
(SILENCE)
しーん…
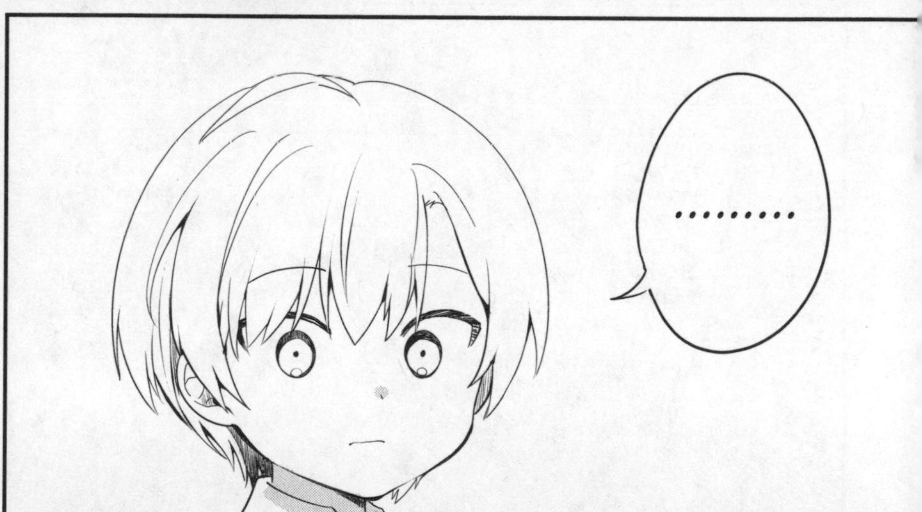
....

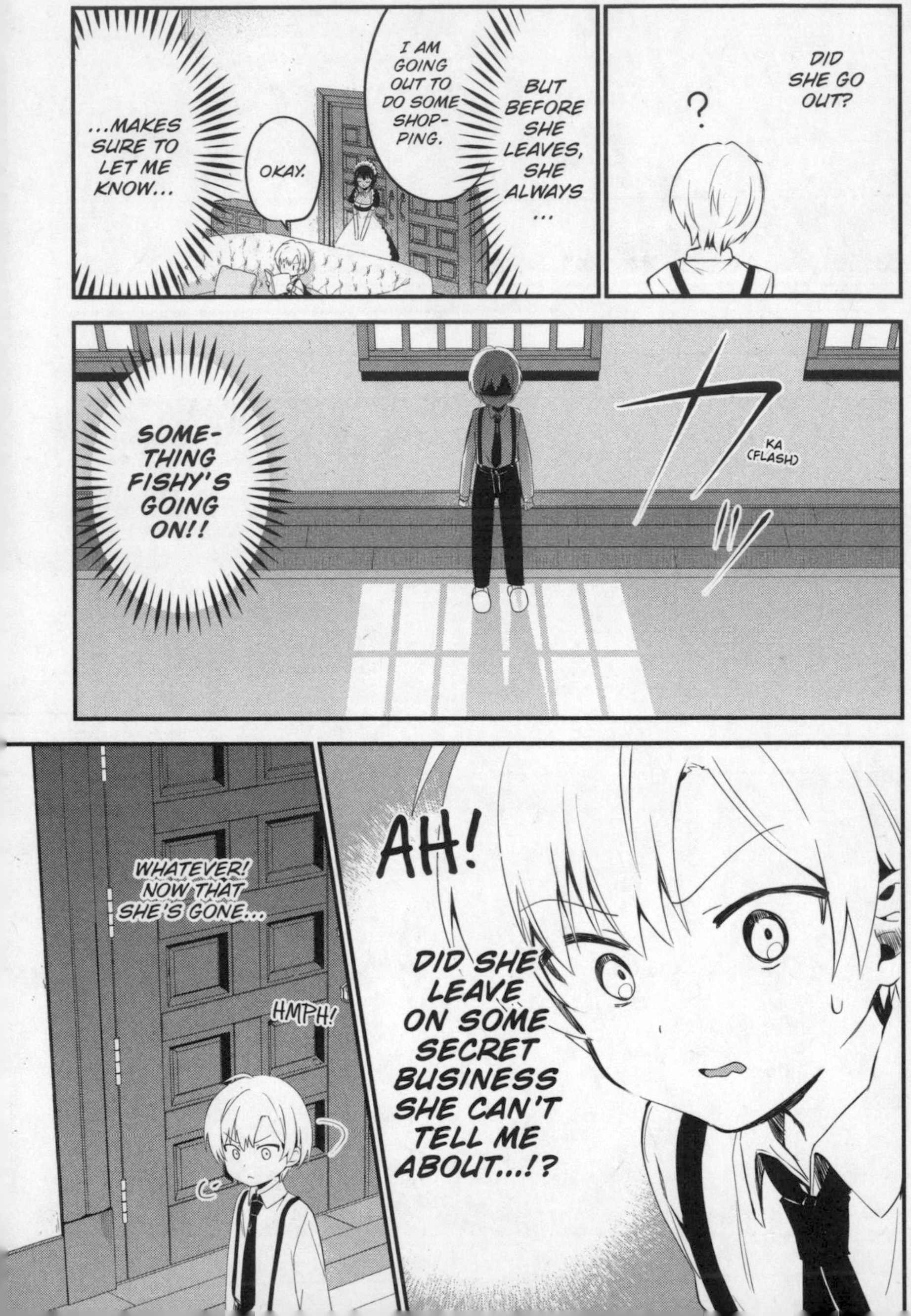
DID SHE GO OUT?
?
BUT BEFORE SHE LEAVES, SHE ALWAYS ...
I AM GOING OUT TO DO SOME SHOP-PING.
OKAY.
...MAKES SURE TO LET ME KNOW...
KA (FLASH)
SOME-THING FISHY'S GOING ON!!
AH!
DID SHE LEAVE ON SOME SECRET BUSINESS SHE CAN'T TELL ME ABOUT...!?
HMPH!
WHATEVER! NOW THAT SHE'S GONE...

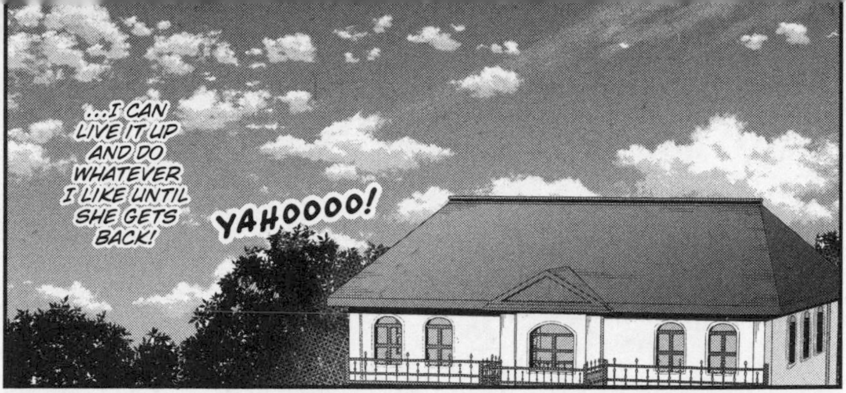
...I CAN LIVE IT UP AND DO WHATEVER I LIKE UNTIL SHE GETS BACK!
YAHOOOO!

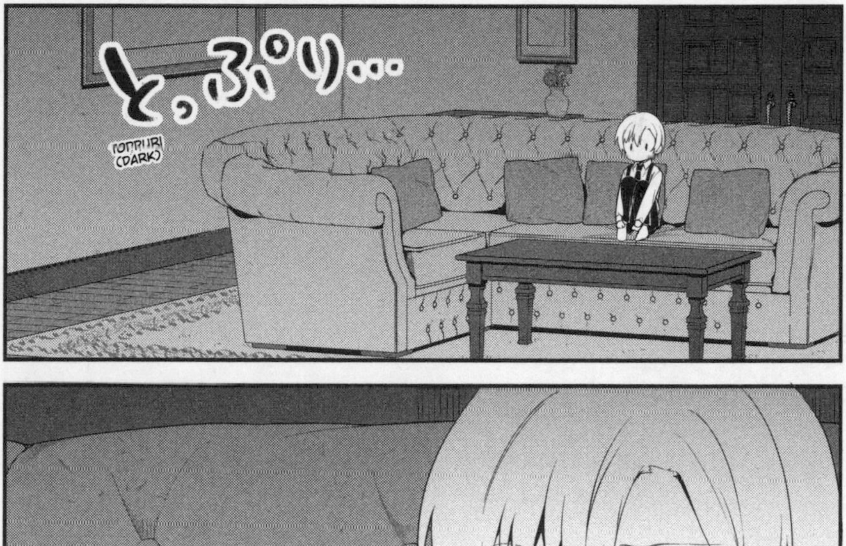
とっぷり...
DOPPURI (DARK)

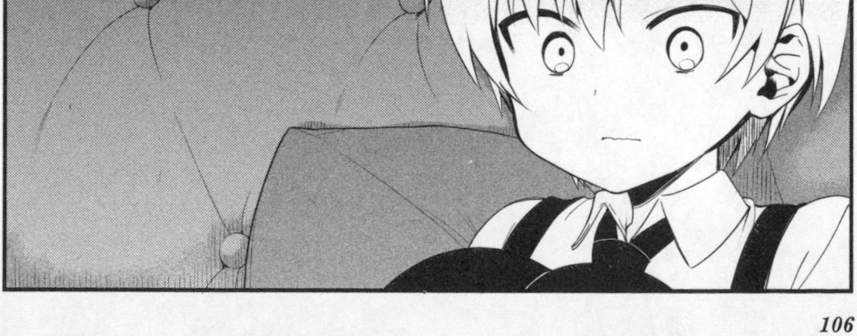

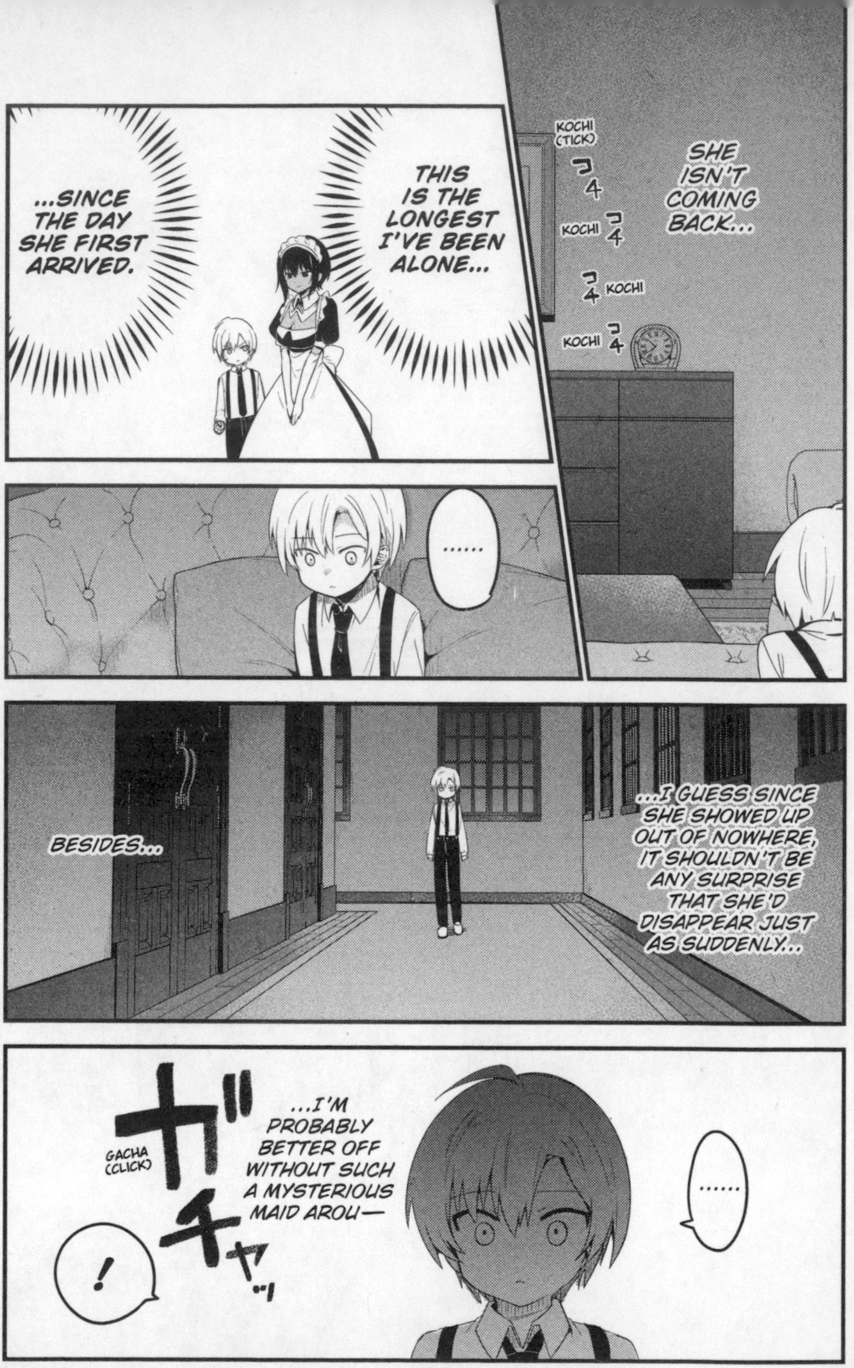

KOCHI (TICK)
コチ
KOCHI コチ
コチ KOCHI
KOCHI コチ
SHE ISN'T COMING BACK...
THIS IS THE LONGEST I'VE BEEN ALONE...
...SINCE THE DAY SHE FIRST ARRIVED.
......
...I GUESS SINCE SHE SHOWED UP OUT OF NOWHERE, IT SHOULDN'T BE ANY SURPRISE THAT SHE'D DISAPPEAR JUST AS SUDDENLY...
BESIDES...
......
...I'M PROBABLY BETTER OFF WITHOUT SUCH A MYSTERIOUS MAID AROU—
ガチャッ
GACHA (CLICK)
!

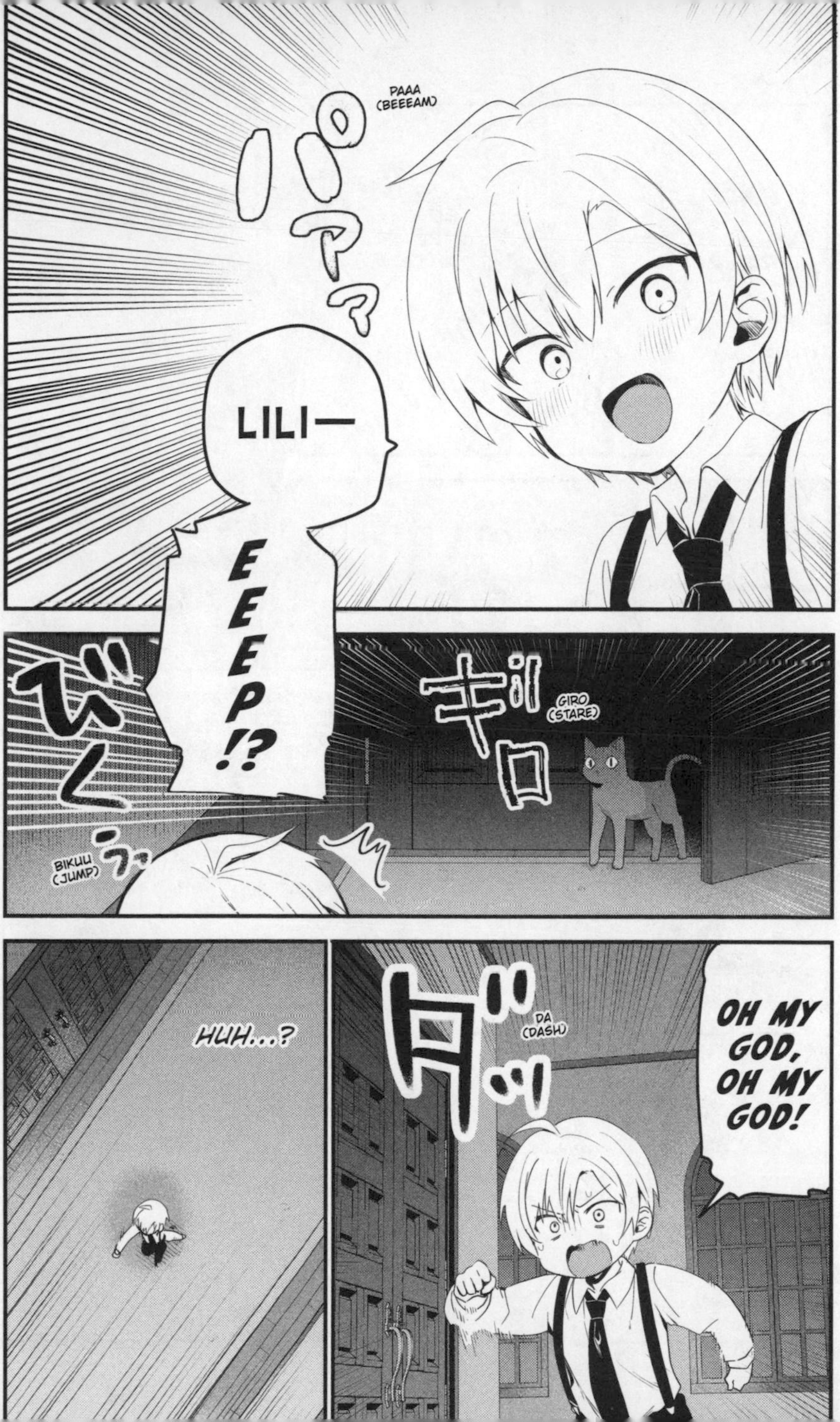
パァァ
PAAA (BEEEAM)
LILI—
ギロ
GIRO (STARE)
EEEP!?
びくぅ
BIKUU (JUMP)
ダッ
DA (DASH)
OH MY GOD, OH MY GOD!
HUH...?

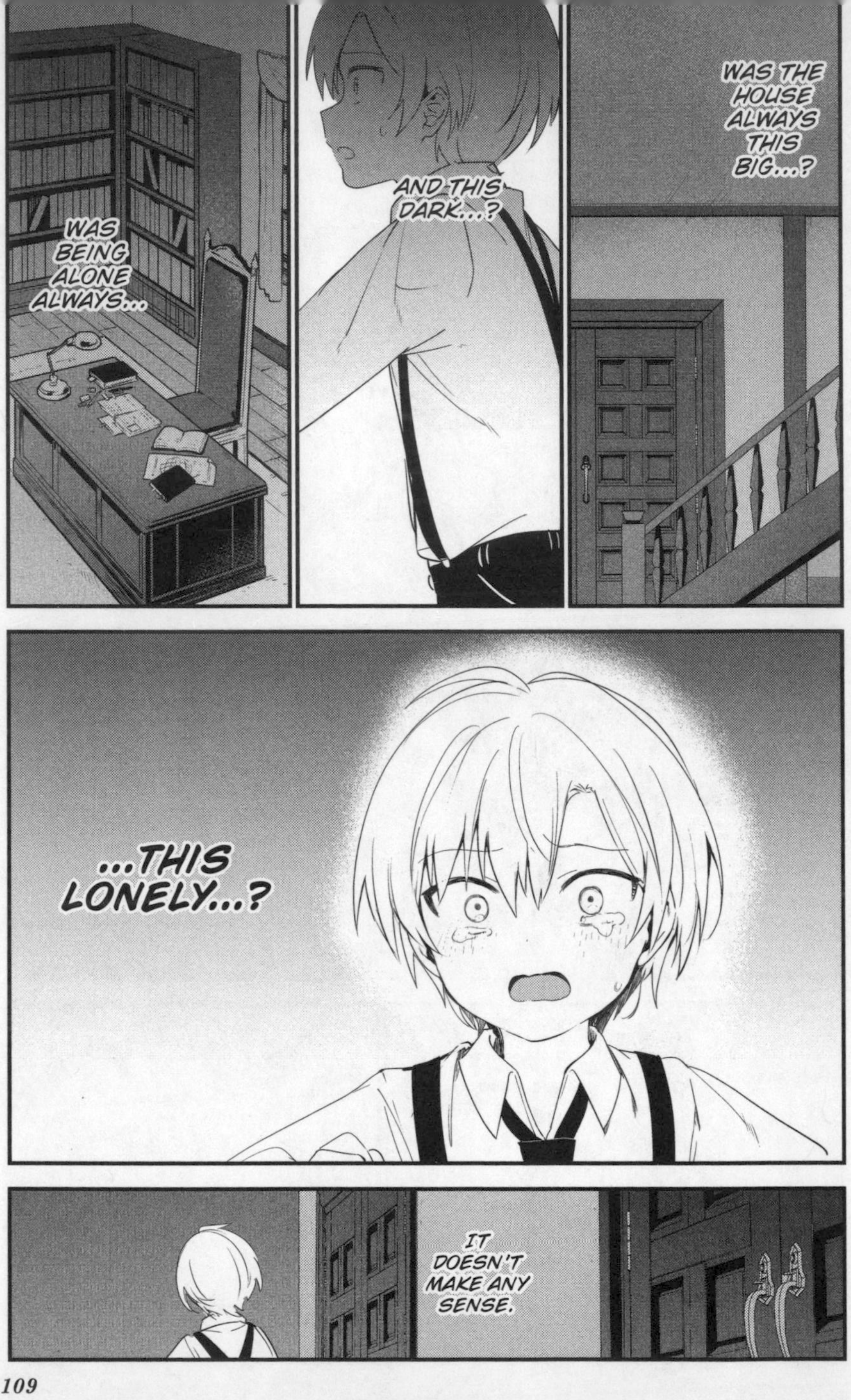
WAS THE HOUSE ALWAYS THIS BIG...?
AND THIS DARK...?
WAS BEING ALONE ALWAYS...
...THIS LONELY...?
IT DOESN'T MAKE ANY SENSE.

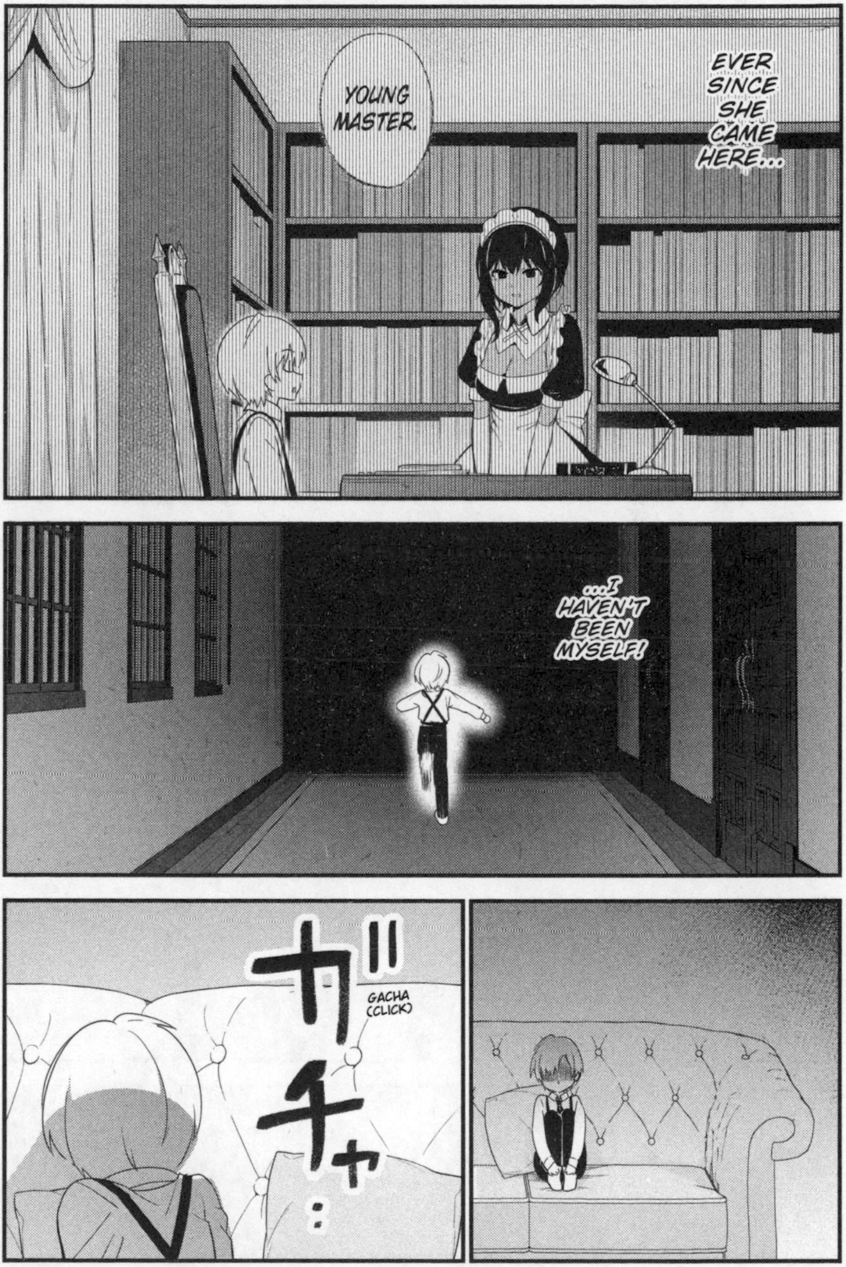
EVER SINCE SHE CAME HERE...
YOUNG MASTER.
...I HAVEN'T BEEN MYSELF!
ガチャ‥
GACHA (CLICK)

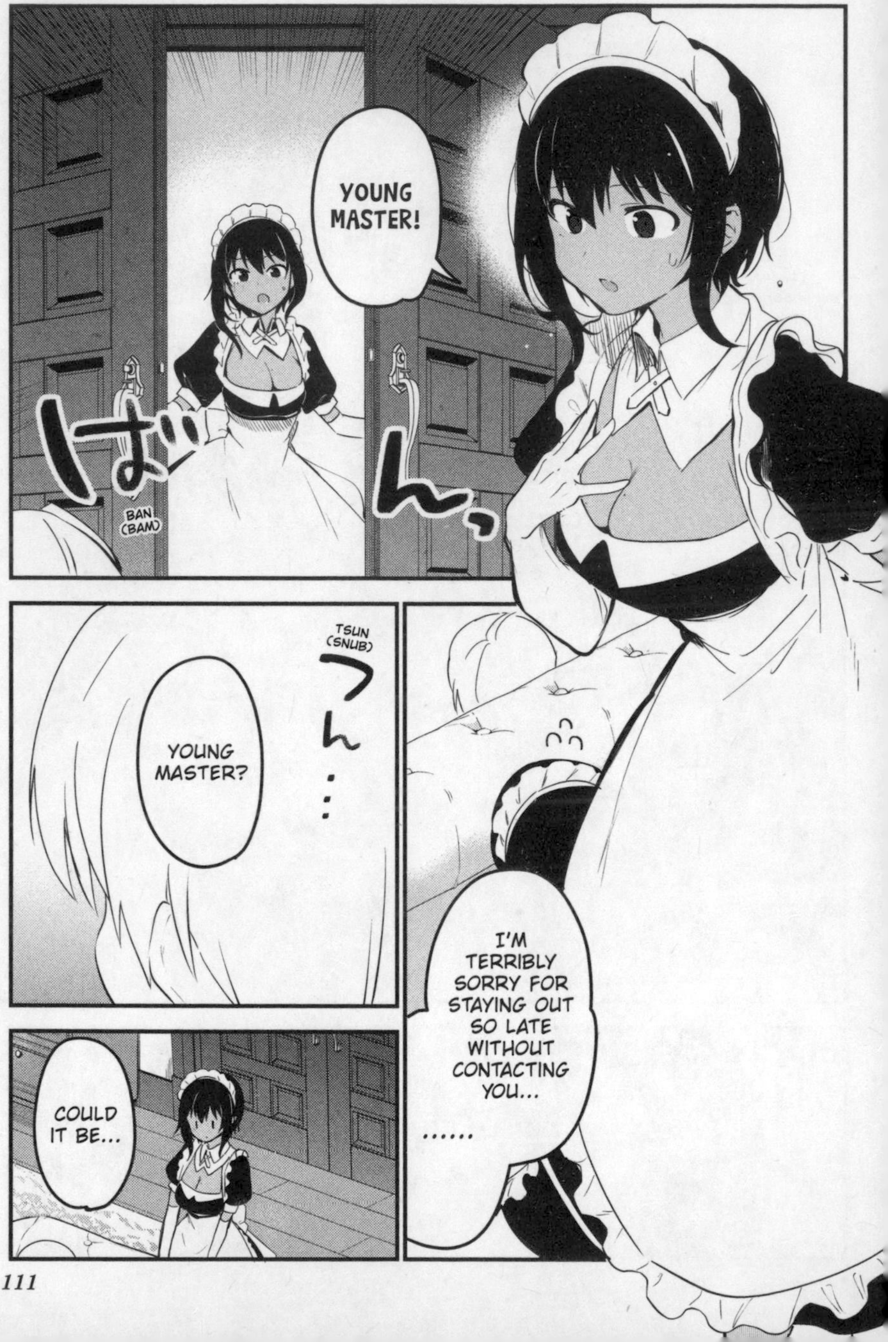
YOUNG MASTER!
ばん
BAN (BAM)
I'M TERRIBLY SORRY FOR STAYING OUT SO LATE WITHOUT CONTACTING YOU...
......
つん...
TSUN (SNUB)
YOUNG MASTER?
COULD IT BE...

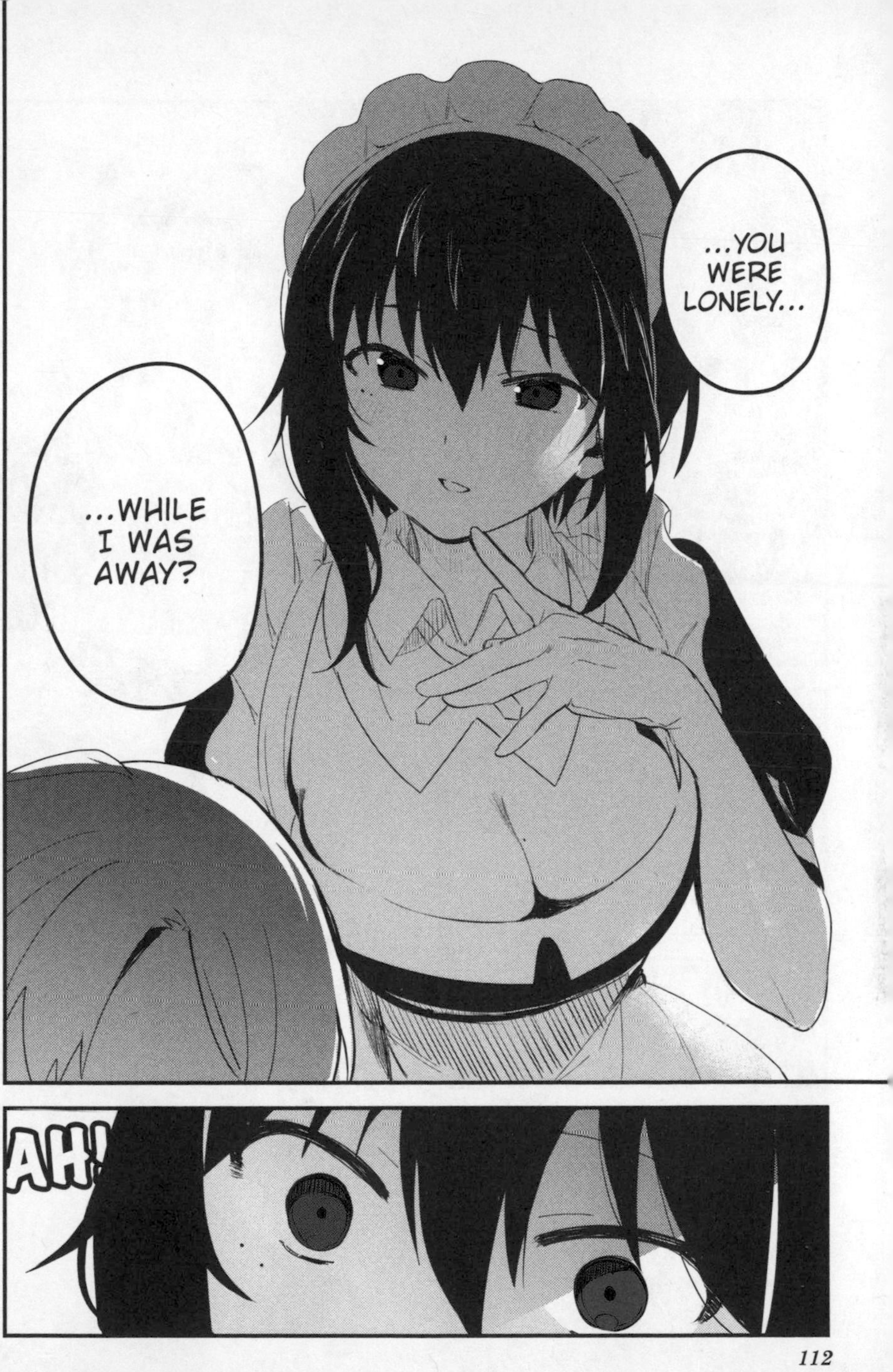
...YOU WERE LONELY...
...WHILE I WAS AWAY?
AH!

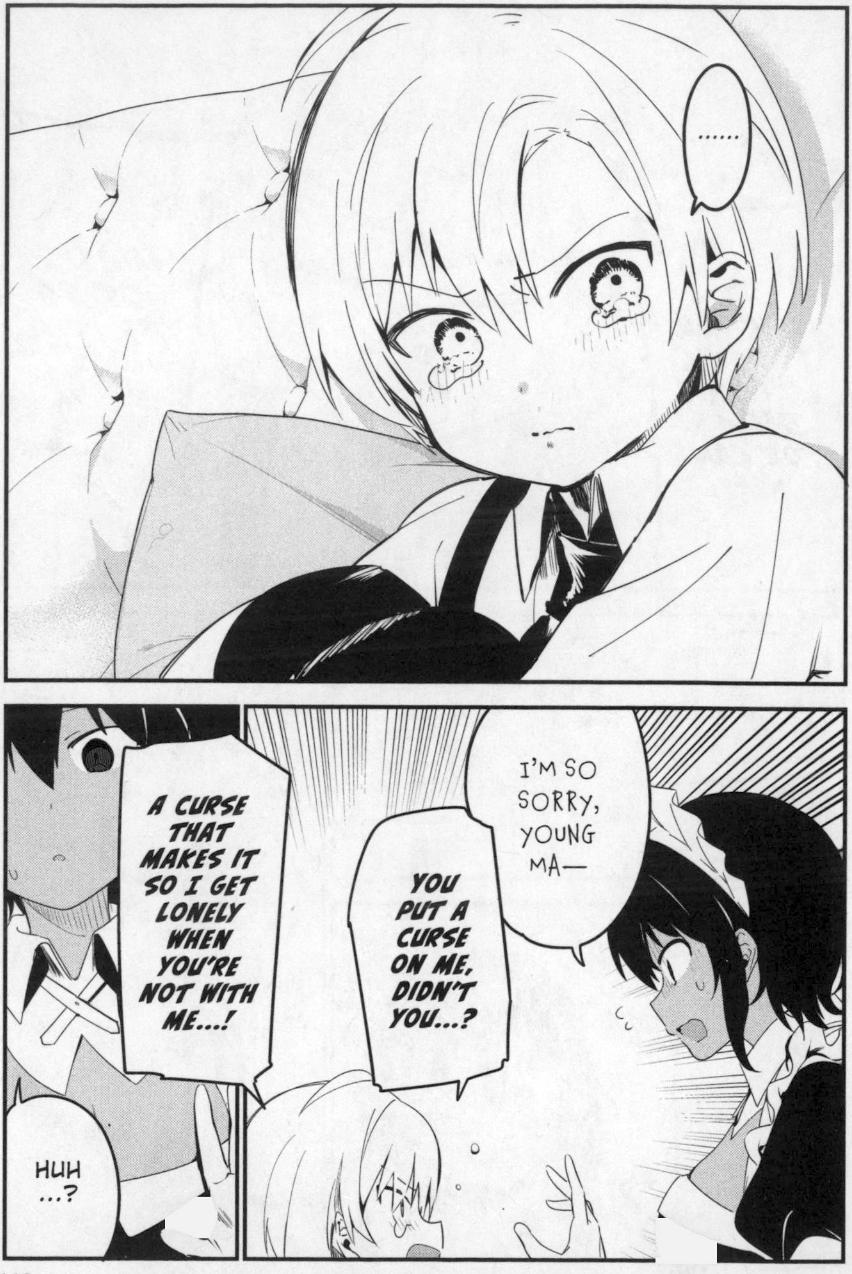
......
I'M SO SORRY, YOUNG MA—
YOU PUT A CURSE ON ME, DIDN'T YOU...?
A CURSE THAT MAKES IT SO I GET LONELY WHEN YOU'RE NOT WITH ME...!
HUH ...?

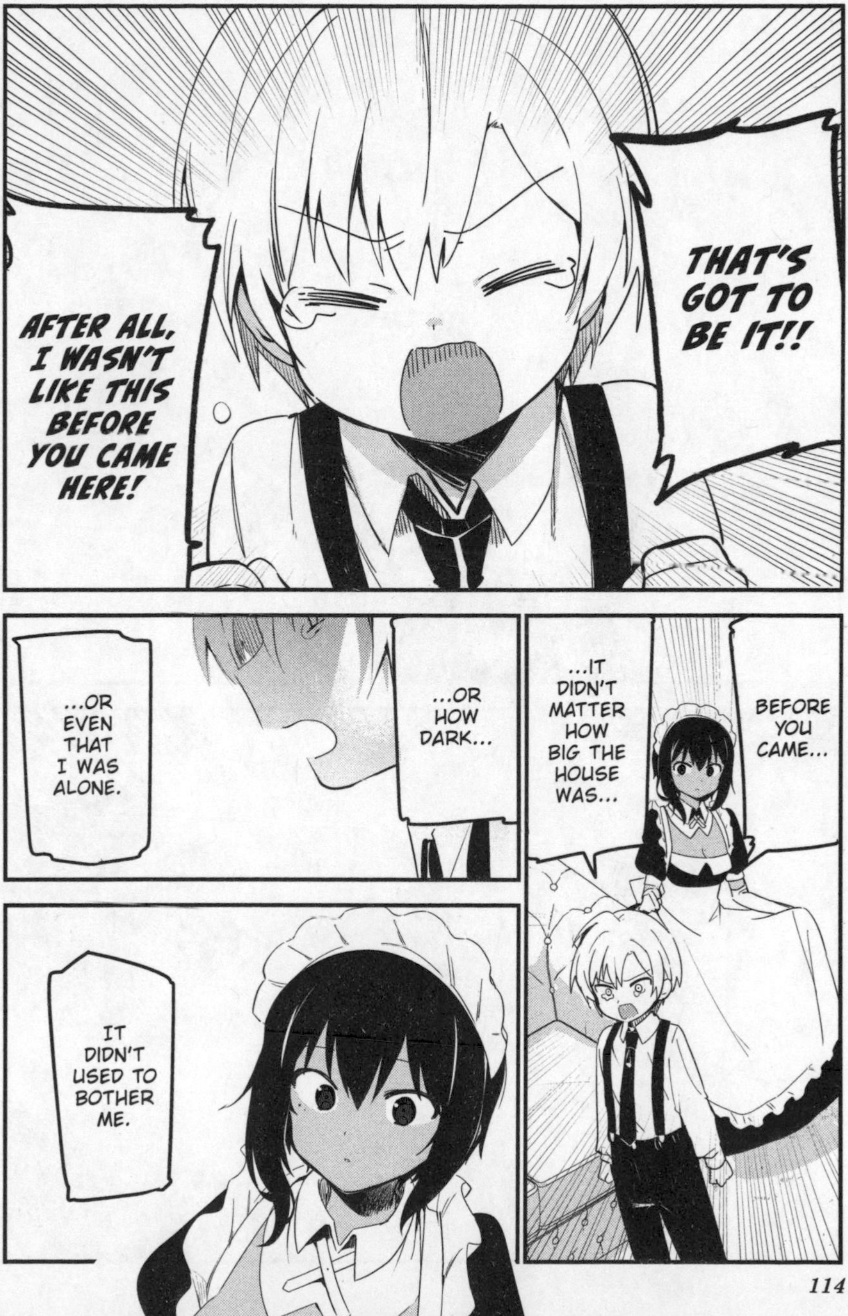
THAT'S GOT TO BE IT!!
AFTER ALL, I WASN'T LIKE THIS BEFORE YOU CAME HERE!
BEFORE YOU CAME...
...IT DIDN'T MATTER HOW BIG THE HOUSE WAS...
...OR HOW DARK...
...OR EVEN THAT I WAS ALONE.
IT DIDN'T USED TO BOTHER ME.

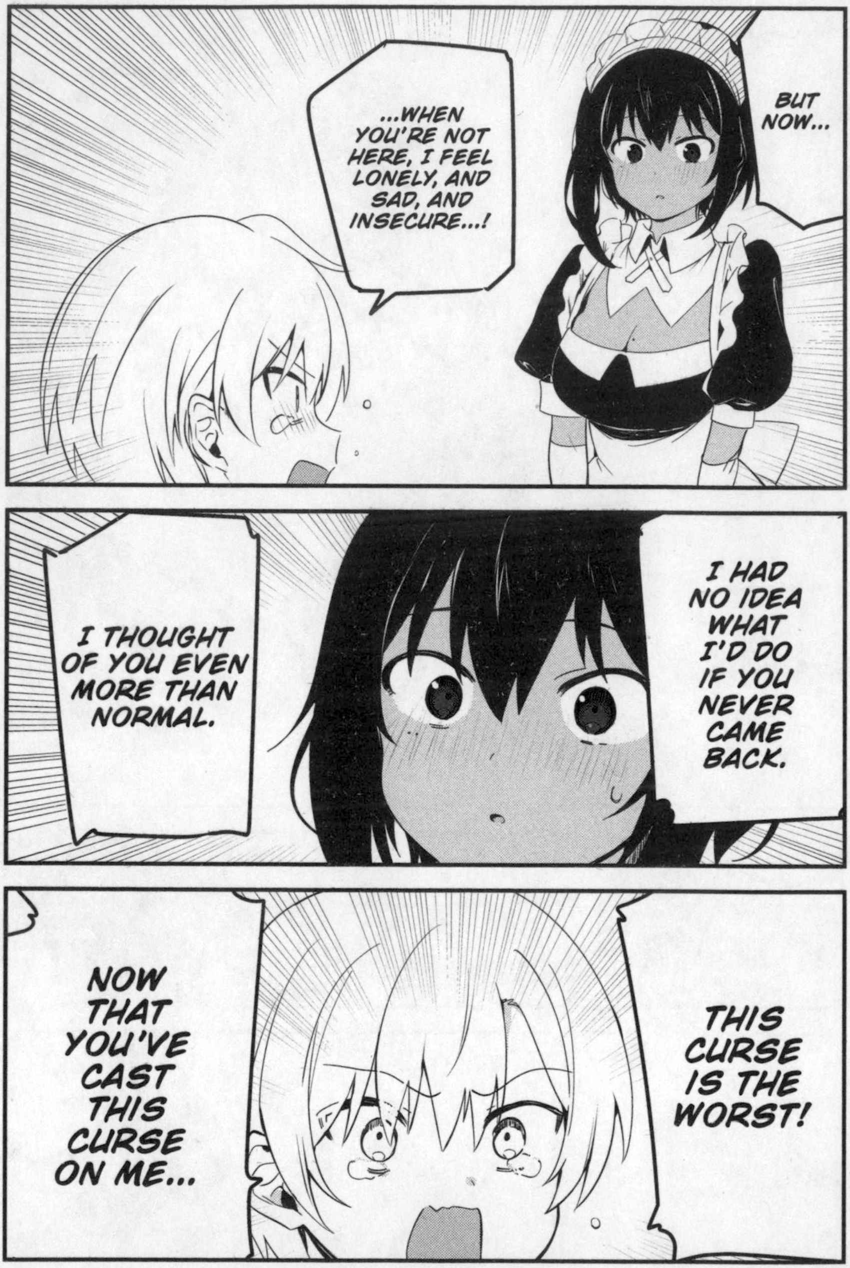
BUT NOW...
...WHEN YOU'RE NOT HERE, I FEEL LONELY, AND SAD, AND INSECURE...!
I HAD NO IDEA WHAT I'D DO IF YOU NEVER CAME BACK.
I THOUGHT OF YOU EVEN MORE THAN NORMAL.
NOW THAT YOU'VE CAST THIS CURSE ON ME...
THIS CURSE IS THE WORST!

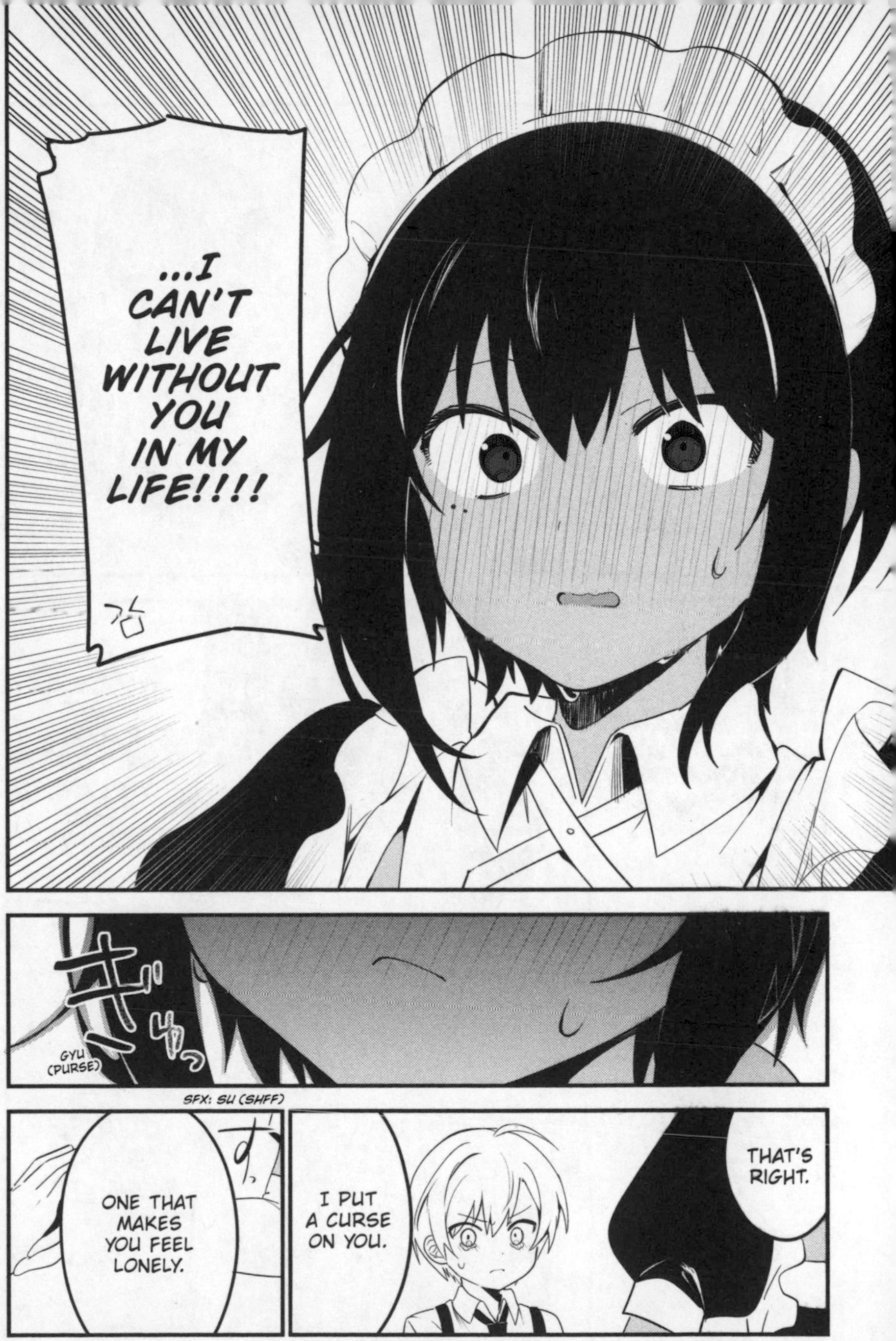
...I CAN'T LIVE WITHOUT YOU IN MY LIFE!!!!
GYU (PURSE)
SFX: SU (SHFF)
THAT'S RIGHT.
I PUT A CURSE ON YOU.
ONE THAT MAKES YOU FEEL LONELY.

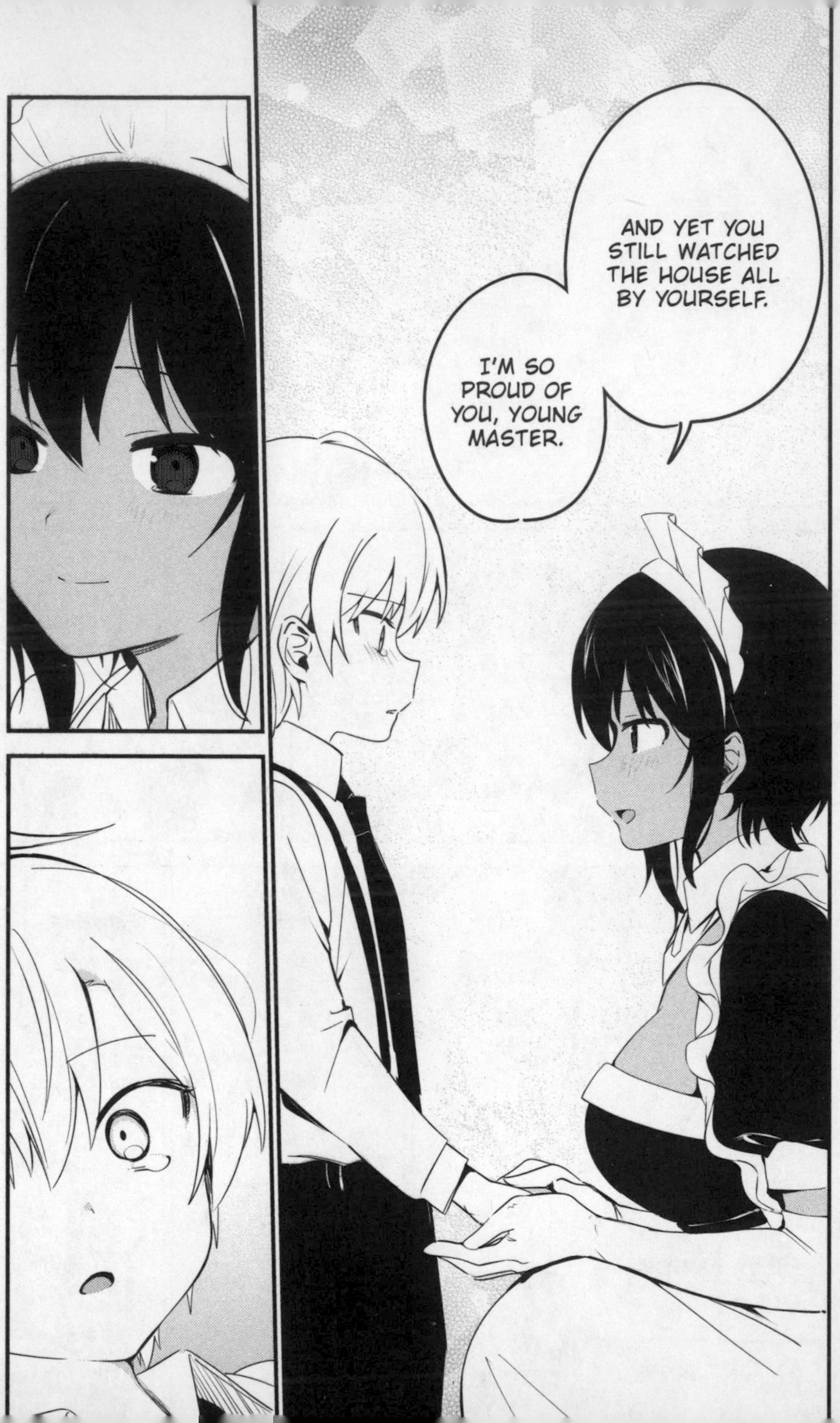
AND YET YOU STILL WATCHED THE HOUSE ALL BY YOURSELF.
I'M SO PROUD OF YOU, YOUNG MASTER.

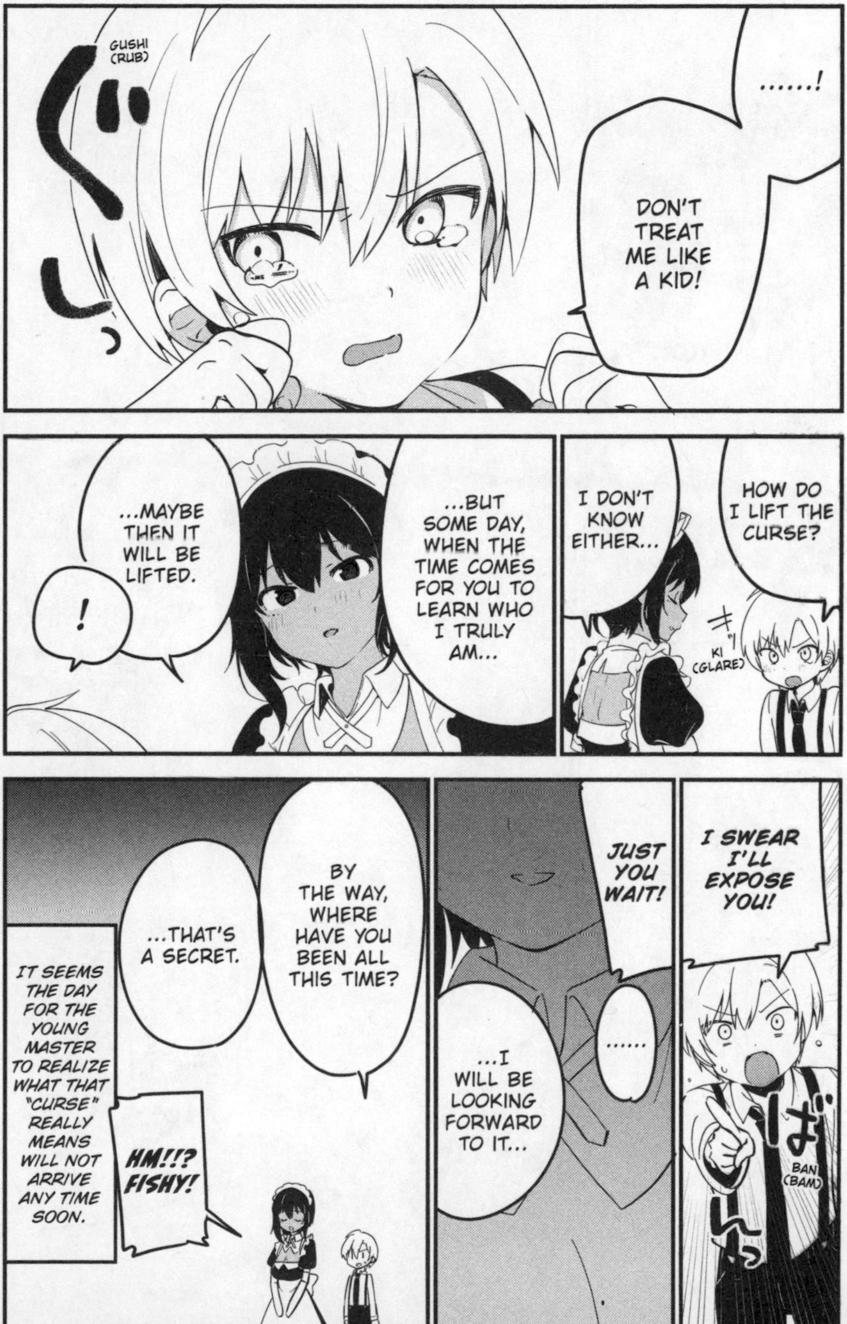
......!
DON'T TREAT ME LIKE A KID!
GUSHI (RUB)
HOW DO I LIFT THE CURSE?
I DON'T KNOW EITHER...
KI (GLARE)
...BUT SOME DAY, WHEN THE TIME COMES FOR YOU TO LEARN WHO I TRULY AM...
...MAYBE THEN IT WILL BE LIFTED.
!
I SWEAR I'LL EXPOSE YOU!
BAN (BAM)
JUST YOU WAIT!
......
...I WILL BE LOOKING FORWARD TO IT...
BY THE WAY, WHERE HAVE YOU BEEN ALL THIS TIME?
...THAT'S A SECRET.
HM!!? FISHY!
IT SEEMS THE DAY FOR THE YOUNG MASTER TO REALIZE WHAT THAT "CURSE" REALLY MEANS WILL NOT ARRIVE ANY TIME SOON.

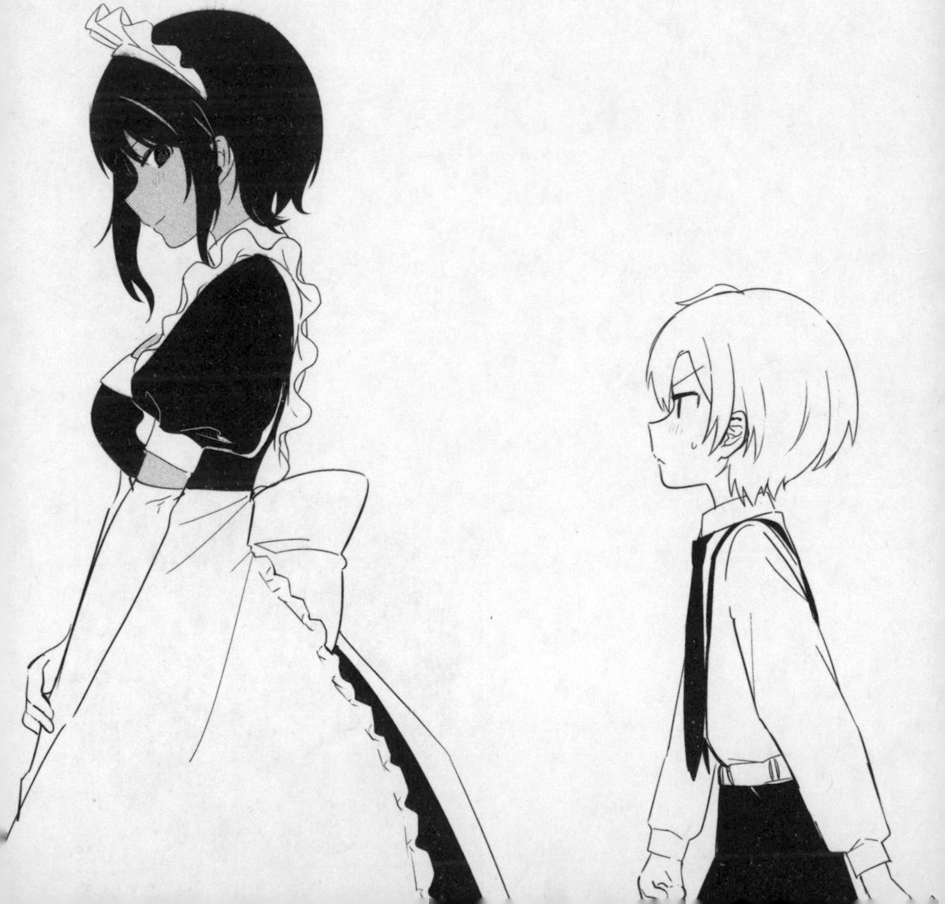

The Maid I Hired Recently Is Mysterious

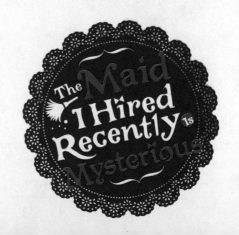

BONUS STORY

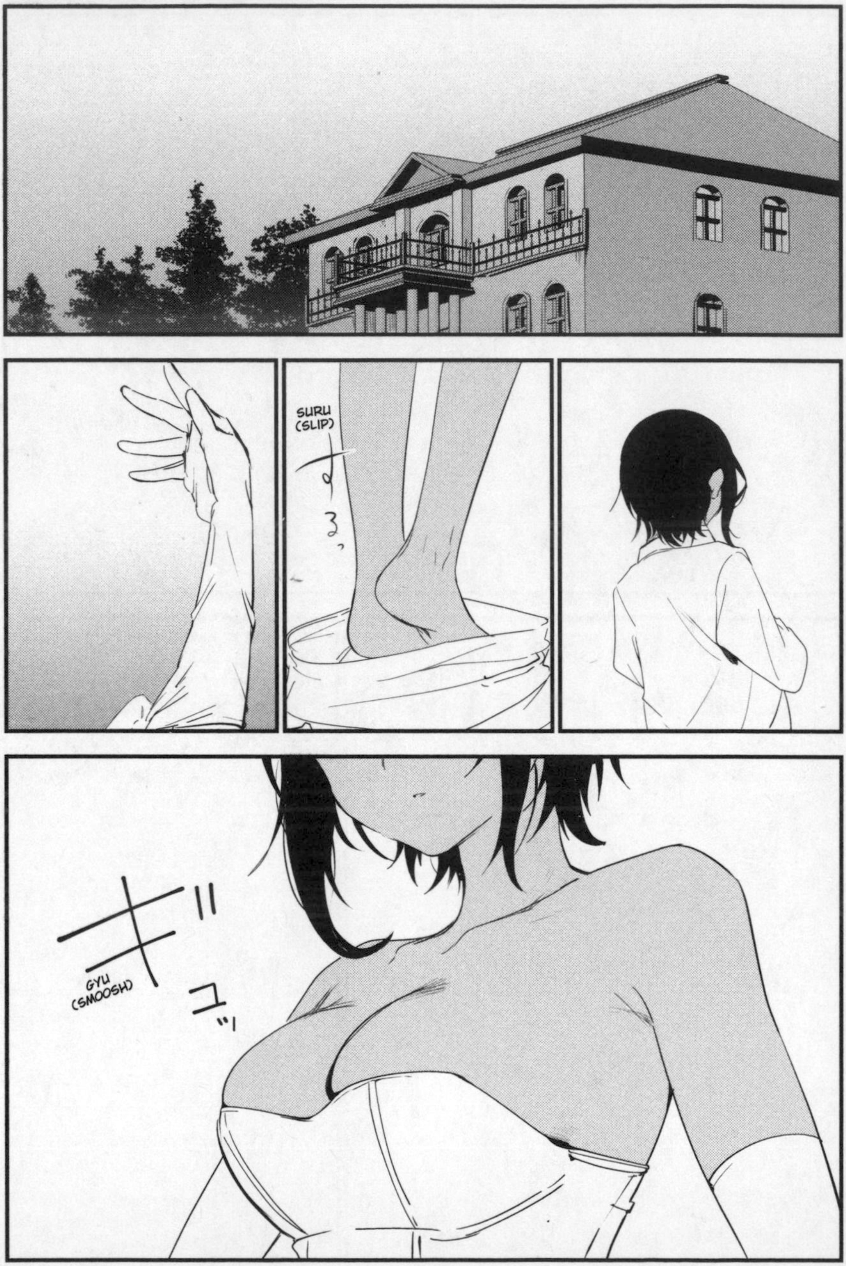
SURU (SLIP)
GYU (SMOOSH)

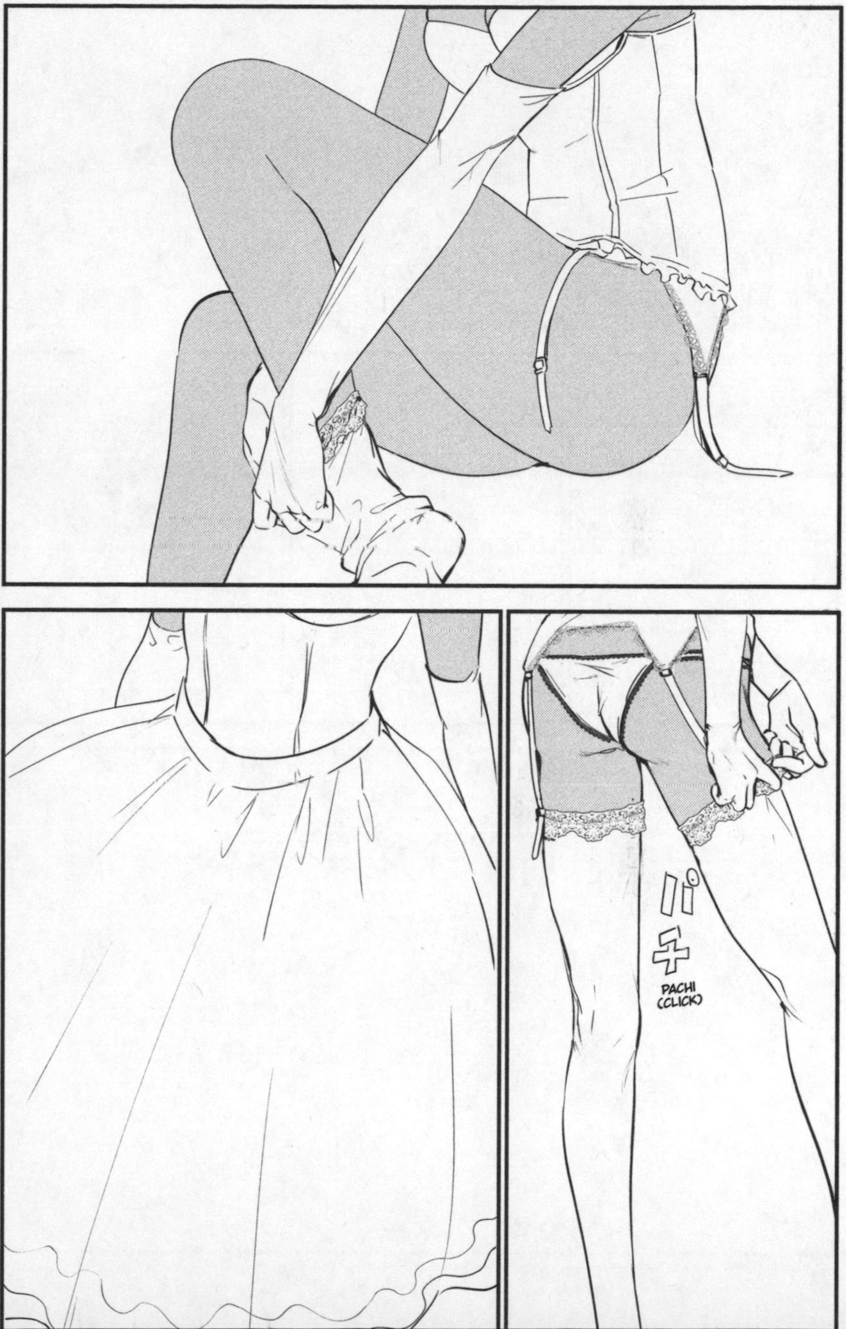
パチ
PACHI
(CLICK)

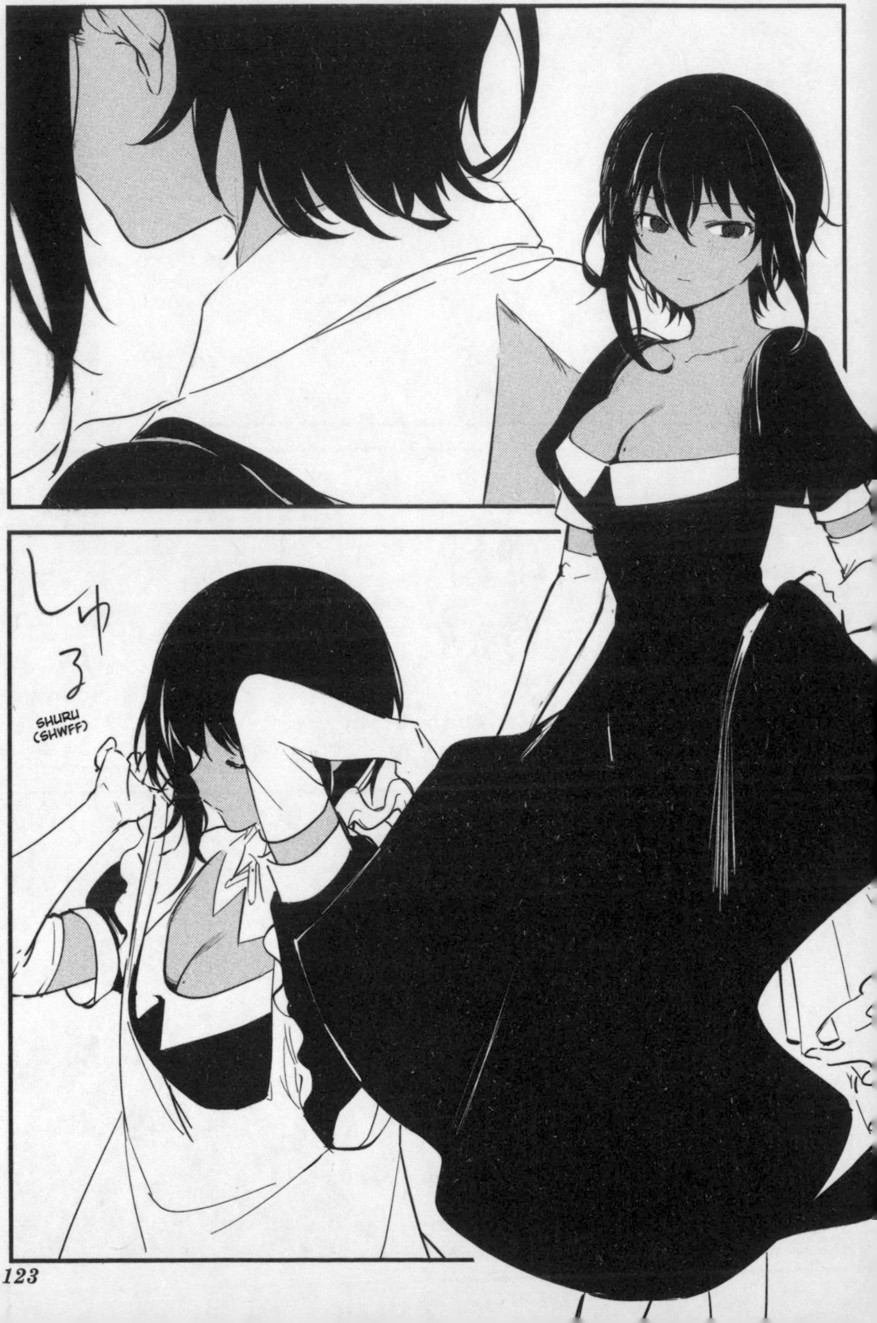
しゅる
SHURU
(SHWFF)

キュッ
KYU (TUG)
すちゃ
SUCHA (SNUG)

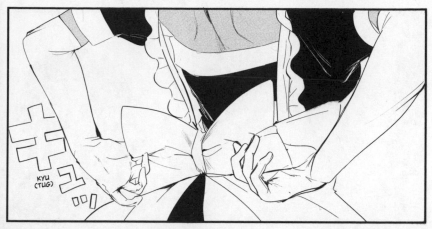

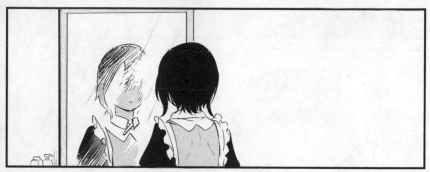

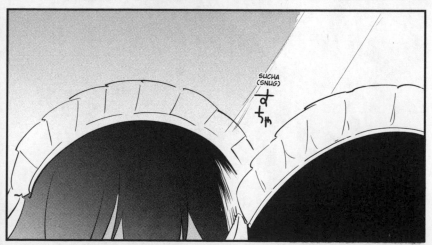

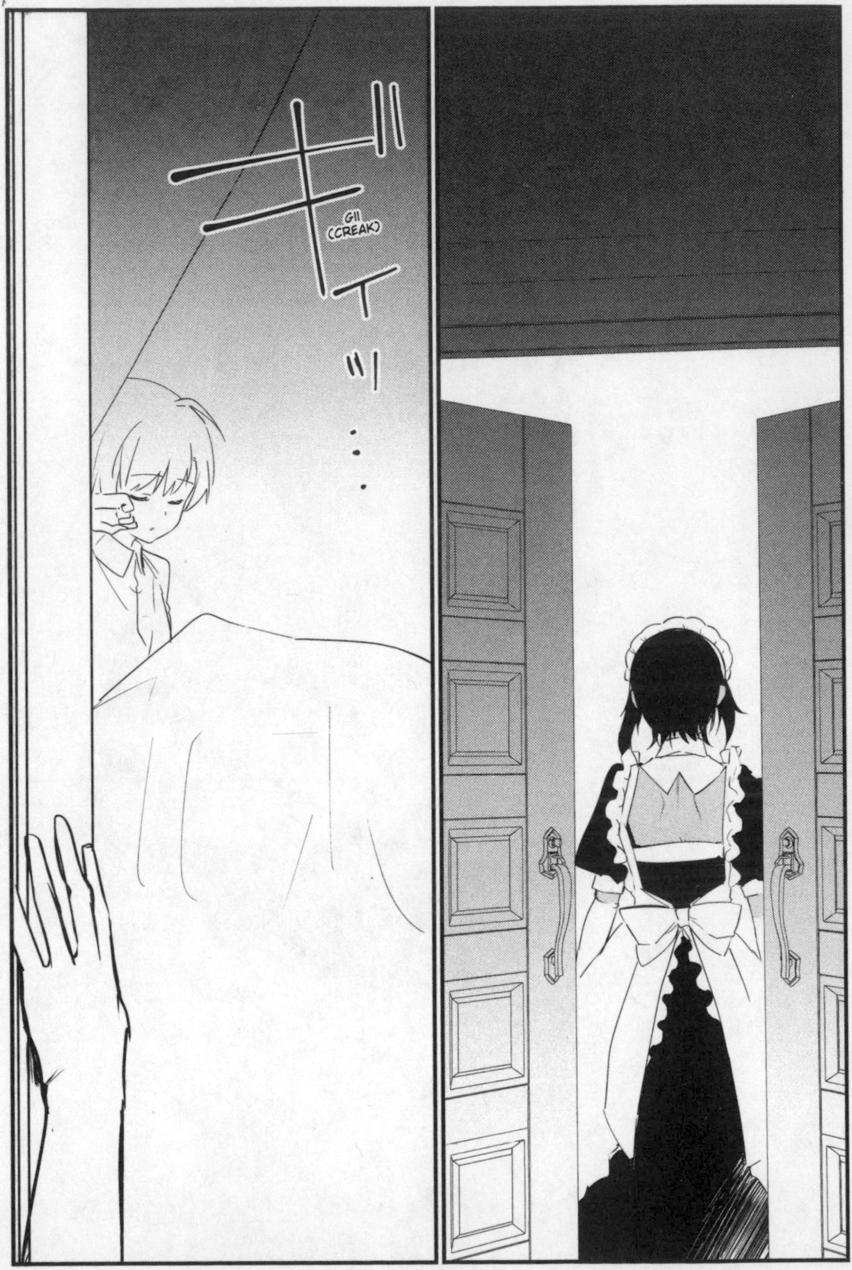
ギイ ッ…
GII (CREAK)

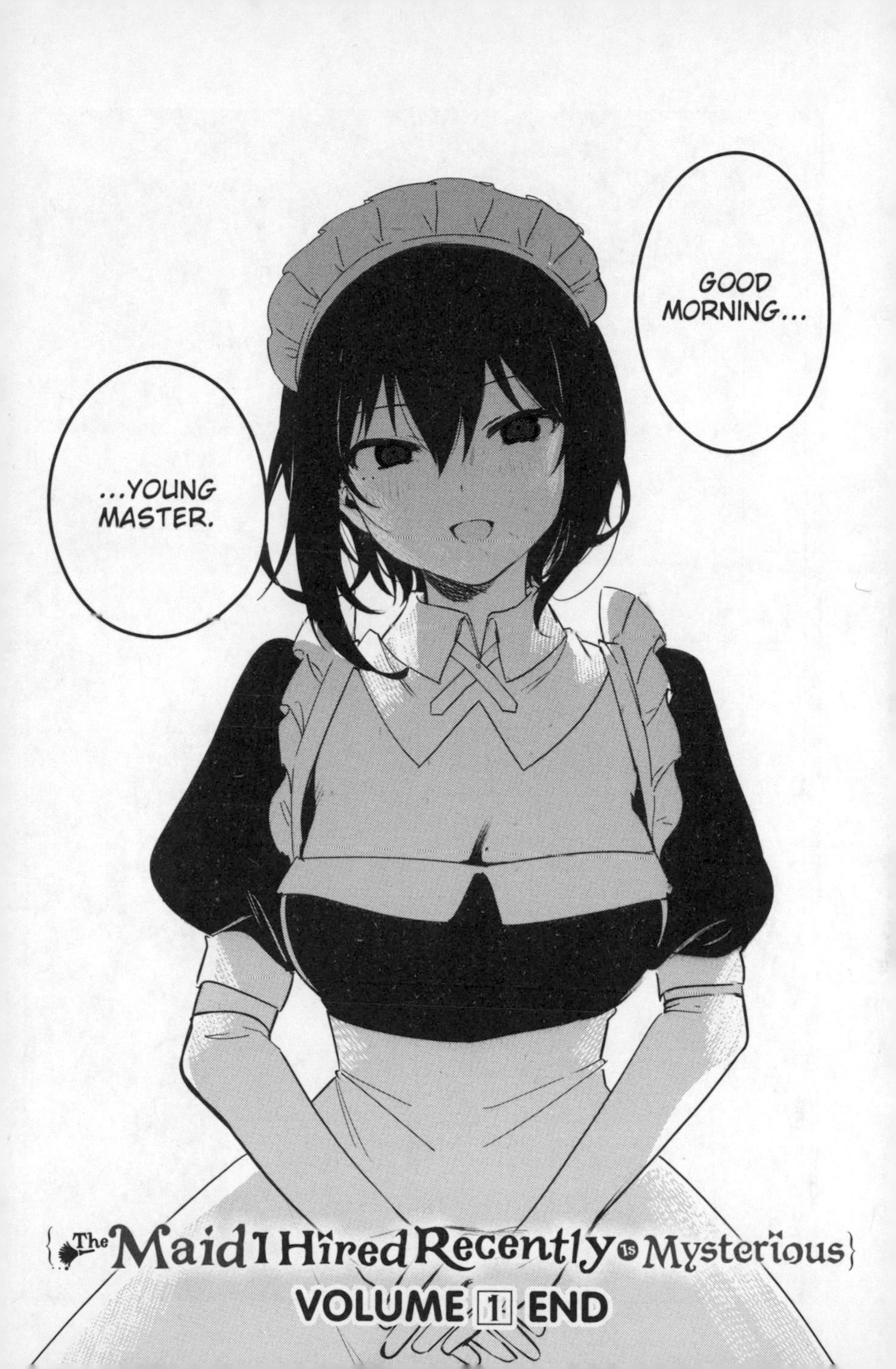
GOOD MORNING...
...YOUNG MASTER.
The Maid I Hired Recently Is Mysterious
VOLUME 1 END

THANK YOU FOR ALL YOUR HELP:

- REIA-SAN   - MY FAMILY
- MY EDITOR   - EVERYONE WHO HAD A HAND IN THIS
- MY DESIGNER   - ALL MY READERS

THANK YOU!!

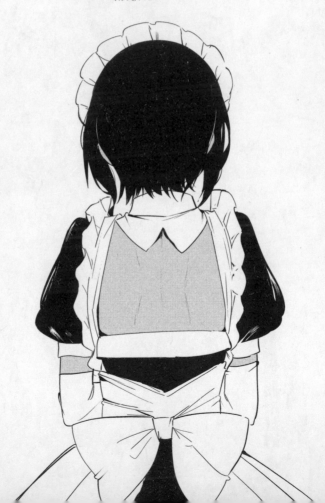

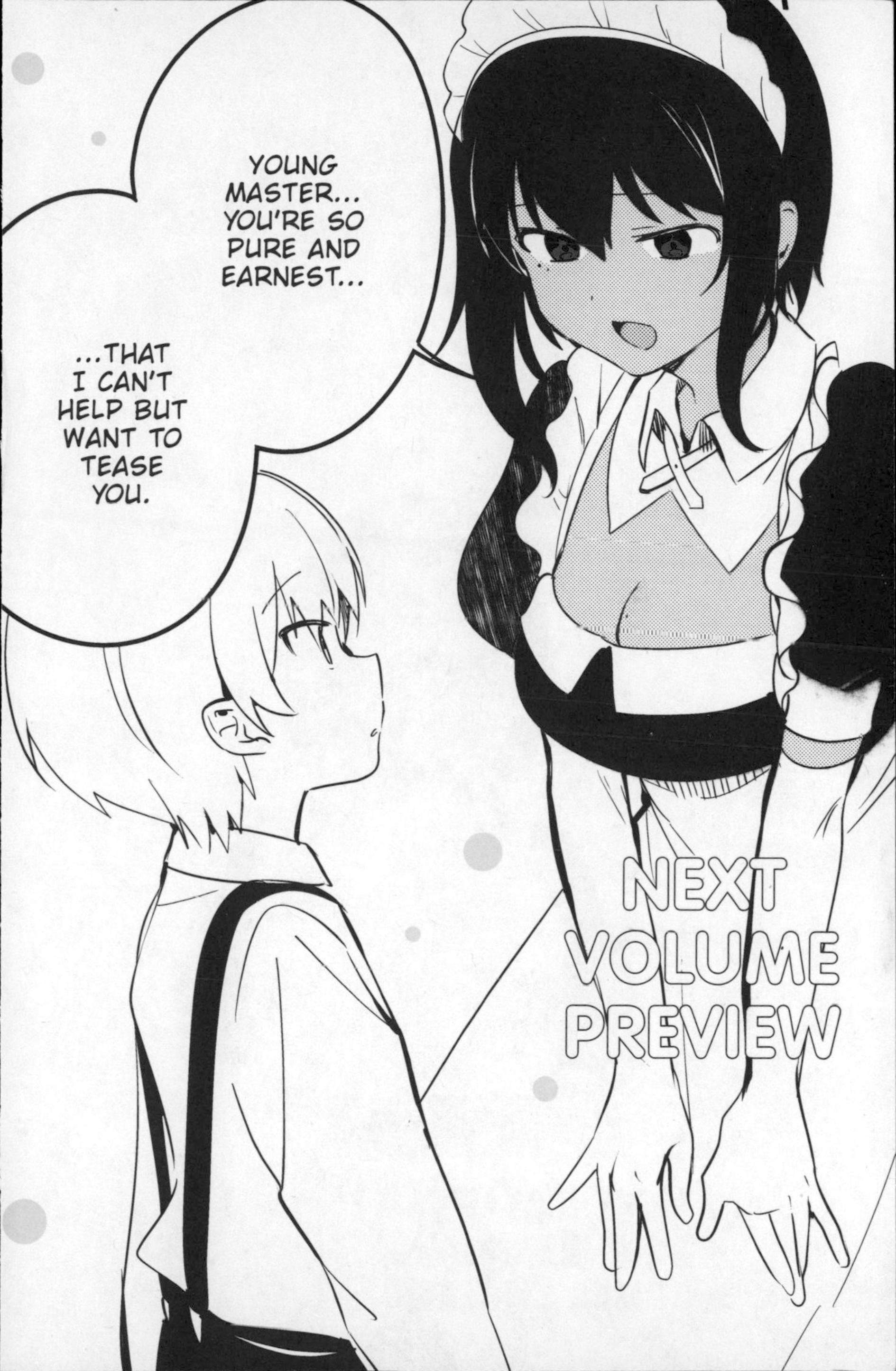
YOUNG MASTER... YOU'RE SO PURE AND EARNEST...
...THAT I CAN'T HELP BUT WANT TO TEASE YOU.
NEXT VOLUME PREVIEW

THE SECRET OF THIS MYSTERIOUS MAID COMES EVER CLOSER TO DISCOVERY.

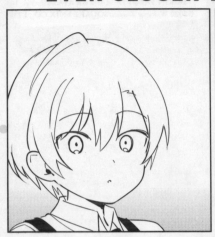

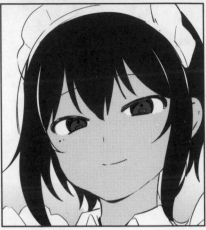

The Maid I Hired Recently Is Mysterious 2

ON SALE IN FALL 2021!

EVEN THOUGH MY HEAD'S SO FULL OF THOUGHTS ABOUT YOU... YOU'D STILL CALL ME... EARNEST!?
YES... VERY...

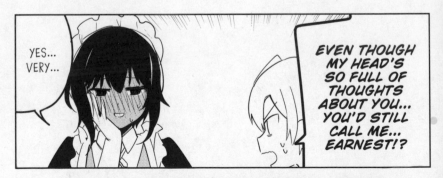

AND THE DISTANCE BETWEEN THESE TWO PURE AND INNOCENT SOULS BECOMES SMALLER AND SMALLER.

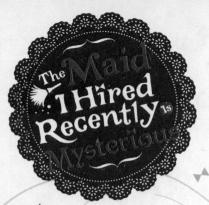

The Maid I Hired Recently Is Mysterious

1 Wakame Konbu

Translation: Christine Dashiell

Lettering: Brandon Bovia

First published in Japan in 2020 by SQUARE ENIX CO., LTD. English translation rights arranged with SQUARE ENIX CO., LTD. and Yen Press, LLC through Tuttle-Mori Agency, Inc.

English translation ©2021 by SQUARE ENIX CO., LTD.

Yen Press
150 West 30th Street, 19th Floor
New York, NY 10001

Visit us at yenpress.com
facebook.com/yenpress
twitter.com/yenpress
yenpress.tumblr.com
instagram.com/yenpress

First Yen Press Edition: June 2021

Yen Press is an imprint of Yen Press, LLC.

The Yen Press name and logo are trademarks of Yen Press, LLC.

The publisher is not responsible for websites (or their content) that are not owned by the publisher.

Library of Congress Control Number: 2021935580

ISBNs: 978-1-9753-2476-6 (paperback)
978-1-9753-2477-3 (ebook)

10 9 8 7 6 5 4 3 2 1

WOR

Printed in the United States of America